An Introduction
to Modern
Philosophy

An Introduction to Modern Philosophy

Garrett Thomson

UNIVERSITY OF WISCONSIN—OSHKOSH

Wadsworth Publishing Company
Belmont, California
A Division of Wadsworth, Inc.

Philosophy Editor: Kenneth King
Editorial Assistant: Gay Meixel
Production Editor: The Book Company
Print Buyer: Diana Spence
Designer: John Osborn
Copy Editor: Steven Gray
Cover: Harry Voigt
Compositor: Kachina Typesetting
Printer: R. R. Donnelley & Sons Co.

*This book is printed on acid-free paper that meets Environmental Protection Agency
standards for recycled paper.*

1 2 3 4 5 6 7 8 9 10—97 96 95 94 93

Library of Congress Cataloging-in-Publication Data
Thomson, Garrett.
    An introduction to modern philosophy / Garrett Thomson.
      p.   cm.
    Includes bibliographical references and index.
    ISBN 0-534-19734-5
    1. Philosophy, Modern—17th century.   2. Philosophy, Modern—18th
century I. Title.
B801.T47   1992
190'.9'032—dc20
                                  95-595
                                    CIP

To June

Contents

Preface   iv

INTRODUCTION
1

The Medieval Period   1
The Modern Period   5

Part One
The Rationalists
7

BIOGRAPHY
Descartes (1596-1650)
9

CHAPTER 1
*Descartes: The Method of Doubt
and the Cogito*
12

Comments on the Three Stages   14
What Is Descartes's Method of Doubt?   15
Some Criticisms of Descartes's Scepticism   16
The Cogito as the End of Doubt   17
The Interpretation of the Cogito   19
A Famous Criticism of the Cogito   21

CHAPTER 2
Descartes: God
24

The Classification of Ideas   24
The Idea of God   26

The First Proof of the Existence of God   26
The Second Argument for the Existence of God   30
The Cartesian Circle   31
False Beliefs   32

CHAPTER 3
Descartes: Mind and Body
35

Thinking Substance   35
The Existence of Material Things   37
The Nature of Matter   37
Rationalism and Science   38
Primary and Secondary Qualities   39
The Real Distinction   40
The Nature of Descartes's Dualism   44
Some Criticisms of Dualism   44
The Causal Analysis of Mind   46
Materialism   47

BIOGRAPHY
Spinoza (1632-1677)
49

CHAPTER 4
Spinoza: God and Substance
51

A Preliminary Overview   52
Spinoza's Proofs   53
A General Review   56
Finite Modes   57

CHAPTER 5
Spinoza: The Nature of the Mind
62

God's Causality and Science   62
The Infinite and Eternal Modes   63
The Attributes   64
Extension and Thought   65
The Mind and the Body   66
The Mind as the Idea of the Body   67
All Things Have Souls   67
Materialism   68
No Ownership of Ideas   68
The Reality of Finite Minds   69

CHAPTER 6
Spinoza: Theory of Knowledge
71

Kinds of Knowledge   71
Truth and Falsity   73
Determinism and Free Will   74

BIOGRAPHY
Leibniz (1646-1716)
77

CHAPTER 7
Leibniz: Truth and Reason
80

Truth   81
Finite and Infinite Analysis   81
Primitive Concepts   82
Substances and Complete Concepts   83
The Principle of Sufficient Reason   84
Contingent Truths and Existence   85
Contingency and God's Free Choice   86
Contingency and Sufficient Reason   86
The Principle of the Best   87

CHAPTER 8
Leibniz: Monads
89

Relations   89
Substance   91
The Principle of the Identity of Indiscernibles   91
Monads   92
Monads and Causality   93
Monads and Mirrors   94
Points of View   95
Preestablished Harmony   95

CHAPTER 9
Leibniz: God and Space
97

The Ontological Argument   97
The Cosmological Argument   98
The Argument from Preestablished Harmony   99

Existence   99
Extension   100
Matter   101
Space and Time   102

CONCLUSION
Rationalism
105

Consequences of the Principle   106
Some Differences Among Descartes, Spinoza, and Leibniz   106

Part Two
The Empiricists
109

BIOGRAPHY
John Locke (1632-1704)
112

CHAPTER 10
Locke: Ideas and Qualities
115

The Role of Ideas   116
Innate Ideas   116
The Origin of Ideas   117
Simple and Complex Ideas   118
Primary and Secondary Qualities   119
Arguments for the Distinction   120
Some Famous Criticisms of the Resemblance Thesis   121
Locke's Theory of Perception   122
Representations and Scepticism   123
Representations and Qualities   125

CHAPTER 11
Locke: The Formation of Complex Ideas
127

Modes   127
Substance in General   128
Substance and Empiricism   129
A Problem with the Notion of Pure Substratum   130
Relations: Causality   131
Identity and Diversity   131
Personal Identity   132

Locke's Rejection of Other Theories   133
Some Well-known Criticisms of Locke   133

CHAPTER 12
Locke: Language and Knowledge
136

Locke's Theory of Language   136
Some Popular Criticisms   137
General Words: A Problem   138
Another Problem: Classification   139
Real and Nominal Essence   139
Definition   140
Natural Kinds   141
Real Essence and Substance in General   141
Knowledge: Some Preliminaries   142
Locke and Descartes   143
The Agreement Between Our Ideas   144
Degrees of Knowledge   145
The Extent of Knowledge   145

BIOGRAPHY
George Berkeley (1685-1753)
147

CHAPTER 13
Berkeley: The Denial of Matter
149

Abstract Ideas   149
Ideas of Sense   151
The Argument From Illusion   151
How Berkeley Uses This Argument   153
Another Argument   153
A Criticism of the Argument From Illusion   154
An Alternative View of Perception: Direct Realism   155
Primary and Secondary Qualities   156
Sensible Objects   158
External Objects   159
Material Substance   160

CHAPTER 14
Berkeley: God and Minds
163

Answers to Some Objections   163
Common Sense   164

Unperceived Objects   165
A Causal Argument for God   166
Another Argument for God: Continuity   168
A Nonstandard Interpretation   168
The Spirit or Mind   169
Other Minds   170

BIOGRAPHY
David Hume (1711-1776)
173

CHAPTER 15
Hume: Ideas and Impressions
176

Ideas and Impressions   178
Simple and Complex Perceptions   178
Association   180
Belief   181
Some Problems   181

CHAPTER 16
Hume: Causation
183

Relations of Ideas and Matters of Fact   183
The Causal Relation   184
Universal Causal Axiom   185
The Idea of Cause   185
A Brief Overview   186
Particular Causal Inferences: Inductive Scepticism   187
The Need for Uniformity   189
The Five Strands   190
The Naturalistic Explanation   190
The Two Definitions of Cause   192

CHAPTER 17
Hume: Material Bodies and Identity
195

The Senses and Reason   196
Imagination   197
Constancy and Coherence   197
Identity   198
Constancy   198
Mental Substance   199

Personal Identity 200
Some Problems 200

CONCLUSION
Empiricism
203

Some Comparisons 205
Development 206

Part Three
Kant
209

BIOGRAPHY
Immanuel Kant (1724-1804)
213

CHAPTER 18
Kant: The Transcendental Aesthetic
215

Kant's Aims 215
Transcendental Idealism 217
The Transcendental Aesthetic 217
The Metaphysical Exposition of Space 218
The Argument from Geometry 219
Non-Euclidean Geometry 219
Time 220
Arithmetic 221

CHAPTER 19
Kant: The Analytic of Concepts
223

Concepts 224
The Metaphysical Deduction 225
The Transcendental Deduction 225
The Transcendental Unity of Apperception 227
Objectivity and Experience 228
Noumenal Psychology 230

CHAPTER 20
Kant: The Analytic of Principles
232

The Schematism	232
The First Analogy	234
Another Argument	235
Substance	235
Causation	236
A Necessary Order	236
The Second Analogy	237
The Third Analogy	238
Refutation of Idealism	238
Transcendental Idealism	239
Phenomena and Noumena	240

CHAPTER 21
Kant: The Transcendental Dialectic
243

Paralogisms	244
The First Paralogism: Substance	244
The Second and Third Paralogisms	245
The Antinomies	246
The First Antinomy: Time	247
Time and Reason	247
The Solution	248
The First Antinomy: Space	249
The Second Antinomy: Simples	249
The Third Antinomy: Freedom	250
The Fourth Antinomy: God	252

Suggested Reading   256

Notes   259

Glossary   264

Index   269

Preface

The seven philosophers Descartes, Spinoza, Leibniz, Locke, Berkeley, Hume, and Kant are usually considered to be the major figures of the Modern period (1600–1800). These thinkers grappled with and shaped philosophical problems that are still alive today.

In teaching Modern Philosophy I have found that, in the absence of a comprehensive secondary text, much class-time can be taken up with clarifying the ideas of these philosophers, leaving little room for philosophical discussion of wider issues. This book developed as a response to the needs of my students: it is a general introduction to the claims and arguments of the seven philosophers and is designed to be accessible without being philosophically naive. It contains explanations and critical analyses of their central arguments in metaphysics and epistemology. The book is intended to be read as a companion text to the original works of the philosophers.

The book is organized into three parts:

Part One: Rationalism: Descartes, Spinoza and Leibniz;

Part Two: Empiricism: Locke, Berkeley and Hume;

Part Three: Kant.

The idea that Modern philosophy can be divided into three neat, self-contained groups—the Rationalists, the Empiricists, and Kant—is open to criticism. However, this framework needs to be understood, even if it is ultimately to be rejected. This book presents the reasons why Modern philosophy has been thus portrayed, but at the same time it points out the shortcomings of such a portrayal.

A major purpose of Modern Philosophy courses is to stimulate students to think about certain basic philosophical issues. I have sought to achieve this by connecting the views of the philosophers of the period with some basic contemporary discussions.

At key points the book also presents standard critical assessments of the views and arguments of the philosophers. Offering a companion to the great philosophers without presenting some critical assessment of their ideas would mislead students as to the critical nature of philosophy itself.

Where appropriate, I have attempted to inform students of different, contrasting interpretations of the original texts, but without entering the quagmire of detailed exegesis.

In addition to the book's general introduction, each part has its own introduction and conclusion. There is a brief biography of each of the seven philosophers. At the end of each chapter, two sets of questions appear: self-test questions, to help readers assess their comprehension of the chapter; and discussion questions, to help connect the material in the chapter to wider philosophical issues.

I am indebted to the scholarly work of many writers. I am very grateful to my wife Renata, who helped to edit the manuscript. I would also like to thank Steven Cohen, who gave detailed comments and suggestions on earlier versions of this manuscript. I have benefited greatly from the comments of Drs. Martin Gunderson, Dan Kolak, Adrian Moore, Marshall Missner, and Philip Turetzsky. My thanks to the reviewers of the manuscript: Dennis E. Bradford, State University of New York College at Geneseo; William J. Donlan, Salem State College; Don Garrett, University of Utah; David Owen, University of Arizona; and O. A. Robinson, Central Methodist College. I would also like to thank Colleen Harkins, Jesus Illudian, Nathalie Moore, Ken King, George Calmenson, and the Wadsworth team.

Introduction

The Modern period in philosophy, which roughly spans the years 1600–1800, is traditionally seen as encompassing profound changes in European thinking about the universe and humanity's place in it. These changes were vital to the development of contemporary Western culture and science, and hence twentieth-century life. Despite their dramatic nature, these changes were in fact part of a long process that involved freeing people from the authoritarian tradition of the Church.

The Medieval Period

It is difficult for most of us living now to appreciate the dominating effect of the Church on Europeans during the Medieval period (the years 400–1400). The Church had tremendous wealth and the most imposing buildings, and it was scarcely distinguishable from the king, the state, and the law. Its traditions were thought to be the key to the damnation and salvation of souls. It was the dominating institutional influence on the thinking and feelings of all Europeans; it shaped their view of man's place in the cosmos; and deviation from church doctrine was heresy. While the majority of people labored long hours in the fields and spent much of their time hungry, a small minority did have access to learning; but it was offered exclusively in church institutions, such as monasteries and the few existing universities.

Early Medieval European learning was also influenced by the powerful heritage of the Roman Empire. Scholars were familiar with the Roman poets and prose writers, and all scholarly writing and discussion was conducted in Latin.

This dual influence meant that early thinkers labored to reconcile the traditions of Christian orthodoxy and Roman thought. Because Plato had influenced Roman philosophy, these early attempts to reconcile Christian and non-Christian thought basically aimed to harmonize Christianity with elements of Platonism, as understood by Roman commentators. The most famous of these early writers was St. Augustine (354–430), whose work was definitive until the thirteenth century.

In contrast to the influence of Rome, there was little direct knowledge in early Medieval Europe of the intellectually richer culture of ancient Greece or of the Greek language. This culture was so rich and varied that its rediscovery and absorption into Medieval Europe transformed European thinking by slowly freeing it from the dogma of the Church. The injection of Greek culture into Christian Europe produced many slow changes over the course of what later became known as the Renaissance. The Medieval Renaissance of the twelfth and thirteenth centuries was mainly triggered by the rediscovery of important Greek texts, especially some of the works of Aristotle. The great Renaissance of the fifteenth and sixteenth centuries was in part a response to a flood of translations of many ancient Greek poets, playwrights, scientists, and philosophers.

The slow changes of the Medieval Renaissance began during the twelfth century, following the rediscovery and translation into Latin of some of the more important ancient Greek texts, such as those of Euclid and Ptolemy and especially Aristotle's works in logic and scientific method. These works had been unknown in Europe for many centuries, and their rediscovery gave a new direction and impetus to Medieval learning.

During this period—thanks largely to the Moors living in Spain, who had preserved much of the Aristotelian legacy—Greek thought directly influenced the European tradition. The logical and scientific works of Aristotle, and the interpretations of these by the Arabic thinkers, Avicenna and Averroes, were especially influential. These works emphasized the importance of observation, experiment, and logical argument, as opposed to abstract speculation, an emphasis that had been lacking in the earlier Roman-Platonic tradition.

During the thirteenth century, as more and more of Aristotle's writings were translated, Medieval scholars began to hold his works in awe, recognizing their breadth and depth. This is why Aristotle was called "the master of all those who know." In the thirteenth century Aristotle's works became the common texts for teaching philosophy, with emphasis on his instruction in formalized logical argument.

This reassertion of Aristotelian thought was the seed that, in the Modern period some four centuries later, bore as fruit the formation of science. At first, however, this change expressed itself primarily in attempts to reconcile the revelations of Christianity with the wisdom of Aristotle, to show that faith and reason are in fact in harmony. This new approach to theology, attempting to show that theological claims are consistent with the demands of reason, was especially notable in the work of St. Thomas Aquinas (1226–1274), whose *Summa Theologica* became the main textbook for instruction in theology.

By the fourteenth century, rational thought began to make claims independent of Christianity. The attempt by Aquinas to demonstrate a harmony between faith and reason was denied, especially by William of Ockham (1300–1349), who argued that religious claims must be accepted purely on faith. Ockham also rejected traditional Medieval metaphysics and scholastic theology, arguing that nonrevealed knowledge must be based on experience. In the fourteenth century, Ockham's approach became more influential, especially at the Universities of Paris and Oxford. In other words, science and philosophy slowly separated from theology.

The idea that learning and knowledge could be quite independent of the Church took firmer root in the fifteenth and sixteenth centuries, following the development of the printing press (1450) and the exploration of new continents (1480s onward), both of which enlarged the conception of the known world. These developments gave rise to new breeds of professional men who were devoted to learning but worked outside the ecclesiastical institutions. They began to form a small European community, exchanging ideas through letters and travel. These new men of learning set off a stampede of translations of classical Greek works, apart from those of Aristotle, and liberated the humanistic forces of the Renaissance. For example, the rediscovery of Greek drama in the Renaissance later gave birth to opera, because it was thought that Greek plays had been sung. Partly as a consequence of the growing confidence and liberating influence of the learned men of the Renaissance, two revolutions were quietly brewing.

The first revolution occurred within the Church in 1517, when Luther nailed his 95 theses to the door of a church in Wittenburg. Scandalized by the commercialization and dogmatism of the church, Luther campaigned publicly for its reform. His work was printed and read widely in Germany. Finally Luther gave up the idea of reforming the Catholic Church from within and set up a new church, which led to the proliferation of Protestant Christian sects around Europe. In 1531, for example, Henry VIII formed the Church of England. What had previously been an unthinkable heresy became the new orthodoxy, and the church splintered. This was the first revolutionary challenge to the authority of the Church.

The second revolution took shape through the work of Copernicus, who laid the foundations for the development of modern science. Copernicus produced arguments that the earth revolved around the sun. Thereby he challenged the traditional belief that the planets and stars revolved around the earth, which was assumed to be at the center of the universe. This traditional conception had previously been sanctioned by the combined authority of scripture, Aristotle, and St. Thomas Aquinas. As support for the Copernican revolution gathered strength during the sixteenth century, the Medieval conception of physics, based largely on the writings of Aristotle, was badly eroded; finally, in the seventeenth century, it was overthrown.

The latter half of the sixteenth century saw the beginnings of the Modern era and the steady supplanting of Aristotelian scholasticism by modern science and philosophy. This replacement of Aristotle's investigative method by scientific inquiry, culminating in the work of Sir Isaac Newton (1642–1727), is marked by several important and deep changes:

1. Authority was replaced by observation and reasoning. Up until the late sixteenth century, a common form of scholarly argument for a thesis was to amass relevant supportive quotations and references from authoritative sources such as classical texts, especially those of Aristotle. However, astronomy and mathematics required a different type of demonstration, and their development was therefore important to the process of replacing arguments from authority with direct observation and reasoning. Francis Bacon urged thinkers to reject arguments based on authority and to base their conclusions on experiment and observation. This kind of change gave birth to what is now called *epistemology*—the philosophical study of knowledge itself. It became important to discover the foundations of knowledge, to ensure that learning should not have a false basis. Self-conscious reflection on the sources and standards of knowledge is one of the hallmarks of the Modern period.

2. There was a radical change in the way natural phenomena were explained. Aristotle had distinguished four types of causes: material, formal, efficient, and final.[1] He had argued that the most basic of these four was the final or teleological type of cause. In other words, Aristotle asserted, explaining things in terms of their purpose is the fundamental form of explanation. Many Medieval thinkers took this Aristotelian claim to an extreme and tried to explain natural events, like the falling of stones or the motion of planets, in terms of their divine purpose. Gradually this teleological view of explanation was replaced by a mechanistic view of causation and of the physical universe.

3. Thinking in terms of qualitative analogies was replaced by purely quantitative reasoning. The Medieval mind had conceived of the universe as a hierarchical organic whole, with different levels of being. Between these levels of being, between the macrocosmic universe and the microcosm man, there existed affinities or correspondences. Accordingly, the universe and natural events could be understood as analogous with the human body or a living organism. Thus, for example, storms were viewed as expressions of divine anger; and the relation between the king and the nation was conceived as being patterned on the relation between God and His creation. During the sixteenth century, this way of thinking was replaced by a quantitative paradigm. Galileo was prominent and influential in the attempt to quantify nature. According to him, science should concern itself exclusively with the measurable properties of the world, such as size, shape, and motion. As science developed, the hierarchical view of the universe was undermined and eventually replaced by the scientific paradigm, according to which all natural things exist on the same level, subject to the same physical laws and differing only in quantitative ways. These changes in the mode of thought occurred gradually and in sporadic fits and starts.

The Modern Period

Each era embodies a certain approach to knowledge that rests on deep assumptions that even the best thinkers of the time can hardly articulate, let alone critically examine. These presuppositions are best seen in the aims of the thinkers of the time—in the questions they ask and regard as important, rather than in the detail of their answers.

The spirit of the age began to change during the Modern period (1600–1800), primarily because scientific discoveries undermined the idea that we should acquire knowledge by appealing to authorities. The development of science contained two models of knowledge, however, and both were attractive to thinkers in the Modern age. The first is typified by insistence on the importance of experimentation and observation, on the idea that conclusions based on carefully made observations are less susceptible to error. The second model is based on the example of mathematics, on the idea that reasoning logically from self-evident truths yields mistake-free conclusions. The latter approach was modeled on the work of the ancient Greek mathematician Euclid.

We can give a simplified portrait of Modern philosophy by distinguishing two currents of thought about knowledge, based on these two models: Empiricism and Rationalism. Whereas Empiricists emphasize the empirical, observational source of knowledge, the Rationalists stress the rational nature of knowledge. The Empiricists see the senses and the Rationalists think of reason as the primary source of all knowledge.

According to this picture of modern philosophy, there were three principal Empiricists, all of whom lived in the British Isles:

John Locke	(1632–1704)
George Berkeley	(1685–1753)
David Hume	(1711–1776)

During the same general period, there were three principal Rationalists, all of whom lived on the continent of Europe:

René Descartes	(1596–1650)
Benedict Spinoza	(1632–1677)
Gottfried Leibniz	(1646–1716)

Furthermore, according to this portrait, although Locke stated the principles of Empiricism, he did not realize their full implications, and Berkeley and Hume progressively took these Empiricist principles to their logical conclusion. Similarly, according to the picture, although Descartes laid down the basic principles of Rationalism, he was not entirely consistent in the way he applied them, and Spinoza and Leibniz improved upon Descartes's foundations by taking Rationalism to its logical conclusion.

This portrait of modern philosophy has one more ingredient: the philosophy of Immanuel Kant (1724–1804). Viewing the extreme positions of both Hume and Leibniz as unacceptable, Kant tried to find errors shared by both; in so doing, he rejected the worst in both traditions and retained the best.

Like any caricature, this picture of modern philosophy distorts the truth by giving prominence to certain features at the expense of others. In particular:

1.   By stressing the similarities between the Empiricists in general, on the one hand, and the Rationalists in general, on the other, this picture neglects the similarities between particular Rationalists and particular Empiricists. For example, it neglects the similarities between Leibniz and Berkeley, both of whom denied the reality of matter, or between Descartes and Locke, both of whom claimed that we can only perceive our own ideas.

2.   Similarly, the picture neglects important differences between particular Empiricists or Rationalists. For example, we might be more impressed by the differences between Descartes and Leibniz than by their similarities. Furthermore, we might find the differences between Descartes and Leibniz more striking than those between Descartes and Locke.

3.   The picture neglects many important philosophers of this period, including Francis Bacon, Thomas Hobbes, Pierre Gassendi, Blaise Pascal, Nicolas Malebranche, Thomas Reid, and Christian Wolff. It also neglects a host of lesser-known writers, who were influential at the time.

In short, dividing modern philosophers into Rationalists and Empiricists is an artificial and oversimplified idea that was imposed on the period after the fact. Remembering this, we should not think of Empiricism and Rationalism as two distinct schools of thought.[2] We should instead regard them as two branches of a family, distinguished by certain emphases and a crisscrossing of resemblances, rather than by strictly distinct principles.

The Rationalists

The three philosophers Descartes, Spinoza, and Leibniz are called Rationalists. What they have in common is not so much shared specific beliefs or doctrines, but a shared emphasis and general direction of thought. The label "Rationalism" is vague and was imposed on the Modern period decades after the fact. Moreover, there are important differences among these philosophers.

The primary emphasis they share is the Principle of Sufficient Reason. All three accept and employ strong versions of this principle, which states that everything must have a rational explanation. Spinoza and Leibniz both understand the Principle of Sufficient Reason as implying that all truths in principle are capable of being demonstrated a priori by reasoning, or rational thought alone. This means that we can have a priori knowledge of the world. Since they claim that all truths can in principle be demonstrated a priori, Rationalists believe that a priori knowledge of the world is in principle possible.

Another emphasis common to the Rationalists follows from the first one: because they hold that all truths can in principle be demonstrated a priori (at least by God), Rationalists stress the superiority of reason as a source of knowledge over sense experience. Sense experience is unreliable or otherwise defective as a source of knowledge; its ideas are confused, incomplete, or misleading, and they must be supplemented or corrected by certain principles validated by reason.

Furthermore, since all reasoning consists of analysis and deduction, Rationalists tend toward the view that all truths are necessary. For this reason, Rationalists have problems accounting for contingency. Again, this is a consequence of their acceptance and use of the Principle of Sufficient Reason, which tends to assimilate causation to logical demonstration.

These common general features of Rationalism should not be taken as indicating a uniformity in their views, even when they are viewed in contradistinction to the Empiricists. The Principle of Sufficient Reason is more explicit and prominent in the work of Spinoza and Leibniz than in that of Descartes, and the principle takes different shapes in the writings of Spinoza and Leibniz; Leibniz, unlike Spinoza, links the principle to a theory of truth and to the proposition. Furthermore, weak versions of the Principle of Sufficient Reason can be found, (although not prominently) in some of the arguments of Berkeley and Locke, later labeled "Empiricists." In particular, Locke and Berkeley claim that the ideas of sense perception must have a cause that lies outside us.

Descartes (1596–1650)

René Descartes was born in France in 1596. Joachim Descartes apparently noticed his son's extraordinary curiosity while the boy was still small, for he referred to him as his "little philosopher." In 1606 he was sent to the Jesuit College de la Flèche, a prestigious school enthusiastically patronized by Henry IV.

Between 1614 and 1616, Descartes studied law at Poitiers, after which he began to travel, hoping "to seek no knowledge other than that which could be found in myself or else in the great book of the world . . . testing myself in the situations which fortune offered me." He rejected the basic idea of his classical education—namely, that one could acquire clear knowledge by studying the Greek and Roman classics.

In Holland he met Isaac Beeckman, to whom Descartes's first work (written in 1618) was dedicated. (This was published posthumously: the brief *Compendium Musicae*.) Descartes then enlisted in the army. After he made a visit to Frankfurt to witness the coronation of Ferdinand II, winter weather delayed his return to the army.

On November 10, 1619, stranded alone in a stove-heated room, Descartes began to explore his own thoughts in earnest. He began to doubt all his beliefs. Hours of intense effort brought him to what he believed was a revelation of the unity of all sciences, of all knowledge. He felt that he was in possession of the foundations of one marvelous new science that would dispel confusions. The same night he had three dreams that he felt were divine indications of his philosophical mission. First he saw himself assailed by phantoms, and then staggering around in a kind of whirlwind that seemed to affect no one else. He awoke with a sharp pain, prayed for protection and forgiveness, and meditated on good and evil for almost two hours before sleeping again. In his second dream, a piercing noise startled him awake, and he saw his room full of sparks. This apparently had happened to him on other occasions, so he was able to fall asleep again. The third dream, though not alarming like the first two, was more complicated. It involved, among other things, several books, one of which was a dictionary, another a collection of poems. Opening the latter book he came to the verse "Quod vitae sectabor iter?" ("What road in life shall I follow?") Descartes felt that the dictionary represented a gathering together of all the sciences, while the poetry book indicated philosophy and wisdom combined.

He understood the first two dreams to be a warning concerning his sinful past, and the third to be an indication of how he should work in the future. Resolving to leave the army and pursue his vocation in philosophy, Descartes also vowed to make a pilgrimage to the Shrine of the Virgin at Loreto.

During the 1620s, Descartes continued traveling, in Germany, Holland, Italy, and France. He spent a couple of sociable years living in Paris and became friends with Mersenne, a Franciscan friar who was to remain in close communication with him and to help with the publication of his works.

In 1629 Descartes decided to settle in Holland, where he is said to have liked the climate and the comparative seclusion. He had a number of friends there but kept his address secret from many and conducted philosophical discussions by letter, devoting one day per week to correspondence. He experimented in optics and physiology, preparing himself to explain the unity of the sciences. He visited universities to talk to mathematicians and medical men, and he studied anatomy with the aid of carcasses purchased for dissection from local butchers. By 1630 he was working on a treatise that he believed would explain "all of physics," thus drawing together his various interests. The first part of this work, called *The World,* included such topics as heat, light, and the nature of stars and planets, while a later section was dedicated to human physiology.

Shortly before it was to be published in 1633, however, he heard of Galileo's condemnation by the Inquisition and cautiously suppressed his own work for fear of being similarly censured by the Church. He wrote to Mersenne of his suppressed ideas: "Though I thought they were based on very certain and evident proofs, I would not wish for anything in the world, to maintain them against the authority of the Church." Later, he may have hoped to communicate to lay people, free of theological prejudice, by writing the *Discourse on the Method for Conducting One's Reason Rightly,* as well as three specimen essays that the *Discourse* was intended to introduce, in French (instead of Latin, as was usual). In 1637 the volume was published anonymously to protect Descartes further.

Between 1638 and 1640, Descartes lived mainly in the countryside near Santpoort. During this period he was joined by his former servant, Helène, who had borne him a daughter, Francine. The child died suddenly in 1640, an event that is said to have been a heavy blow to Descartes. Little more is known about his private life.

Descartes's main work, the *Meditations on First Philosophy,* was published with six sets of objections and his replies to them, in 1641. Two years later he began his celebrated correspondence with Princess Elizabeth of Bohemia, in which they discussed a wide range of topics. In 1644, when he published the *Principles of Philosophy,* it was dedicated to Princess Elizabeth. The *Principles* was intended to be a university textbook and is largely concerned with what would now be called scientific matters. His last work *The Passions of the Soul* was said to have been prompted by his discussions with Princess Elizabeth of the relation of mind to body, and the control of passions.

Descartes had another royal correspondent, Queen Christina of Sweden, who later requested that he come to her court and instruct her in philosophy. For several years Descartes had lived quietly in the countryside, where he spent mornings reading and writing in bed and followed a careful diet that included vegetables from his own kitchen garden. When Queen Christina asked him to come to her court and instruct her in philosophy, Descartes was hesitant, but eventually in September of 1649 he embarked for Sweden. He was obliged to give the Queen philosophy lessons three times a week at 5 A.M., in spite of having long had very different habits. He was lonely and unhappy, and only a few months later he caught pneumonia. He died on February 11, 1650.

CHAPTER 1

Descartes: The Method of Doubt and the Cogito

When Descartes was a young man, his personal quest was to discover the fundamental nature of the universe and human beings and to unify science. Determined to sweep aside veils of ignorance and uncertainty and to bring the truth to light once and for all, he reasoned late into the night, in something like the following way:

> I believe many things, but I have no way of knowing which of my beliefs are really true. Most of my knowledge has been acquired haphazardly, in uncritical, unreliable ways. I must start afresh by subjecting my beliefs to a test of doubt. And yet, to test each belief individually would be an endless task, impossible to complete. Therefore I must challenge everything I have so far accepted as truth at its very roots. I must expose and attack the principles upon which all my opinions have rested. I can then use the principles that survive my test of doubt as a new foundation for knowledge. This rebuilding of my knowledge must be painstakingly methodical; only then shall I be assured of knowing the truth.

Descartes's revolutionary idea consists of using doubt explicitly and systematically as a tool for reaching certainty. The method has three elements:

1. Descartes wishes his doubt to be reasonable and systematic. He is not merely saying that it is logically possible for us to doubt; he is making the

stronger claim that it is reasonable for us to do so. He argues that we do not really know much of what we claim to know.

2. Descartes compares his Method of Doubt to emptying a barrel of apples and then returning to the barrel only the apples that are edible. Doubt functions as a sorting agent; beliefs that succumb to it are rotten and must be discarded. Beliefs that survive the Method of Doubt are worthy of being kept, because they have proved themselves to be clear and trustworthy.

3. The doubt-tested beliefs are to be used later in a reconstruction of Descartes's knowledge. Beliefs that pass the test of doubt are to be used as a secure and certain foundation for the rebuilding of knowledge. They function much as axioms do in geometry.

The process of rebuilding knowledge aims to achieve certainty through rejection of the uncertain. Therefore, many of the beliefs over which the First Meditation casts doubt are eventually vindicated in later Meditations, but only by appeal to truths of reason. Descartes later vindicates belief in the visible by appeal to Reason.

The Method of Doubt as presented in the First Meditation consists of three stages, each stage entertaining a progressively more radical doubt.[3] In the first stage, Descartes remarks that many of his beliefs are derived from sense perception, which has deceived him in the past. He says that it is foolish to trust something that has been known to deceive us. Because our senses can mislead us, especially with small and distant objects, we should not trust them. This consideration alone is insufficient to raise a universal doubt, however, because—although many particular beliefs derived from the senses can be doubted—others still seem certain. Descartes says that he cannot doubt that he has a body and that he is now sitting in front of the fire merely on the grounds that his senses sometimes misled him.

In the second stage, Descartes asks how he can be certain that he is not dreaming. He recalls that he has sometimes dreamed that he is awake and sitting by the fire just as he actually is now. Although dreams are often more chaotic than waking experiences, it can be impossible to distinguish between a dream state and reality. There are no internal criteria or signs by which one can tell whether one is awake or merely dreaming. How can you be SURE that you are not dreaming at this moment? Any given situation COULD be an illusion: it could be a dream. Descartes asserts, however, that this argument is not enough to legitimate a universal doubt, since dreams must be made up of elements from reality, and these simple elements, such as shape, size, number, and time, must be real. And even supposing that you are now dreaming, a priori beliefs like "two plus three equals five" and "a square only has four sides" cannot be doubted and still seem obvious.

To call even these beliefs into question, Descartes introduces the third and most radical stage of his Method of Doubt. This is the hypothesis of the deceiving spirit or evil genius; Descartes supposes that there might be a supremely powerful and intelligent spirit who does his utmost to deceive us. Such a deceiving spirit could cause our powers of reasoning to make mistakes so that we might even be deceived into thinking that two plus three equals five, when in fact it does not.

Descartes is not asserting that such a deceiving spirit actually exists; however, he is asserting that such a spirit could exist and, moreover, that if such a spirit did exist, we would not know it. In other words, the evidence that we now have is entirely consistent with the existence of such a deceiving spirit. We have no positive reason for believing that such a demon does not exist. It seems that the possibility of a deceiving spirit leaves none of our former beliefs free from legitimate doubt, including both a priori and empirical beliefs. At this third stage of the Method, doubt is as universal and radical as it can be. Any beliefs that are immune to this kind of doubt must be certain, and therefore must count as knowledge that can be used as a rational foundation for other knowledge.

Comments on the Three Stages

1. The Argument from Sensory Illusion

It is tempting to argue from the assertion that every single sense experience could be an illusion to the conclusion that all sense experiences could be a collective illusion. However this argument involves a fallacy, because the universal possibility of illusion does not entail the possibility of universal illusion.[4] It is a fallacy of composition to argue that, because each single X is F, the collection of all X's is F. All the same, Descartes does, in fact, argue that all sense-experience collectively could be an illusion—based on his hypothesis of the possibility of a deceiving spirit.

Could we really be so deceived and mistaken? Is it possible that, in spite of what our senses seem to tell us, reality may be quite different? Recently some philosophers, such as Austin, have argued that universal illusion in sense perception is an impossibility.[5] The possibility of the senses deceiving us presupposes that sometimes they do not. Descartes says that he has sometimes caught his senses deceiving him. This is his reason for mistrusting them. But if he knows that they have deceived him, this is because sometimes they have not deceived him. For example, a stick placed in water appears bent, but I know that this is merely an optical illusion only because I can see that the stick is not bent once it is out of the water. If Austin is right, the argument from sensory illusion on its own does not support a very widespread doubt, as Descartes himself attests.

2. The Argument from Dreaming

Similar points can be made about the argument from dreaming. Some philosophers have argued that I could not entertain the possibility of being asleep now unless I had experienced being awake, because the very idea of a dream requires a contrast with waking experience. The possibility of dream experiences requires that some experiences not be dreams.

However, Descartes could insist that this point does not undermine his second stage of doubt, because we are not certain of being able to distinguish the dreaming and waking states. Many people have had vivid dreams that, at the time, they were convinced were real waking experiences. Even if it is impossible that I dream all the time, it is still possible that I am dreaming now.

3. The Deceiving Spirit Argument

Descartes himself admits that the first two stages of doubt lead to a modest scepticism concerning particular sense experience. But the third stage of doubt introduces a radical scepticism about sense experience as a whole and about the powers of reason. For if I am being deceived by an evil spirit, it could be that I am mistaken in thinking that my sense experiences correspond to and are caused by external objects at all. Descartes does not suppose that a deceiving spirit really does exist; he merely points out that there is no evidence in our experience to rule out the existence of such a spirit. The mere possibility of a demon provides grounds to doubt that the external world exists at all. On the other hand, the sense illusion and dream arguments seem to presuppose that it does exist.

What Is Descartes's Method of Doubt?

At this point one might be forgiven for suspecting that Descartes's aim was to prove all human beliefs false; his thinking seems to mock what common sense bids us to accept as true or obvious. Yet even the full title of the *Meditations* indicates that Descartes had a very different intention. Ultimately he sought to demonstrate "the existence of God and the distinction between mind and body." He wished to do this in a rational, scientific way. As a contemporary of Galileo and a gifted mathematician himself, he hoped to replace his uncritical assumptions and the prejudices of sense experience with rational certainty—with truths that could be proved rationally from self-evident premises. In his synopsis to the *Meditations* he explains:

> But although the utility of a doubt so general may not at first be apparent, it is nevertheless very great, in that [such doubt] delivers us from all sorts of prejudices, and prepares for us a very easy way of accustoming our mind to detaching itself from the senses and finally, in that it brings it about that it is no longer possible that we can have any doubt about that which we afterwards discover to be true.[6]

When Descartes says that we should treat our beliefs as though they were false, he does not mean that they are false. He means that we should suspend judgment as to their truth, rather than hesitantly believing them. According to Descartes, believing involves both having an idea in one's mind and also judging that idea to be true. To assent to the idea of p is to believe p; to deny the idea of p is to disbelieve p. When one doubts p, however, one suspends judgment as to the truth or falsity of p. To doubt a belief is not to deny or to disbelieve it; it is to suspend judgment.

In effect, Descartes's Method of Doubt amounts to withholding the judgment that anything in the external world corresponds to or causes an idea in the mind. It presupposes that ideas are the immediate objects of cognition and that the external world is known only mediately through these ideas. In other words, Descartes claims that we can only directly perceive our own ideas. This claim, which is also vital to the Empiricists, is required by his Method of Doubt.

Some Criticisms of Descartes's Scepticism

Descartes implies that the scepticism raised by his Method of Doubt is reasonable; in response to it, he tries to vindicate some of his former beliefs, as we shall see later. Some twentieth-century philosophers, however, have expressed doubts about the legitimacy of a thoroughgoing scepticism like Descartes's. These philosophers have questioned the legitimacy of doubting the existence of the external world and have challenged some of the assumptions on which doubt or Descartes's scepticism may depend. Not all philosophers agree with Descartes that it is genuinely possible to doubt the existence of the external world.

First, Descartes's Method of Doubt seems to assume that the immediate objects of perception or cognition are ideas in the mind of the perceiver, rather than being truly objects in the real world. He implies that whatever is out there cannot be known by me; I can only know my own ideas. As we shall see in later chapters, some more recent philosophers, including Kant, argue that this claim is suspect. Against Descartes they argue that we directly perceive objects in the external world. If they are right, and if there are good reasons for thinking that the immediate objects of perception are external objects and not mental ideas, then sense experience gives us direct access to the external world and Cartesian doubt is problematic (see Chapters 13 and 20).

Second, when he thinks, for instance, "perhaps an evil demon exists," Descartes assumes that the words used to express such thoughts have meaning. Meaningful language is treated as a given, and is not subjected to the process of doubt to which Descartes is otherwise committed. Descartes seems to be assuming that words can have a purely private meaning by standing for his own ideas. This assumption itself is open to doubt. Many contemporary philosophers hold that meaningful language is essentially a public and social phenomenon—one that cannot be regarded as purely private. The very idea of meaningful language may cast doubt on Descartes's Method of Doubt.[7]

Third, for Descartes, doubt can be purely contemplative. He explains that the

Method of Doubt is restricted solely to theoretical inquiry and is not to be brought into practical matters. Descartes says that no one of sound mind has ever doubted that there really is a world. Nevertheless, he claims that a theoretical doubt about the existence of the world is possible and reasonable. But it has been argued that a solely contemplative doubt that makes no difference in practice is merely an empty verbal utterance. In normal circumstances, when we doubt something, our doubt has at least the potential to affect our behavior. For example, if I doubt that I have turned off the stove, I may return home to check on it. Is the potential for some outward sign of doubt essential in order for the word *doubt* to be meaningful? If it is, what would be an outward sign of doubting that the external world exists? Perhaps all behavior manifests a belief in the existence of the external world. For example, if a person who claims to doubt that the world exists tries to communicate her doubt, she must surely believe that other people exist with whom to communicate. The communication of a universal doubt seems self-defeating.

Descartes's Method of Doubt is presented in the *Meditations* in the first-person singular. Instead of asking questions like "What is known?" and "What can we know?" Descartes asks "What can I know?" Descartes finds himself in the world of his own ideas asking whether anything in the external world matches his ideas. Had Descartes asked a different question, he might not have found himself in this egocentric predicament. For instance, if he had asked "What can we know?" he would have already committed himself to the existence of other minds and possibly also to a common public world in which they live.

Finally, Descartes assumes that knowledge requires absolute certainty and that, whenever there is any room for doubt, one cannot claim to know. This requirement sets a standard for knowledge that is arguably too high. If by "absolute certainty" we mean a circumstance in which doubt is logically impossible, then such certainty may not be necessary for knowledge. Against Descartes it has been argued that knowledge requires reasonable justification, not absolute certainty. This does not mean, however, that we can specify once and for all when it is reasonable to doubt and when it is not. It does mean that knowledge is possible, even if absolute certainty is not guaranteed, because doubt is always logically possible.

Of course, this brief description of some contemporary arguments against Descartes's scepticism is not conclusive. It shows, however, that we should not simply accept Descartes's scepticism without further argument, because the Method of Doubt may itself rest on questionable assumptions.

The Cogito as the End of Doubt

A systematic application of the Method of Doubt has apparently left Descartes with nothing: all of his ideas might be illusions. But in the Second Meditation doubt ends with this thought: a malicious demon could not deceive me into falsely believing that I exist. Even on the hypothesis of a demon who is trying to deceive me, I cannot doubt that I exist without also supposing that I exist. The possibility of a deceiving demon cannot function as a reason for my doubting my own existence. I cannot doubt my own existence, because I can be certain of my own existence merely from the fact that I am doubting. Furthermore, doubting is only one species of thought, and I can be certain of my existence merely from the fact that I am thinking—whatever I am thinking. Therefore, the inference "I doubt therefore I am" can be generalized to "I think therefore I am" or "Cogito ergo sum." The inference "Cogito ergo sum" is often simply called the "Cogito," and we shall follow this general practice.

By the term *thought,* Descartes means a range of mental states such that he who experiences them is immediately aware of them. Thinking thus includes doubting, willing, feeling, and imagining—as well as any other mental activity that the doer is immediately aware of. The Cogito is supposed to guarantee you knowledge of your own existence. One reason it does this is that, if something is thinking, then it follows that this thing exists. Moreover, I can always be certain that I am thinking when I am. I cannot be mistaken about the fact that I am thinking. Descartes often presupposes that conscious states of mind are evident: if I am thinking then I must know that I am. In addition, thought is assumed to be incorrigible; if I believe that I am thinking, then it is true that I am thinking. These two features of conscious mental states mean that I cannot be mistaken or ignorant of any feature of my conscious mental life.

Now we can see the special importance of the Cogito in comparison to other apparently similar inferences. For instance, the following inference is valid and similar in form to the Cogito:

I am walking therefore I am.

What distinguishes this inference from the Cogito is the fact that the Method of Doubt would call into question the premise "I am walking." Although the inference is valid, the premise is open to doubt, and therefore, so is the conclusion. The Cogito, on the other hand, assures one with certainty that one exists, because the inference is valid and the premise "I am thinking" is free from doubt. I cannot doubt that I am thinking because to doubt is to be thinking. Thus, so long as I am conscious of a thought, I can be certain of my own existence.

As we have seen, Descartes often takes conscious states of mind to be both incorrigible and evident. Descartes's theory also implies that I can be certain of the content of my mental states as long as these states are described in the right way. For if a mental state is described in a way that entails the existence of an external object, then I cannot be certain that I am in that state described in that way. I cannot be certain that I am now seeing a table because I cannot be certain that there is a table to be seen. However, the same mental states can be described in a way that does not imply the existence of any external object; and under such a description, the mental states can be known with certainty. I can now be certain that I am having the experience of seeming to see a table, even if there is no real table to be seen. So long as we can and do describe our mental states in a way that does not imply the existence of material objects, we can be certain that we are experiencing those mental states.

The Interpretation of the Cogito

So far we have treated the Cogito as an inference from the indubitable premise "I am thinking" to the conclusion "I exist." The conclusion is supposed to be certain because the inference is valid and the premise is indubitable. But it is disputable whether Descartes intended the Cogito as an inference.

1. The Cogito as a Performance

A sentence like "I exist" verifies itself whenever it is spoken or thought. Similarly, the sentence "I don't exist" is self-defeating; the content of the sentence defeats or undermines the act of asserting it. Hintikka has used the "existential self-verifiability" of the sentence "I exist" to propose a performative interpretation of the Cogito.[8] According to this interpretation, the "I think" part of the Cogito refers to the thought-act of trying to convince oneself that one does not exist. It is in this thought-act that the self-defeating nature of "I don't exist" reveals itself. The certainty of one's own existence is said to consist in the self-defeating nature of the thought-act "I don't exist."

It is important to realize the difference between this interpretation of the Cogito and the interpretation that takes the Cogito to be an inference. According to the standard interpretation of the Cogito as an inference, the Cogito consists of two propositions, "I think" and "I exist," which stand in the logical relation of premise to conclusion. According to the Hintikka interpretation, the Cogito consists of one proposition "I exist." The proposition "I am thinking" is not itself essential if the Cogito is a performance. The act of thinking—not the proposition that records this act—is essential to the Cogito if it is a performance. Furthermore, on the performative model, this act of thinking must consist of the act of thinking to oneself that one does not exist. On this model, we do not have two propositions that stand in the logical relation of premise to conclusion, but a thought-act that relates to one's own existence as process to product. As Hintikka says, "the indubitability of my own existence results from my thinking of it almost as the sound of music results from playing it."

There are several reasons for rejecting the performance interpretation of the Cogito. Descartes discusses the certainty of his own existence not only in the Second Meditation but also in the *Principles of Philosophy* and *The Search After Truth*. But it is only in the Second Meditation that the thought in the Cogito is a thought about his own existence. The performance interpretation is implausible for the other presentations of the Cogito. Moreover, as we have already seen, the term *think* or *cogito* is used by Descartes very broadly to cover a wide range of conscious mental states. The word *cogito* refers to any mental state of which we are immediately aware. If the Hintikka interpretation is correct, the term must refer to the act of professing to oneself that one does not exist. But Descartes does not use the word *cogito* in this narrow way when he says "Cogito ergo sum." In the *Principles* he says, "We can draw the same conclusion from all the other things which come into our thought; namely that we who think them exist."

2. The Cogito as an Intuition

Some interpreters have seen the Cogito as a simple appeal to intuition. For Descartes, intuition is similar to seeing with the intellect: the mind can just immediately see or intuit that certain self-evident truths (such as "a triangle has three sides") are true. Descartes says in the *Rules for the Direction of the Mind* that each person can intuit his own existence. The certainty of the Cogito has been taken by some commentators to be a matter of merely intuiting that one exists. However this interpretation ignores the presentation of the Cogito as an inference between two propositions—that is, as an inference from "I am thinking" to "I am."

We can deny that the certainty of the Cogito is simply a matter of intuition without also having to neglect the role that intuition has to play in the inference from "I am thinking" to "I am." If the Cogito is an inference, it still requires intuition of the fact that one is thinking. The premise "I am thinking" must be intuitively certain if the conclusion "I am" is to be certain. According to Descartes, intuition is also required for seeing that the conclusion does in fact follow from the premise.

3. The Cogito as an Inference

If the Cogito is an inference, what inference is it? In the *Second Replies,* Descartes denies that the Cogito is a syllogistic inference involving the premise "Everything that thinks exists." He denies this because this general proposition is only known from what the individual perceives in himself—namely, that it is impossible that he should think if he does not exist. Thus we may suppose that Descartes is willing to admit "It is impossible to think without existing" as a presupposition of the Cogito. Clearly Descartes regards the connection between thinking and existence as a necessary one. Moreover, the presupposition "It is impossible to think without existing" does not make any reference to anything in the external world. It can be intuitively grasped without being subject to doubt. On the other hand, the statement "Everything that thinks exists" might be taken as an existential claim, and then it would not be immune from doubt.

We may conclude that the Cogito is an inference having the indubitable premise "I am thinking." Given the intuitive supposition "It is impossible to think without existing," the conclusion "I exist" is also indubitable. But although this is the preferred interpretation of the Cogito, it is not without problems. It is difficult to render this interpretation consistent with several passages in Descartes's writings—for instance, the following passage from the *Second Replies*. In the *Second Replies,* Descartes says, "He who says 'I think therefore I am or exist' does not deduce existence from thought by a syllogism, but by a simple act of mental vision, recognizes it as if it were a thing known per se."[9]

A Famous Criticism of the Cogito

Some commentators, including Russell,[10] have objected to the occurrence of the word "I" in the premise "I am thinking." According to Russell, Descartes has no right to the premise "I am thinking," but only to the weaker claim "there is a thought."

This objection to Descartes's Cogito can be expressed in the form of a dilemma. Either we have an idea of what is meant by "I" where this is an idea of an "I" that has thoughts but is not identical with those thoughts; or we do not have this idea, and the "I" is simply identical with those thoughts. Either way, the Cogito does not work. If we accept the first alternative, the premise "I am thinking" will yield the conclusion "I exist." But according to this alternative, "I am thinking" is not a suitable premise for the Cogito. The premise of the Cogito is put forward as indubitable, but according to Russell, "I am thinking" is not indubitable. It is open to doubt whether there is an "I" that thinks and is not identical with these thoughts. Hume, for instance, challenges the notion of a self distinct from thoughts and perceptions. Since the idea is open to doubt, it is illegitimate for the word "I" to appear in the premise of the Cogito.

If we admit this and accept the second alternative, there is no justification for the word "I" to appear in the Cogito at all. If what is meant by "I" is simply the occurrence of thought, then the premise should be "there is thought." But from this premise, the conclusion "I exist" cannot be inferred.

Descartes could make two responses to this challenge. First of all, there is good reason for using the word "I" in the premise "I am thinking." The reason is that thinking, like green, is a property, and if there is a property there must be something which has this property. That which has a property Descartes calls a substance. There cannot be thinking without there being something that thinks, just as, if there is green, there must be something that is green. The existence of a property requires the existence of a substance or thing that has this property.

Although this response is reasonable, it is not clear that Descartes is entitled to make it since the Method of Doubt should lead him to question whether thinking really is a property. He should not merely assume that it is a property, given his scepticism. Second, Descartes is careful to point out just after the Cogito that he has not yet reached any conclusion about the nature of this "I" that thinks. When Descartes concludes that he can be certain he exists, he has not committed himself to his nature except that he thinks. Descartes seeks to establish what his essential nature is in the Second Meditation. By the end of that Meditation, he concludes that he is a thing whose essence is to think. However, he does not assume this in the Cogito.

Conclusion

If we practice the Method of Doubt, we shall call into question many of our former beliefs. It is then important to find a way of removing these doubts. Whatever beliefs survive the Method of Doubt will be certain and these will be an appropriate new foundation for knowledge.

The most powerful reason for doubt is the possibility of a malicious demon. But even this hypothesis cannot lead me to doubt my own existence and doubt that I am having an idea while I am having it. According to Descartes, these two beliefs, then, can serve as foundations in the reconstruction of knowledge.

The next step is for Descartes to discover his own nature. In the Second Meditation, he concludes that his essence is to think; Descartes reaches this conclusion from the certainty of the Cogito. Later we shall return to this step in Descartes's argument.

Having proved that he exists and that he is a thinking thing, Descartes must show that some of his ideas are true. He must show that some of his ideas correspond to objects in the external world. At the beginning of the Third Meditation, Descartes says that what assures him of the certainty of the Cogito is that he perceives clearly and distinctly that, in order to think, he must exist. So the certainty of the Cogito suggests to Descartes a general criterion of certainty and truth. He claims that it can be a general rule that whatever we perceive clearly and distinctly is true. But in order to guarantee that our clear and distinct ideas do represent something real, Descartes seeks to prove the existence of God. Once the existence of God has been proved, we can be certain that clear and distinct ideas are true, because God would not deceive us about what seems evident. Thus Descartes's proof of the existence of God is the next necessary step in his path towards rebuilding knowledge upon secure foundations.

At the end of the First Meditation Descartes is locked into the prison of his own current ideas, unable to know anything beyond them. If his later attempts to secure certainty and knowledge of the external world by proving the existence of God fail, he will be saddled with radical scepticism. Of course, one way to avoid this scepticism is to challenge Descartes's starting position—that is, his Method of Doubt.

Study Questions

1. How and why does Descartes try to doubt whatever can be doubted? What is his Method of Doubt?

2. For what reason does Descartes suppose that a deceiving spirit might exist?

3. Is Descartes certain that the external world does not exist?

4. How does Descartes distinguish between doubt and disbelief?

5. Why is Descartes certain that he exists?

6. What is the Cogito?

Discussion Questions

1. Is Descartes being reasonable in seeking foundations for knowledge?

2. Is it really possible to doubt the existence of the external world?

Descartes: God

At the beginning of the Third Meditation, Descartes is certain of his own existence, that his nature is to think, and of his ideas or modes of consciousness. But he is not certain that anything exists in the external world to correspond to those ideas. In order to show that knowledge of the external world is possible, Descartes seeks to prove the existence of God. He must prove the existence of God from knowledge that he has already shown to be certain—that is, from his knowledge of his own ideas. Descartes has two major proofs for the existence of God, and both of these spring from the fact that he, Descartes, has an idea of God.

Once Descartes has proved God's existence, he can show that some of his ideas represent reality. If God exists, then the hypothesis of an evil genius is certainly false, because God would not permit an evil genius to deceive him. Indeed, the hypothesis of an evil genius was the main reason for doubting the existence of an external world. Second, if he can be sure that God does exist, then Descartes can treat his faculties of judgment as reliable. He can be sure that he has a true belief whenever he assents to a clear and distinct idea. In this way, the idea of God as guarantor forms a bridge that enables Descartes to pass from knowledge about his own ideas to knowledge about the external world.

The Classification of Ideas

In the Third Meditation, before undertaking to prove God's existence, Descartes attempts to classify his ideas in order to discover which of them may properly be called true or false.[11] This is an appropriate time for us to examine his theory of ideas.

Descartes does not use the term *idea* discriminately. At different times the word stands for mental capacities and abilities, for concepts, for mental episodes (like the experience of pain), for mental acts such as willing, believing and fearing, and for the content of these acts and episodes. Although Descartes uses the term *idea* to cover all of these, many differences are involved in such a broad range of phenomena. For instance, the ability to perceive heat should be distinguished from an actual sensation of heat, and this is quite different again from the concept of heat itself. Descartes himself notes one possible ambiguity of the term *idea*. In the Preface to the *Meditations,* he claims that the term stands for both the act of understanding and also "what is represented by this act"; he says that the act of understanding should be distinguished from what is understood.

The distinction between an act and the object of that act is important for Descartes's claim that ideas considered in themselves cannot, strictly speaking, be false. In the Third Meditation, where Descartes makes this claim, he uses the term *idea* in a more specific sense than usual, to indicate the content or object of a mental act, which he likens to the picture of an object. The acts of willing *p,* fearing *p,* imagining *p,* desiring *p,* and judging "that *p*" share a common object or content, which Descartes calls the idea of *p.* But these acts differ in what is done to that object. The act of desiring or imagining *p* is neither true nor false. Similarly the idea of *p* is neither true nor false. Only the judgment "that *p*" can be either true or false.

Although Descartes recognized some of the problems of his terminology, it still creates confusions. This is perhaps most apparent in his famous theory of innate ideas. In the Third Meditation, he says that some of his ideas seem innate, some seem acquired, and others seem fictitious or devised by his mind's own invention.[12] He is careful to point out that he has as yet no clear view of the actual origin of any of these ideas. They could all be innate or fictitious, rather than acquired from anything external to the mind. In particular, the fact that some ideas do not depend on the will does not necessarily mean that they proceed from external objects. Although it is natural to suppose that these involuntary ideas or sensations are caused by external objects, this is not certain, because they might be caused by some unconscious faculty of the mind, as are dreams.

The preceding passage in the *Meditations* suggests a threefold classification of ideas, according to their origin. But it is clear from Descartes's other writings that this is misleading. In a sense, all ideas are innate. To Mersenne, Descartes wrote "I hold that all ideas that involve no affirmation or negation are innate."[13] Ideas are innate not in the sense that they have been hanging in some mental picture-gallery since a person's birth, but in the sense that it is in the nature of the mind to produce them. The ideas of color, sound, or pain are innate in the sense that the mind has an innate ability to experience or feel them. The distinction between innate and acquired ideas is not that some ideas (like the idea of God) are innate and others (like the idea of color) are acquired. The distinction is that, as a capacity, all ideas are innate and that, as an experience or mental event, they are adventitious (see *Notes Against a Program*).[14] The possibility of having ideas of various types (such as color) is innate, while the actual having of particular ideas is not. All ideas are innate for Descartes in the sense that mental capacities are not acquired through experience. When later Empiricist philosophers, like Locke, attacked the doctrine of innate ideas, they were arguing against the possibility of innate knowledge—knowledge not acquired through sense experience (see Chapter 10). They were not arguing against the possibility of innate mental capacities, and in fact were confused over this point.

The Idea of God

Descartes's arguments for the existence of God develop from the premise that he, Descartes, has this idea. In order for anyone else to be convinced of God's existence, therefore, it would be necessary for them also to be convinced that they too have an idea of God.

The idea of God is of a perfect, eternal, infinite creator. Some of Descartes's contemporaries denied having this idea. Descartes gave one swift reply to their claim: one need not know that one has this idea in order to have it. To have an idea of God, one is not obliged to conceive of God, for this idea might simply be an innate capacity to conceive Him. Furthermore, if a person denies having an idea of God, Descartes can reply that, if the person understands the words he is using to make this denial, then he does have an idea of God.

Nevertheless, Descartes does offer to demonstrate that there is an idea of God. Typical of his ingenious economy of thought, Descartes uses as a premise the already certain fact that he doubts. To doubt is to lack a perfection, and from the fact that he doubts, Descartes concludes that he is imperfect. Because he has an idea of imperfection, he concludes that he also has an idea of absolute perfection, and hence of an absolutely perfect being—God. However, this argument fails because it trades on an ambiguity in the term *idea*. If I know that I am imperfect, it may follow that I know the meaning of the term *perfect,* but it does not follow that I have a coherent concept of an absolutely perfect being, nor that I have an idea of absolute perfection.

Early commentators on Descartes (like Gassendi[15]) have argued that, even if we use the word *God* meaningfully, this does not show that we have an idea of an infinite perfect being. A finite mind cannot comprehend an infinite being. Descartes's rather unsatisfactory reply was to distinguish understanding and comprehension. He says that we do have a clear and distinct idea of an infinite being, but not an adequate or complete idea of God's being infinite. We understand that God is an infinite being, but we do not comprehend how he is infinite.

The First Proof of the Existence of God

The first proof of the existence of God, which occurs in the Third Meditation, is basically a causal proof.[16] Since Descartes is only certain of his own ideas or modes of consciousness at this stage of inquiry, he can use only that knowledge as the premise of his proof. In effect, he argues that the idea of God must have been caused by God.

The idea of God must have a cause, for nothing comes of nothing. Descartes accepts the principle that everything must have a cause as self-evident. This claim, called the Principle of Sufficient Reason, is one of the foundation stones of Rationalism and is a basic assumption in the thought of Leibniz and Spinoza. Descartes claims that this Principle of Sufficient Reason implies another proposition—one that we can call the Principle of Adequate Reality—which he formulates as follows: "There must be at least as much reality in the total efficient cause as in the effect." In other words, if A has less reality than B, then B cannot have been caused by A. Although Descartes says that this Principle of Adequate Reality is self-evident, he supports it with analogies. He says, for example, that heat cannot be induced in a substance except by something at least as hot. He also claims that the Principle of Adequate Reality is implied by the Principle of Sufficient Reason. For, if the effect has more reality than its cause, then the surplus reality would have no cause, and this would contravene the idea that everything must have a cause.

Descartes explains the notion of degrees of reality as follows. Substances have more reality than properties, because the existence of properties depends on the existence of substances. Thus, heaviness exists only insofar as heavy things or substances exist. In this sense, substances have more reality than properties. In a similar way, God has more reality than any finite substance, because the level of being (or degree of reality) of God is such that finite substances depend for their existence on God. This in itself does not show that God exists; rather, it means that the idea of God is a representation of a substance that has a higher degree of reality than any finite substances. A unicorn has a higher degree of reality than the color white, even though unicorns do not actually exist; similarly, the fact that God has a higher degree of reality than finite things does not show that God actually does exist, but rather it shows what His position is in the scale of being if He does exist. From what has been said so far, we can conclude that there are at least three levels of being or degrees of reality: the lowest, properties; the middle, finite substances; and the highest, God, an infinite substance.

To prove that God does exist, Descartes applies the Principle of Adequate Reality to his ideas—in particular, to his idea of God—but he does so in a rather strange way. He applies it to the content of his ideas rather than to their status as modes of consciousness. As modes of consciousness, all my ideas are equal; they are all properties of a finite substance, namely my mind. In this respect my ideas of whiteness, of myself and of God are not different from each other: as my ideas they are properties of my mind, and as such all belong to the lowest of the three levels of being. Despite this, these ideas do differ in their content or in what they represent. My idea of white represents a certain property of finite things; my idea of a unicorn represents a finite substance; and my idea of God represents an infinite and all-perfect substance.

Descartes inquires into the origin of his ideas, especially his idea of God, by applying the Principle of Adequate Reality to the content of his ideas. He says that an idea needs a cause with at least as much reality as the content of that idea. In other words, every idea must have a cause equal in reality to what it is an idea of. If A has a lesser degree of reality than B, then an idea of B cannot have been caused by A. Descartes supports this application of the Principle of Adequate Reality of ideas with an appeal to the idea of a complex machine (in the *Principles* I.17). If a person has an idea of a complicated machine, we may ask from where he obtained this idea. Either he has seen such a machine made by someone else or he has the sophistication or complexity of mind to have thought of it himself. The existence of such an idea requires a cause of adequate complexity. This is the kind of consideration that led Descartes to believe that the cause of an idea must have at least as much reality as what the idea represents. This is what makes the idea of God so special. Only God Himself has a sufficient degree of reality to cause the idea of God. Descartes says that a finite being such as himself could not be the cause of his idea of God, because finite beings possess less reality than God and thus are not adequate to cause the idea of God. Since Descartes has an idea of God, he concludes that God must exist.

As for the idea of external objects, Descartes says "that they might have possibly proceeded from myself."[17] The idea of an external substance or object could be invented by the mind, because the mind itself is a finite substance.

We can summarize Descartes's first argument for the existence of God as follows:

1. I have an idea of God.

2. This idea must have a cause.

3. There cannot be less reality in the cause than in the effect.

4. If the cause of my idea of God were anything but God, there would be less reality in the cause than in the effect (because the degree of reality of an idea is determined by what it is an idea of).

---

5. Therefore, God exists.

The first premise was discussed in the previous section. Descartes would support the second premise with the Principle of Sufficient Reason and the third with the Principle of Adequate Reality. The fourth premise is the Principle of Adequate Reality applied to the content of ideas, or to what they represent.

When he explains the Principle of Adequate Reality and how it should be applied to the content of our ideas, Descartes uses terminology that is unusual for us today. He contrasts the objective and formal properties of ideas. The terms *objective* and *formal* are not being used in their usual contemporary sense. Descartes uses the phrase "the objective properties of an idea" to stand for the content of the idea or what the idea is of. The objective properties of an idea are its representative properties—the properties it has as a representation. My idea of a unicorn has the objective property of being of the idea of a substance, even though unicorns do not exist.

The objective or representational properties of an idea are contrasted with its formal properties. The formal properties of an idea are the properties it has as a mode of consciousness. If I now think of Christopher Columbus arriving in the New World in 1492, the formal time of the thought is the time at which I have the thought—that is, 1992. The objective time of this thought is 1492.

As we have seen, Descartes argues that the Principle of Adequate Reality should be applied to the content of ideas or to what they are ideas of. Descartes expresses this point by saying that the principle should be applied to the objective rather than to the formal properties of ideas.

What should we make of this first argument for the existence of God? First, there is an ambiguity in the notion of "degrees of reality." Whereas modes logically depend on the existence of substances, created substances only causally depend on God. Consequently there is no uniform property of reality that things possess in varying degrees. Modes depend on substances in quite a different way from that in which created substances are supposed to depend on God.

We might also challenge Descartes's Principle of Adequate Reality on other grounds. But, more important, even if we grant that principle to Descartes, there are problems with the way he specifically applies it to ideas. In order for Descartes to arrive at his desired conclusion—namely, that the idea of God must be caused by God—it is not sufficient for him to apply the principle to ideas merely as modes of consciousness (that is, to their formal properties). As a mode of consciousness, the idea of God has the same degree of reality as any other idea; it is merely a property of a substance, a mind. As a mode of consciousness the idea of God, like any other idea, need only be caused by a finite substance; it could be invented by the mind. In order to reach his desired conclusion, Descartes must apply the Principle of Adequate Reality to the content of his ideas (that is, to their objective properties). This is the crucial turning point of his argument, yielding the required premise 4: the cause of an idea must have as much reality as what the idea is of. But why should we accept this special application of the principle? In answer to this, Descartes only has the analogy with the idea of a complex machine, which is a weak argument.

The analogy with complex machines can be used to articulate another problem with the argument. We should distinguish the blueprint of such a machine, which requires skill in the making, from a child's drawing of the machine, which does not. Our idea of God might be like the child's drawing rather than like the blueprint. Descartes's argument requires that we have a positive idea of an infinite being. But perhaps our idea of God is not like that. For instance, it could be the idea of a being who does not have the imperfections and limitations that we have. Such an idea might be drawn from knowledge of our own limitations and imperfections. The having of such an idea would not require the existence of God as its cause. This might be called a negative idea of God. Following this line of argument, even if we accept the special application of the Principle of Adequate Reality outlined above, we can deny that it proves the existence of God.

The Second Argument for the Existence of God

In the Fifth Meditation, Descartes offers a simpler proof for the existence of God. Whereas the first argument was a causal one, the second is an ontological argument—one based on the nature of God's essence. The essence of a thing consists of its distinguishing properties, of what is necessarily contained in the idea of that thing. The essence of a triangle is to have three enclosed angles and three sides. An idea of a thing that did not include this property could not be the idea of a triangle.

Usually knowledge of the essence of a thing does not inform us of the thing's existence: the essence of a triangle is compatible with the nonexistence of triangles. Descartes argues that, although we usually distinguish existence and essence, in the case of God His essence involves His existence. The idea of God is of a being with every perfection. Descartes thinks that existence is a perfection, and from this it follows that the essence of God must involve His existence. If God did not exist, He would lack a perfection, which is impossible:

1. By definition, God has all perfections.

2. Existence is a perfection.

   _____

3. Therefore, God exists.

The primary criticism of this argument, made famous by Kant, is that the second premise treats existence as a property. But according to Kant, existence is not a property of things. The sentence "Henry is blind" attributes the property of blindness to an individual, but the sentence "Henry exists" does not attribute any property to an individual. According to Kant, to deny that Henry exists is not to deny that he has a certain attribute or property, like blindness. This criticism was anticipated by Gassendi, who says in the *Objections,* "something which does not exist is neither perfect nor imperfect." If existence is not a property, then it is not a perfection and so premise 2 is false.

There is a reply to this argument, but it is unclear whether Descartes would have made it. The reply offers us a way of treating existence as a property by introducing an ontological category of possibly existent things. In Descartes's terminology, these possibly existent things would be called "eternal and immutable essences"; today, they are sometimes called "possible objects" or "pure objects." Possible objects do not actually exist unless they have the property of existence; existence, according to this reply, is a property that some possible objects (namely, those that exist) possess. A unicorn is, according to this view, an object that does not have the property of existence. On the other hand, the possible object God necessarily has existence, because that is part of its essence.

Today many philosophers consider the notion of a pure or possible object that either does or doesn't have the property of existence untenable. This is because pure or possible objects that do not exist cannot be clearly distinguished from each other. There are no clear criteria for their identification or individuation. To use an example from Quine, we cannot decide whether the possible bald man in the doorway is the same as or different from the possible fat man in the doorway.[18] For identity, it is necessary that we be able to tell when two predications are made of the same thing, but we cannot do this with possible objects. If the idea of pure objects is not tenable, there is no case for treating existence as a property of some of these objects and no reason to think that Descartes's ontological argument can be saved from Kant's objection.

Another criticism of Descartes's ontological argument is also made by Kant. In effect, Kant argues that, even if we admit that existence is a property, this will still not make the ontological argument valid. Descartes claims that the concept of God is such that God has necessary or eternal existence, which means that God is not a created being who will someday cease to exist. Kant argues that, even if the idea of God is such that God has the property of necessary existence, this does not show that God actually exists. Kant's point is that no definition of a concept can be used to prove that instances of that concept exist. Even if the concept of God includes the idea of His necessary existence, this does not show that God exists. To take a different example, we could invent the concept "existing Santa," defined as a Santa Claus who exists. By definition, the concept of "existing Santa" includes the property of his existing. Kant's point is that the mere definition of "existing Santa" does not prove that Santa actually does exist; similarly, even if the concept of God includes the idea of his necessary existence, this does not demonstrate that God exists. It merely tells us that, if He does exist, He exists necessarily.

The Cartesian Circle

Earlier, Descartes seemed to be locked in the realm of his own ideas, unable to show whether any of them represented external reality. Having now proved the existence of God, he can be sure that henceforth, when he assents to a clear and distinct idea, he will have a true belief. For God would not deceive us about what seems clear and obvious to us. Descartes has often been accused of arguing in a circle here. Arnauld expresses the circle as follows: "[W]e can be sure that God exists only because we clearly and evidently perceive that He does; therefore, prior to being certain that God exists, we should be certain that whatever we perceive clearly and distinctly is true."[19] Since Descartes uses the principle "whatever is distinctly and clearly perceived is true" in his proof of God, he cannot also use God to establish the truth of that principle. To do that would be to argue in a circle.

To show why Descartes did not argue in a circle, we should return to the nature of doubt. According to Descartes, one "cannot but assent" to a clear and distinct idea while thinking it: he says of these ideas "we cannot think of them without at the same time believing them to be true." Clear and distinct ideas cannot be doubted while we have them. This seems to contravene the Method of

Doubt, although in fact it does not. It seems to contravene the Method of Doubt because among the ideas doubted were clear and distinct ones; for instance, the proposition "2 + 2 = 4" forms a clear and distinct idea, but mathematics came under the ambit of doubt. In fact, however, the Method of Doubt does not involve doubting clear and distinct ideas at the time of thinking them. In doubting the propositions of mathematics, Descartes does not raise specific doubts about the proposition "2 + 2 = 4" but rather about the class of mathematical propositions as a whole. The Method of Doubt does not involve doubting particular clear and distinct ideas, but a general systematic scepticism about the reliability of our judgments and faculties as a whole.[20]

We can now see how Descartes can refute the charge of circularity. Descartes never offers the existence of God as grounds for accepting the truth of particular clear and distinct intuitions (that is, direct and immediate perceptions). According to him, the clarity of intuition is good enough. So when Descartes uses the truth of particular clear intuitions to prove the existence of God, he is not arguing in a circle.

Although clear and distinct beliefs cannot be doubted at the time of our having them, there remains the "metaphysical possibility" that the faculty of intuition as a whole might be mistaken. The existence of God is used by Descartes to allay this general and systematic doubt. God is introduced to establish the principle that "what is clearly and distinctively perceived is true." God is introduced to meet general systematic doubts about the truth of clear and distinct ideas. This is not circular. Descartes uses the truth of particular clear and distinct ideas to establish the existence of God, and thus to vindicate the general trustworthiness of intuition as a whole. Suppose that I am having a clear and distinct idea now. While I am having this idea, I am sure that it is true. But there is a problem: holding on to the idea is difficult, and when it is not intuited anymore I can no longer be sure that it is true. However, this problem is solved once I know that God exists, because then I can be sure of my clear and distinct ideas, even when I am not intuiting or having them. Descartes says to Burman that the proof of God can be grasped in a single thought. Once we clearly perceive that God exists and that He is no deceiver, we can allay systematic doubts about intuition in general.

False Beliefs

Having proved the existence of God, Descartes can now be certain that the *correct employment* of his faculties will not lead him into false belief. Descartes says that God would not have given him a faculty that leads him astray; God would not deceive him, because deception involves imperfection. But now, Descartes faces a new problem: if his faculties are given to him by a benevolent God, how is it that Descartes can ever be mistaken? In the Fourth Meditation, Descartes tries to answer this question by explaining what error is. An understanding of error is an important part of Descartes's program, since such an understanding would enable us to avoid error, in so far as we can.

Descartes does not intend to investigate why God created him as an imperfect being, for Descartes thinks it would be rash and fruitless to inquire into the aims of God. Instead, Descartes intends to investigate which human limitation causes errors. His conclusion is that error arises from the relation between the will and the understanding. These are two general faculties of the mind. The understanding is the faculty that produces ideas. Although our understanding is limited, this in itself does not cause error. Ideas themselves are neither true nor false. They have to be judged as true in order for there to be any possibility of error; and in order for them to be judged, the will has to assent to or dissent from the ideas of the understanding. The will (or faculty of free choice) is limitless and is not in itself the cause of error. Error originates, according to Descartes, because "my will extends more widely than my understanding, and yet I do not restrain it within the same bounds, but apply it to what I do not understand." In other words, error comes about because the will is limitless while the understanding is limited, and because the will assents to ideas that are not properly understood.

Summary

Having demonstrated that he exists, starting from the realization that he can be sure he is having an idea when he is having it, Descartes aims to show that material things outside himself also exist. He tries to do this in three steps. First, he attempts to prove the existence of God. Second, since God is not a deceiver, Descartes uses God's existence to establish the principle that his own clear and distinct ideas are true. Third, this principle gives Descartes a way to distinguish between true and false ideas and thereby to establish the existence of the external world.

Descartes's attempted proof of the existence of God is an important hinge in his enterprise of reconstructing knowledge on secure and certain principles. If the proofs are not successful, Descartes has no way to establish the principle that clear and distinct ideas are true, and no means to combat the scepticism induced in the First Meditation.

Study Questions

1. Why does Descartes try to prove the existence of God?

2. Does Descartes think that some, all, or none of our ideas are innate?

3. Why is Descartes certain that he has an idea of God?

4. What is the Principle of Adequate Reality, and how does Descartes use it?

5. What is the ontological argument?

6. How does Descartes attempt to explain the possibility of error or false beliefs? Why does he need to do this?

7. What does Descartes mean by "clear and distinct ideas"?

Discussion Questions

1. Why should we call Descartes a Rationalist?

2. Could there be any evidence for the principle that clear and distinct ideas are true?

3. Is existence a property?

4. What is an idea?

CHAPTER 3

Descartes: Mind and Body

According to the full title of the *Meditations,* one of Descartes's main aims is to show that the mind and the body are distinct entities. To demonstrate this, Descartes attempts to prove that the essential nature of the mind or of mental substance is different from the essential nature of the body and of material substance. Descartes's main arguments for the distinction between mind and body are given in the Sixth Meditation, which also contains his proof of the existence of material objects. Before looking at the Sixth Meditation, we must return to the Second Meditation, where Descartes inquires into the essential nature of the mind.

Thinking Substance

In the Cogito, Descartes affirms the certainty of his own existence. But he has not yet affirmed the existence of his own body, for the existence of external things is still in doubt. To be faithful to his own Method of Doubt, Descartes must be careful not to affirm too much. He must not mistake the indubitable knowledge of the Cogito for something less evident. So, Descartes's next step is to find out just what he has shown to exist in the Cogito. That is, his next step is to discover what he is, or what his essential nature is. At this stage of his inquiry, the one thing that Descartes knows for certain about himself—apart from the fact that he exists—is that he thinks. So in the Second Meditation, Descartes concludes that he is a thinking being and that his essence is to think.

By *essence* Descartes means the properties that a substance must have. If a substance ceases at any time to have its essential properties, it ceases to exist.

From the fact that he is thinking, Descartes infers that there must be some substance that is thinking, and that he, Descartes, is that substance. He then argues that his essence is to think, because it is inconceivable that he should not think. This part of Descartes's argument appears to be invalid. He seems to move directly from a consideration of the Cogito—from the truth of

1. "I cannot conceive of myself not thinking."

to the conclusion

2. "I cannot exist without thinking," or "Thinking is essential to me."

This argument trades on an ambiguity in the statement "I cannot conceive of myself not thinking." The conclusion requires the strong claim that it is absolutely inconceivable that I should cease to think at any time, because thinking is essential to my nature. But premise 1 is true in a much weaker sense—namely, that the proposition "I am not thinking now" is something one cannot truly think. Although it is obviously true that I cannot correctly think that I am not now thinking, this is not equivalent to saying that I must conceive of myself as a being who thinks at all times because thought is essential to my nature.

Although Descartes takes the bare reasoning of the Cogito to show that his essence is to think, the latter claim is best understood in terms of his metaphysical assumptions rather than in terms of the previous argument. For instance, Descartes assumes that the "I" proved to exist in the Cogito—that is, Descartes himself—is a substance or thing with one and only one essential property or attribute. He also assumes that there are only two essential attributes: thought (or consciousness) and spatial extension. Hence, he concludes that there are only two created substances: mind and matter. An essential property is one that substance necessarily possesses; thus, minds cannot exist without thinking or being conscious, and matter cannot exist without being extended in space. This helps to explain Descartes's belief that he is a mind or a thinking substance.

Descartes also assumes that any property a substance possesses must be a mode or modification of its essential attribute. All the properties of minds, or thinking substance, can only be different types of thought or different ways of thinking. All the properties of matter must be explicable in terms of the essence of matter, extension. This assumption helps explain the thesis of Descartes's Sixth Meditation that the mind is distinct from the body, and that matter—in particular, the brain—cannot think. It also helps explain his treatment of physics as geometry.

Given these metaphysical assumptions, it is easier to understand Descartes's line of argument in the Second Meditation. He assumes that the "I" of the Cogito is a substance and that any property that the "I" might lack cannot be its essence. He then tries (and fails) to show that he might lack every property except thought and consciousness. He fails to show this because he can only demonstrate that he cannot doubt that he is thinking while he is thinking.

It is important to remember what Descartes claims to have proved in the

Second Meditation. In reply to some comments of Hobbes, Descartes insists that he does not prove the distinctness of mind and body until the Sixth (and last) Meditation. Only then does Descartes claim that thinking is the sole property essential to him and that he is essentially nonmaterial. These strong claims are propounded in the Sixth Meditation.

The Existence of Material Things

We can now proceed to the themes of the Sixth Meditation and Descartes's reconstruction of knowledge. When he was practicing his Method of Doubt, Descartes could only be sure what the content of his own mind was—but not that anything in the external world caused or corresponded to that content. He could not be sure that his ideas of the external world were true. But now he has proved the existence of God and has deemed it certain that "God is liable to no errors or defects" and hence is no deceiver. Because He is no deceiver, God would not wish us to be led into error. Thus we can be sure that our clear and distinct ideas are true.

Descartes acknowledges that the mere existence of mental images and sensations gives us indubitable reason to think that there is an independent external world corresponding to them. Nevertheless, we have a very strong natural tendency to believe in the existence of such a world and to believe that our ideas are caused by it; and this tendency survives the scrutiny of reason. In other words, if, in general, sensations were not caused by such a reality, we would be deceived by God, which is impossible. Descartes carefully notes that this does not mean that all bodies are as we perceive them to be, since particular perceptions are obscure and confused in many respects. But his general principle that clear and distinct ideas are true furnishes us with a way of avoiding error. We must always suspend our assent to ideas that are unclear and indistinct. As we saw in Chapter 2, according to Descartes, the determination to give assent to an idea (or to judge it to be true) is a matter for the will.

The Nature of Matter

Descartes's principle that clear and distinct ideas are true has implications that conflict with popular opinion. This is especially apparent in his treatment of matter. According to Descartes, the only properties of matter are those that can be explained in terms of the fundamental attribute, extension. Extension is the essence of matter, and any other property that a substance has can only be a mode of that essential attribute.

The essence of a thing consists of the property without which that thing would cease to exist. So in order to prove that the essence of matter is extension, Descartes argues that a body can lose any of its properties, except extension, without ceasing to be a material body. At *Principles* II.11, Descartes argues that a body can lose its hardness, weight, color, and heat without ceasing to be a body. But it cannot lose its extension; and consequently extension is the essential attribute of material bodies.

This conception of matter as extension has some radical consequences. First, it implies that a vacuum is impossible. Descartes argues that matter as extension and physical space are identical; hence, there can be no empty space. He also argues that a vacuum is impossible because, if there is nothing between two bodies, they must be in contact (see *Principles* II.18). Second, his conception of matter also implies that there are no indivisible atoms. All parts of matter must be extended, and anything that is extended is, like space, infinitely divisible (see *Principles* II.20). Third, Descartes holds that all properties of matter must be explained in terms of matter in motion. But since there is no vacuum for bodies to move into, "the only possible movement of bodies is in a circle." As one part of matter moves, it pushes another out of the place it enters, and this pushes another and so on, until a body enters the place left by the first body "at the very moment the first body leaves it." Fourth, Descartes's view of matter excludes force and solidity as basic. However, he does hold as a truth that two things cannot be in the same place at the same time, so matter occupying one part of space excludes other matter from occupying the same place. But as Leibniz points out, this seems inadequate to explain how different bodies exert different degrees of resistance and have different degrees of density.

Descartes's ultimately geometrical conception of physical science leads him to picture the material world as one continuous, infinite, extended whole, moving as in a whirlpool. This anticipates and influenced Spinoza's later view that there is only one substance. According to Descartes, while there are an indefinite number of mental substances, there is only one extended substance—the material universe as a whole. Particular physical objects themselves should not, strictly speaking, be called substances but only modes of the one extended substance. This means that objects can be distinguished only by differences in motion and matter at different places. Objects are differentiated on the basis of the ways in which matter moves.

Rationalism and Science

In claiming that matter is extension, Descartes supports his mathematical view of science, since extension and motion are obviously quantifiable and measurable. This means that they are clear and distinct ideas. Descartes also claims that all physical phenomena can be explained by the motion of matter, and thus that all scientific explanation is purely mechanical.

It is important to note the historical context and influence of Descartes's physics and his view of science. Descartes's mechanistic account of the physical universe is an important step in the development of science. For example, he explicitly rejects the possibility of attributing purpose to matter in order to explain the motion of physical objects (for example, the claim that objects move because they fear a vacuum). Although Descartes is not unique in this respect, his scientific work was very influential partly because he tries to apply the principles of mechanistic explanation to such a wide range of natural phenomena, including planetary motion, light, the motion of the tides, and functions of the human body such as the circulation of the blood and respiration.

Descartes's vision of the unity of all the sciences and of all knowledge is founded on his belief that he had discovered in geometry a model and a method for arriving at truth with certainty. The ideas of geometry are clear and distinct. Furthermore, in geometry one thing is deduced from another. Descartes thinks that the basic principles of science can be deduced a priori in a similar fashion. For example, he asserts that principles like "God always preserves the same quantity of motion in matter" and "What is once in motion always continues to move" can be deduced by reasoning.

However, Descartes also thinks that observation and sense experience are necessary to show how particular effects depend on such general principles. Descartes does not claim that all truths can be demonstrated by reasoning alone.

Primary and Secondary Qualities

There is one further important consequence of Descartes's view of matter—namely, that heat, sound, taste, colors, and flavors, which Locke later called the secondary qualities, are not properties of objects at all. Instead, they are only confused ideas that exist in the mind due to its interreaction with the body. Strictly speaking, extended substance is not colored at all. When we perceive a tree as colored, some variation in the extended properties of the tree causes the idea of green in us. The tree itself is not colored but only has the power to cause in us the idea or sensation of color. The tree itself has only extended properties.

One of Descartes's reasons for holding this view is that secondary qualities are not clear and distinct ideas. To judge that the tree is itself green is to assent to a confused idea. In thinking that secondary qualities are confused ideas, Descartes is most probably comparing them to the quantifiable ideas of extension and motion. He thinks that it is unintelligible to judge that the object itself is colored, just as it is unintelligible to judge that pain belongs to an object that causes us to feel pain (*Principles* I.68). It is an error to believe "that if a body is hot, it has some property just like my idea."

Another reason for Descartes's view is his belief that secondary qualities have no role in an adequate physiological account of perception. Perception can be fully explained in terms of the effect on the mind of matter in motion. Furthermore, Descartes's conception of physical reality is of the world as it really is or as it is independently of observers. This notion of the world as it really is contrasts sharply with the concept of the world as it seems to us. Given such a contrast, it is natural to exclude colors and other secondary qualities from the world as it really is, since our experience of colors depends on physiological factors that are peculiar to us as a species. For example, dogs do not see color. The so-called primary qualities, on the other hand, seem far less variable from one species or individual to another. For these reasons, color and other secondary qualities are often excluded from a scientific picture of the world as it really is, whereas the primary qualities like shape, size, and motion are included.

Descartes's views about color, heat, and so on anticipate Locke's later discussion, except that for Locke solidity is a primary quality belonging to the real physical world, whereas for Descartes solidity is not a mode of the extended world but rather an idea that exists only in our minds, because solidity is not a spatial or geometrical property.

Although Descartes interprets his belief in God as vindicating his belief in an external world, we can see how philosophical thinking has changed his view of the world. Prior to doubting the existence of the world and embarking on the Method of Doubt, Descartes had good reason for believing that material objects were colored. Moreover, prior to doubting, Descartes believed in the existence of material bodies on the unclear and untrustworthy evidence of his senses. Now he can be sure that they exist, because he has rationally proved their existence—and he can be sure that they are not colored.

It is important to remember that Descartes holds a representationalist theory of perception, according to which our ideas of sense represent external objects. He holds that seeing consists of the infallible perceiving of ideas, which represent material objects. The immediate objects of perception, according to this view, are mental ideas rather than physical objects. Thus we can be more certain of the contents of our own minds than of the existence of physical objects. Both features of this view were later challenged by Kant and others, who held that the immediate objects of perception are physical objects and that we cannot be more certain of the content of our minds than of the existence of an external world (see Chapters 19 and 20).

The Real Distinction

In the Second Meditation, Descartes tries to show that his essence is to think. As we have seen, this attempt either fails or requires a dubious metaphysical framework. In the Sixth Meditation, Descartes offers a different argument to show that his essence consists solely in thinking, or that the one and only attribute without which he cannot continue to exist is consciousness. This new argument involves the principle that clear and distinct ideas are true—a principle that was not available to him at the time of the Second Meditation, when he had not yet proved the existence of God. The new argument notes that, when we think of the self as a conscious being, we clearly and distinctly perceive that consciousness is all that the self needs in order to exist as a substance or complete thing. Because clear and distinct ideas are true, Descartes infers that his essence consists solely in the fact that he is conscious.

Furthermore, Descartes also claims to have a clear idea that he, as a conscious being, is really distinct from his body and could exist without it. He takes this to be adequate proof that the mind is distinct from the body.

Descartes introduces two other arguments to support his contention that the mind and the body are distinct.

1. The Argument from Doubt

This argument occurs in the *Discourse on the Method,* Part IV, as follows:

1. I cannot doubt that I (as a mind) exist.

2. I can doubt that my body exists.

   _____

3. Therefore, I (as a mind) am distinct from my body.

The argument relies on the Principle of the Indiscernibility of Identicals. This principle states that identicals, like water and H_2O, must have all properties in common. If water had a property that was not shared by H_2O, then the two could not be identical. In more technical terms, if X is the same object as or is identical with Y, then any predicate F that is true of X must also be true of Y. Descartes relies on this principle when he argues as follows: if my mind is identical with my body, then what is true of the one must also be true of the other; but there is one thing that is true of my mind but not true of my body—namely, that I cannot doubt that it exists.

We can reformulate the argument from doubt more accurately as follows:

1. If two things are identical, then they must have all their properties in common.

2. My mind has the property that I cannot doubt that it exists.

3. My body does not have this property.

   _____

4. Therefore, my mind and my body are not identical.

Descartes's argument does not work, however, as can be seen from a hypothetical example. Water and H_2O are identical, but the preceding argument could be applied to them. A person who is ignorant of chemistry could argue as follows:

1. If water and H_2O are identical, then they must have all their properties in common.

2. Water has the property that I do not doubt that it exists.

3. H_2O does not have this property, because I do doubt that it exists.

   _____

4. Therefore, water and H_2O cannot be identical.

Since we know that water and H_2O are identical, there must be something wrong with this argument; it must be unsound. Furthermore, Descartes's argument from doubt has the same basic logical form as this unsound argument, so it too must be unsound.

The two arguments are not sound, because they involve psychological phenomena like doubting, believing, and wanting, which form what are called "nonextensional contexts." A context is simply a part of a sentence. For example, "is red" and "John believes that" are contexts that when combined with suitable phrases, make a complete sentence. Many inferences that are valid for extensional contexts are invalid for nonextensional or intensional contexts. This is one of the crucial differences between them.

In an extensional context, when we substitute for a word any other word that picks out or refers to the same thing, the substitution will not change the truth or falsity of the whole sentence. For example, "has a beard" is an extensional context, because—if the sentence "Lincoln has a beard" is true, and if Lincoln and the sixteenth president of the United States are the same person—then the sentence "The sixteenth president of the United States has a beard" will also be true. Substituting the phrase "the sixteenth president of the United States" for the word "Lincoln" will not change the truth value of the sentence; consequently, the context "has a beard" is extensional. Because of this, the following argument is logically valid:

1. Lincoln has a beard.

2. The sixteenth president of the United States is the same person as Lincoln.

---

3. Therefore, the sixteenth president of the United States has a beard.

In an intensional context, on the other hand, when we substitute a word with any other word that picks out or refers to the same thing, the substitution may change the truth of the whole sentence. For example, suppose that "Dan believes that Lincoln has a beard" is true; now, even if Lincoln and the sixteenth president of the United States are the same person, the sentence "Dan believes that the sixteenth president of the United States is bald" may not be true. Substituting the phrase "the sixteenth president of the United States" for the word "Lincoln" may change the truth of the sentence; consequently the context "Dan believes that" is intensional. Because of this, the following argument is not logically valid:

1. Dan believes that Lincoln has a beard.

2. The sixteenth president of the United States is the same person as Lincoln.

---

3. Therefore, Dan believes that the sixteenth president of the United States has a beard.

Furthermore, the following argument, similar in shape to Descartes's, is also invalid:

1. Dan believes that Lincoln has a beard.

2. Dan does not believe that the sixteenth president of the United States has a beard.

   _____

3. Therefore, Lincoln is not the sixteenth president of the United States.

Like belief and desire, doubt is intensional. It should therefore not be a surprise that Descartes's argument from doubt is invalid and fails to prove that the mind and the body are distinct. We cannot logically infer, from a subjective doubt about X and a lack of doubt about Y, that X and Y are objectively nonidentical.

2. The Argument from Divisibility

In the Sixth Meditation, Descartes contends that he is a complete and indivisible thing. But matter, being extended, is always divisible. Hence, Descartes concludes that he, as a thinking thing, must be different in kind from all matter, including his own body:

1. The mind is an indivisible thing.

2. All material objects must be spatially extended.

3. Anything that is spatially extended is divisible.

   _____

4. Therefore, the mind is not a material object.

As we shall see later, Kant criticizes this argument in the Paralogisms and rejects premise 1. Kant argues that, even though a single consciousness is a unity, it is a mistake to treat consciousness as though it were an object. In effect, Kant rejects the claim that the mind is a thing or substance at all.

Even if we think that the mind is a substance or thing, we may also question Descartes's claim that it and consciousness are indivisible. People who have split brains, brain disorders, strokes, and split personalities are sometimes described as having a divided consciousness.

The Nature of Descartes's Dualism

Descartes holds that a person is a mind or a mental substance whose sole essence is to be conscious. The mind is distinct from the body and can exist independently of it. This view is often called "mind/body dualism" and is opposed by Materialists, who claim that mental states are identical to brain states.

Descartes holds that anything that is spatially extended is material and therefore is infinitely divisible. He also affirms that the mind is not made of matter and is not infinitely divisible. This implies that the mind is not spatially extended. The same conclusion also follows from Descartes's view of essence. The essence of matter is to be extended, and all properties of matter are ways of being extended. Similarly, the essence of the mind is to be conscious, and all properties of the mind are modes of consciousness. For Descartes, all properties of a thing with a given essence are modifications of that essence (*Principles* I.53 and I.56). This implies that no property that essentially belongs to one thing can nonessentially belong to another. In other words, Descartes holds that the mind is not spatially extended. For this reason, some commentators think that Descartes conceives of the mind as a nonspatial entity.

Although Descartes argues that the mind is distinct from the body and can exist without it, he also holds that there is a special close causal relationship between the two in living humans. Otherwise, the embodied person could not claim that his or her body was in any way his or hers. In particular, Descartes claims that "my soul is not in my body as a pilot in a ship." By this he means that the mind is able to move the body directly and that the mind feels pains and other sensations in the body.

Descartes holds that there is a two-way causal interaction between the mind and the body. In sense perception, neural impulses in the brain affect the mind. For instance, in the process of seeing an object, lightwaves reflected from that object affect the eye, the optical nerves, and hence the brain; these changes in the brain cause us to have visual sensations in the mind. When we act voluntarily, acts of the will (which are a form of mental activity) cause physical changes in the brain, and these in turn cause the muscles and body to move.

Some Criticisms of Dualism

There are several problems with mind/body dualism, the kind of theory Descartes embraced. We shall briefly examine some of these problems, as well as one of the main arguments in favor of a Materialist view of the mind.

1. The Problems of Interaction

Descartes's dualism makes the two-way interaction between the mind and the brain mysterious in two ways. First, we can never have direct experience of this interaction. Second, the two types of substance, mind and matter, are utterly different in kind, and this makes interaction between them obscure, placing some doubt on the whole idea of dualism. These problems were known to Descartes, and he made some attempt to overcome them. In particular he postulated the pineal gland as the locus for mind/body causation. This, however, does not remove the obscurity: how can mental substance, which is apparently not in space, interact with spatially extended matter?

There are further problems. If nonspatially located acts of will cause changes in my brain, this must be thought of as a form of magic or psychokinesis. Why is only my brain and, in particular, my pineal gland affected by this psychokinesis? Why is it that, for instance, I cannot directly will my eyes to change color by psychokinesis? Why does my mind, which is not in space, enjoy causal relations solely with my body, and in particular my pineal gland, but not with other objects? These are questions that Descartes's dualism invites us to ask but to which he gives no answer.

Spinoza, Leibniz, and Berkeley accept the claim that radically different kinds of substances, such as mind and matter, cannot interact. Their acceptance of this claim has some importance in their later denials of ontological dualism.

2. The Problem of the Identity of Mental Substances

In the *Critique of Pure Reason* (B319), Kant points out that two material objects that are otherwise identical can be distinguished and identified at different times only by their position in space. He claims that substances or objects are distinguishable because of their spatio-temporal position. Kant claims that, if minds—as bodiless persons—do not have a spatial position, there can be no way to distinguish between two qualitatively similar disembodied minds. For Kant, this puts into question the thesis that nonspatial minds are substances or objects.

In effect, Kant claims that the concept of substance has no content and objective meaning except in application to both space and time (see also A349). In the Paralogisms, Kant criticizes Descartes's dualism for assuming that the mind can be regarded as a substance or object at all. Kant rejects Descartes's assumption that the word "I" can refer to a mental substance. We shall examine Kant's arguments in more detail in Chapter 21.

3. The Problem of Other Minds

Descartes's dualism also faces problems in relation to the knowledge of other minds. How can I know that other beings are conscious? If I am only acquainted with other people's behavior, how can I know that a mind is causing that behavior? For all I know, their behavior could be caused by two or even more mental substances. Alternatively, their behavior might have purely physical causes—in which case, according to Descartes, they could not be conscious beings at all, no matter how sophisticated or similar to my own their behavior was. They would instead be like robots.

It might seem absurd to suggest that I do not know whether others have feelings and sensations, and yet Descartes's dualism does suggest this. It does so by implying that behavior is irrelevant in settling the question of whether others are conscious or not. All that is relevant is the presence of a nonmaterial mind, which, in the case of others, cannot be perceived.

Descartes regards the human body as a machine (albeit a machine made by God). Such a view accords with his mechanistic conception of matter. Descartes also thinks that nonhuman animals lack minds and that their behavior in principle could be explained entirely mechanistically, on analogy with a machine. But if nonhuman animals are only complex machines, what reason do I have for thinking that other humans are not machines? In the *Discourse on the Method*, Descartes tries to answer this question by appealing to language. He says that a machine could never produce different arrangements of words so as to give an appropriately meaningful answer to what is said in its presence (AT VI, 56). Intelligent language users have the capacity to respond in an indefinite range of contexts. Descartes's reply to the problem of other minds is that we can know that other people have minds because they use language intelligently.

Even leaving aside the possibility of computer and animal languages, Descartes's reply does not really answer the problem of other minds. It assumes that the only explanation of intelligent language use is the existence of a nonmaterial mind. It does not answer the question: if I see another using language, how do I know that there is a mind causing that behavior? Perhaps such behavior could be caused by the presence of many minds, or perhaps it has purely physical causes. Descartes obviously thinks that intelligent linguistic behavior cannot have a purely physical cause, but how can he know this?

The Causal Analysis of Mind

What is the mind? Does Descartes's reply that the mind is a nonmaterial substance answer this question? Evidently it does not. Reifying mental states (that is, treating them as objects) does not explain what they are. What consciousness is remains a mystery, even if we regard consciousness as a special kind of object. In other words, we need to distinguish ontological questions about the mind (such as "Is the mind distinct from matter?" and "Is the mind a kind of object?") from questions about the character of the mind (such as "What is it to be conscious?" and "What is it to perceive and think?"). Descartes's dualism tries to answer the first type of question but not the second. In effect, he regards consciousness as if it were simple and unanalyzable.

Ryle makes a similar point graphically by comparing Descartes's view of a person to the image of a ghost in a machine.[21] Descartes's mechanistic view of matter treats the body as a machine; his view of the mind is as of a ghostly entity. Ryle argues that we cannot explain what, for example, seeing is by appeal to this ghost in the machine model. We cannot explain how human beings see by claiming that minds see; this merely repeats the problem at one remove. The problem of what seeing is is not solved by reifying the mind or treating it as an object. What it is for a Cartesian mind to see is just as puzzling as what it is for a human being to see.

Some twentieth-century philosophers argue that the only satisfactory answer to the question "What is the mind?" is given by a causal analysis of mental states. According to this kind of analysis, any type of mental state is characterized purely in terms of its causal role—its effects on behavior, on other mental states, and on the body. A mental state is thus a general and complex causal disposition.

What fundamentally distinguishes conscious creatures, like people, from inanimate objects, like stones, is not the presence or absence of a nonmaterial substance, the mind. Rather, it is that we can perform purposive actions, like walking, and whole ranges of very complex tasks, like recognizing a face.

According to this kind of analysis, as a matter of fact, we do recognize types of mental states by the actions and reactions they typically cause: joy is recognized by certain behavior patterns and physiological reactions and by its relation to other mental states; the desire to keep dry in the rain is recognized by other appropriate actions and reactions.

A causal analysis links mental states to their potential outer manifestations, which are public and objective, as well as to other mental states. In so doing, it must be contrasted with Descartes's own analysis, which tends to treat mental states as essentially private and subjective. By linking mental states to possible actions and physiological reactions, as well as to other mental states, the causal analysis of mind avoids the problem of other minds that confronts dualism. Because the causal analysis links mental states to potential actions and to physiological reactions, it allows us to take account of evidence that others are conscious and that they feel pain or anger, just as we can have good evidence for other unobservables. Mental states are characterized by their causal role and not as the states of a nonmaterial substance.

Materialism

Earlier we distinguished ontological questions about the existence of the mind (such as "Is the mind distinct from matter?") from questions about the character of the mind. The causal analysis does not in itself answer ontological questions about the mind; thus, in itself, it is compatible with ontological dualism. It tells us about the character of mental states, but not whether the mind is immaterial or not.

However, some twentieth-century philosophers have used a broadly causal analysis of mental states to argue for Materialism—the view that mental states are nothing but brain states. According to the causal analysis, mental states are capable of causing actions or appropriately complex behavior. Recent philosophers, like David Armstrong,[22] have appealed to neurological and physiological theory to argue that all actions and physiological reactions are in fact caused solely by the central nervous system or brain. Armstrong concludes that mental states are brain states. His argument can be summarized as follows:

1. Mental states are whatever is capable of causing intentional actions.

2. All intentional actions are caused solely by activity in the brain.

3. Therefore, mental states are brain states.

In short, Armstrong argues that the mind is whatever has a certain causal role; but as a matter of fact, the only thing that has that role is the brain; and therefore the mind is the brain.[23]

This alternative view to Descartes's also helps us separate two elements in Descartes's view of the mind. Descartes does not think that the nature of the mind is its causal role, and consequently he tends to treat mental states as purely private and would deny Armstrong's premise 1. There is also another relevant element of Descartes's view of the mind. Because of his ontological dualism, he would reject Armstrong's premise 2. Descartes's claim that the mind is a substance that exists distinct from matter would lead him to deny that actions are caused solely by brain states.

Study Questions

1. How does Descartes claim to know that his essence is to think or to be conscious?

2. What does Descartes mean by *essence*?

3. Why does Descartes think that material objects are not really colored?

4. Why does Descartes deny the possibility of a vacuum?

5. How does Descartes rely on the Principle of the Indiscernibility of Identicals to show that the mind is distinct from the body?

6. Why does doubting form an intensional context, and why is this point important for one of Descartes's arguments for dualism?

7. What is the difference between dualism and Materialism?

8. What is the problem of other minds?

Discussion Questions

1. How would Descartes react to the claim that some computers can think?

2. Are there any good reasons for thinking that substances must be public-ally identifiable?

Spinoza (1632–1677)

Baruch de Spinoza was born in the Jewish community of Amsterdam in 1632. His early education was almost entirely religious, but his later teachers included Manasseh ben Israel, a major figure in seventeenth-century Judaism who was also well connected in the secular world. It was probably he who introduced Spinoza to non-Jewish philosophy, languages, mathematics, and physics.

In 1654, after the death of his father, Spinoza went to live with Francis Van Den Ende, an ex-Jesuit bookseller who gave instruction in Latin and science, the philosophy of Descartes, and the underground worlds of free thought and politics.

In 1656 Spinoza was excommunicated from the synagogue and began using the Latin version of his name, Benedict. His family disowned him, and he abandoned his earlier plans for a commercial career. He chose instead the trade of making and polishing lenses for spectacles, microscopes, and telescopes. His skill in this was what first attracted the attention of such contemporary figures as the mathematician Christian Huygens and the philosopher Leibniz.

From 1660 to 1663, Spinoza lived in Rijnsburg, a village near Leiden that contained the headquarters of the Collegiant sect. The Mennonites and Collegiants, who were opposed to rigid orthodoxy, formed study groups, which Spinoza joined. His earliest known work, the *Short Treatise on God, Man and His Well-Being,* was probably written for these friends. It remained undiscovered until the nineteenth century.

Spinoza was apparently working on the *Ethics* intermittently from 1662 to 1675. He attempted to publish it in 1675, but the effort was resisted by theologians. In the meantime, with the help of Ludovicus Meyer, he published in 1663 the *Principles of the Philosophy of René Descartes,* with an Appendix by Meyer on Spinoza's metaphysical thoughts. During the same year, he moved to Voorburg, a small village near The Hague. He may have been seeking both peaceful surroundings and the proximity of powerful protectors.

In 1670 he moved to The Hague and spent the rest of his life there. During his last years, apart from working on the *Ethics,* Spinoza also wrote a Hebrew grammar, a scientific treatise on the rainbow, and the *Tractatus Politicus.*

Spinoza seems to have had many friends and correspondents, and he had the reputation of being gentle, humane, and unpretentious. On behalf of his friends he could also become passionately indignant, to judge from a report of one incident in 1672. After the French invasion of the Low Countries, an Orange mob killed his friends, the de Witt brothers, in the street. In a rage, Spinoza made up a placard with the words *"Ultimi barbarorum,"* intending to confront the murderous mob with it. His landlord, fearing that he too would be killed, locked Spinoza inside the house until the danger subsided.

In 1677 Spinoza died of consumption, probably complicated by chronic inhalation of glass dust—an occupational hazard of lens grinders. His greatest work, the *Ethics,* was published the following year. He seems unlikely to have been disappointed at the lack of recognition he received during his lifetime. Among his reflections was the thought that "Riches, fame, or honor, satisfaction of libidos or basic drives . . . only distract us." The highest good, for Spinoza, was "knowledge of the union which the mind has with total Nature."

CHAPTER 4

Spinoza: God and Substance

Spinoza's aim in the *Ethics* was to present a new ethical system founded on metaphysics and a philosophy of mind. He repudiated Descartes's claim that mind and body are two distinct substances that causally interact. Spinoza saw the mind in union with the whole of nature and believed that an understanding of this oneness was the highest possible good. In his time Spinoza was denounced as an atheist, and much of his work was vehemently condemned, especially by the Jesuits. In retrospect, this bears testament to the originality of his thought.

Spinoza presents his work in the style of Euclid, with axioms, definitions, and theorems. All of the theorems are supposed to be rigorously demonstrated by deduction from the axioms and definitions. Spinoza's method is very much an integral part of his metaphysics. He does not adopt this Euclidean method merely for the sake of clarity or to achieve the mathematical certainty that Descartes sought. In following proofs in logical sequence, he says, the "mind will to the utmost extent reflect nature." In other words, Spinoza believes that nature has a logical order and that proper knowledge of it constitutes a deductive system, because in principle any statement of fact can be logically deduced and all truths are necessary rather than contingent. In accordance with his own method, he produces logical demonstrations that attempt to reflect the proper logical order of the world. Furthermore, Spinoza argues that all knowledge and all truths are essentially part of a single system; this is the seed of his pantheism—the claim that God is literally everything.

Spinoza's deductive method reflects his view that all truths can be demonstrated and are necessarily (rather than contingently) true. Further, it reflects his view that ideas or thoughts and physical facts are merely two aspects of substance, rather than two kinds of substance. Spinoza's methodology is also essential given his mathematical model of knowledge. A mathematician works by a priori reasoning, without recourse to observation. For Spinoza, ideally, this method of procedure could be extended to every area of knowledge. Since all truths are necessary and in theory can be shown by demonstration, Spinoza's view of knowledge denies the need for experimentation in principle.

A Preliminary Overview

The most basic point in Part I of the *Ethics* is that there can be only one substance. Spinoza calls this single substance "God" or "Nature." He does not regard God as an entity separate from the Universe, and in this sense Spinoza departs from traditional theism and rejects the Judeo-Christian notion of God. He also rejects Descartes's idea of God as the primary substance, with mind and matter conceived as two created substances. For Descartes the attributes of thought and extension define the two distinct substances of mind and matter, while for Spinoza these are just two of the infinite attributes of the One Substance, God.

In Spinoza's terminology, substance "is in itself," while derivative modes "exist in" something other than themselves. Our concepts of, for instance, a meter, yellow, and swimming are notions of dependent existents: a meter must be a meter of some material; yellow must be the color of some object; and swimming must be the swimming of some person or animal. Substance, for Spinoza, exists in itself, independent of anything further.

To understand Spinoza's view of substance, we need to appreciate the relation between substance and causation. Spinoza defines substance as "what is in itself and is conceived through itself."[24] The second part of this definition is important: why should substance be conceived through itself, as well as existing in itself? The bald answer is that whatever exists in itself must also be conceived through itself. At proposition 8 in Part I of the *Ethics,* Spinoza says that something is conceived through itself when knowledge of it does not involve or depend on knowledge of anything else. He is referring especially to knowledge of causes, for he takes it as axiomatic (axiom IV) that knowledge of any effect involves and depends on knowledge of the cause. For example, knowledge of the apple requires knowledge of the tree, which requires knowledge of the earth and the sun (which have nourished that tree), and so on. Because knowledge of the effect depends on knowledge of the cause, the only thing that qualifies as being conceived through itself is something that does not depend on any external causes, and the only thing that does not depend on external causes is Nature as a whole or God.

Spinoza's use of the word *cause* is special. Like other Rationalist philosophers, he assimilates causality to logical implication. A cause is any adequate explanation, and to explain is to show how one idea or proposition logically follows from another. Explanation involves exhibiting the logical connections between ideas or propositions. Consequently, because knowledge of the effect depends on knowledge of the cause, the cause is not logically separable from the effect. Thus Spinoza's philosophy postulates a close tie between existence and explanation or cause, because Spinoza assimilates cause and logical necessity. If something cannot be conceived through itself, it cannot exist in itself. Whenever something has a cause outside itself, it cannot be considered and does not exist in isolation from that cause. The effect and the cause are like two sides of an unsplittable coin.

Furthermore, according to the Rationalist Principle of Sufficient Reason, everything must be explicable as the effect of some cause in this way. Everything must have a sufficient reason or cause for its existence. If causation acts as a logical glue, binding each effect to its cause, then the Principle of Sufficient Reason implies that each thing is bound together with its cause, and that this complex is itself bound to its cause. This binding continues until everything is bound into one.

In the first part of the *Ethics,* Spinoza sets out to prove that substance is its own cause; substance, which exists in itself, does not causally depend on anything else for that existence. Therefore, knowledge of it does not depend on knowledge of anything else external to it; and therefore, it is conceived through itself. According to Spinoza, the only thing that can satisfy this definition of substance is Nature as a whole; and therefore, only Nature as a whole can be properly regarded as a substance or thing. If we were to ask Spinoza "What exists?" he should not answer "Many different things exist, including people, planets, and stars"; instead, he should answer "Only one thing exists, God." Spinoza claims that this answer has supreme ethical significance.

We can summarize this part of Spinoza's argument as follows:

1. Substance is independent.

2. Anything that has an external cause cannot be independent.

_____

3. Therefore, substance does not have an external cause.

4. Everything must have a cause.

_____

5. Therefore substance is its own cause.

6. No finite thing is its own cause.

_____

7. Therefore, substance is infinite.

Spinoza's Proofs

Spinoza tries to prove that substance necessarily exists, that it is God with infinite attributes, and thus that there can be only one. To understand these crucial early propositions of the *Ethics,* it is worth retracing Spinoza's proofs in some detail.

The conclusion of the proofs is stated at *Ethics* I.14: there is only one substance, God. Spinoza reaches this conclusion in two basic steps:

1. He tries to prove that there is at least one substance, which exists necessarily (*Ethics* I.7).

2. He tries to show that there cannot be more than one substance, because substance must be infinite (Ethics I.8 and I.11).

Proposition I.5: There cannot be two substances of the same nature or attribute.

This proposition is important in later proofs. Spinoza says that, if there is more than one substance, they must be distinguishable in some way. He attempts to show that there is no way to distinguish between two substances that possess the same attribute. Obviously, two substances that possess the same attribute cannot be distinguished by their attributes, he says. But neither can they be distinguished by their modifications or modes, because by definition substance must be conceived through itself and not through its modifications. Spinoza believes that this exhausts the alternatives (see *Ethics* I.4), and he concludes that there cannot be two substances with the same attribute.

However, the claim that the alternatives are exhausted is dubious, because two substances might share their attributes or essential properties and yet be distinct because of their spatio-temporal position. For example, two ball-bearings can be qualitatively the same and yet numerically distinct because they can be distinguished by the fact that they do not occupy the same space at the same time.

Proposition I.7: It pertains to the nature of a substance to exist.

According to Rationalist philosophers like Spinoza, everything must have a cause. Spinoza also maintains that a substance cannot be caused by anything external to itself, so it must be its own cause *(causa sui)*. Therefore, existence belongs to the essence of substance; it exists necessarily. A substance cannot be caused by anything external to itself for two reasons. First, if it were so caused, then knowledge of a substance would depend on knowledge of something else, which is impossible because substance must be conceived only through itself. Second, only a substance could be the external cause of another substance. But this is impossible because there cannot be two substances with the same attribute (*Ethics* I.5); and substances with different attributes have nothing in common and thus could not cause one another.

This last point is an implicit criticism of Descartes's mind/body dualism, because Descartes claimed that, even though mind and matter have different attributes, they causally interact.

According to Spinoza, because a substance is conceived through itself, we cannot truly conceive of a nonexistent substance. He also claims that we can conceive of particular tables, rivers, and trees as not existing. Particular finite objects can be conceived as nonexistent, because they are not substances; Spinoza calls them "modes," and they are conceived through something external to themselves—namely, the one substance and its attributes.

Proposition I.8: Every substance is necessarily infinite.

At proposition I.8, Spinoza argues that substances are necessarily infinite with respect to their attribute. It is impossible for a substance to be finite with respect to its attribute, because, if it were, it would have to be limited by something else with the same attribute, and then there would be two substances with the same attribute, which is impossible.

In the notes to *Ethics* I.8, Spinoza gives a more informal argument for the claim that there can only be one substance with the same nature. He takes the example of twenty men. He says that there must be an explanation of why just so many men exist. This explanation cannot lie in the nature or essence of man, he says; but the explanation of why a substance exists does lie in the nature of substance (as shown in *Ethics* I.7). Therefore the men are not substances. Spinoza generalizes this result to say that whatever is a plurality cannot be a substance, because a plurality must have an external cause.

Proposition I.11: God necessarily exists.

At this stage of his argument Spinoza first introduces the idea of God. He defines God as an absolutely infinite substance—that is, a substance that is infinite with respect to each of its attributes and that has an infinite number of attributes.

At proposition 11, Spinoza gives several arguments to show that God, with infinite attributes, necessarily exists. First, he argues that to assert that God does not exist would contradict *Ethics* I.7, which Spinoza has already demonstrated. Second, he argues that there could not be a cause of God's nonexistence. Such a cause could not come from God's own nature, for that would be an imperfection and God is all-perfect. But neither could such a cause come from anything outside God, for a substance of another nature could have nothing in common with God and thus could not cause His nonexistence. Third, Spinoza argues that, if God does not exist, then nothing does. This is because the potential to exist is a power. If finite things existed and God did not, then those finite things would have more power than God. It is impossible that finite things are more powerful than the infinite; therefore, if something exists, then God must exist too. Fourth, Spinoza says that the capacity to exist is a power. The more power belongs to the nature of a thing, the more force it has from itself to exist. The infinite Being has infinite power to exist, and therefore He does exist.

Let us briefly examine these arguments. The argument to show that substances are necessarily infinite after their own kind depends on *Ethics* I.5. It also depends on a very strong form of the Principle of Sufficient Reason: that something will be infinite unless it is prevented from being so by some limiting factor. Similarly, Spinoza's second argument to show that God exists also depends on a strong version of the Principle of Sufficient Reason: that something must exist unless there is a positive reason to prevent it from existing. Spinoza's third and fourth arguments for God's existence depend on the claim that the potential for existence is a power. Consequently they depend on the thesis that existence is a property; this view was challenged in our discussion of Descartes.

Proposition I.14: Except God, no substance can be conceived.

Spinoza tries to argue that there can be no rational reason or explanation for another substance besides God and that, since everything that exists must be capable of explanation, there can be no substance but God or Nature. Any substance besides God would have to be explicable in terms of one of God's infinite attributes, but in that case there would have to be two substances with the same attribute. But this is impossible (see *Ethics* I.5). So there is only one substance, because there exists one substance—God—with all possible attributes, and there cannot be more than one substance with the same attribute (*Ethics* I.5).

A General Review

To prove in Part I of the *Ethics* that there is only one substance—God or Nature—Spinoza has argued first that substance must exist (*Ethics* I.7) and second that, because substance must be infinite (*Ethics* I.8 and I.11), there can only be one (*Ethics* I.14).

To demonstrate that substance must exist, Spinoza argues that substance cannot be caused by anything but itself. To show this, he argues that there cannot be two substances of the same kind (*Ethics* I.5), and that substances of different kinds cannot cause each other (*Ethics* I.6).

To demonstrate that only one substance can exist, Spinoza argues that substance has all (infinite) attributes (*Ethics* I.11); and as proposition 5 asserted, there cannot be two substances with the same attribute (*Ethics* I.5).

It is important to understand how Spinoza's thought differs from Descartes's. In his ontological argument, Descartes tries to show that the existence of a Divine Being distinct from Nature is beyond doubt and necessary. Spinoza, on the other hand, attempts to show that Nature has some of the properties traditionally ascribed to God, like necessary existence. He also tries to demonstrate that Nature is infinite; all of this warrants his calling Nature or the one substance "God."

To conclude, Spinoza seeks to prove that there is only one substance and that nothing can exist independently of this substance. The substance is therefore Nature as a whole. The substance must be infinite and it necessarily exists, so it can be identified with God. In this way, logic and reason have prevailed on Spinoza to reject the Christian dichotomy of God and Nature.

Spinoza has identified what he regards as an important inconsistency in Descartes's philosophy. For Spinoza, Rationalism implies monism—the view that there is only one substance. We can informally reconstruct Spinoza's line of thought as follows: substance, by definition, is an independent existent, so anything with an external cause is not an independent existent and is not a' substance (*Ethics* I.6). But everything must have a cause, so the only thing without an external cause must be the all-inclusive whole (*Ethics* I.11), and there can only be one of those. If there were more than one substance, then each of these would have to be causally unrelated to all others, each like a self-contained universe or a Leibnizian monad (see Chapter 8).

Descartes's alleged inconsistency is that he accepts the traditional definition of substance and the Rationalist view of causation and yet maintains that God is not the only substance. He refers to minds and bodies as "created substances," which according to Spinoza is a contradiction in terms.

Despite his explicit rejection of Descartes's conclusions, Spinoza's views bear some resemblance to Descartes's theory of matter. Descartes believes that the physical universe consisted of a single extended substance in which there was no vacuum or break. This similarity between the views of the two philosophers, however, is less striking than the differences. While Descartes classifies matter, minds, and God as distinct substances, Spinoza argues that matter and mind are only attributes of the one substance, God.

Finite Modes

One difficult exegetical question about Spinoza's system is the status of finite modes—that is, what we normally call individual things—such as particular persons and physical objects. Clearly these are not substances for Spinoza; they are merely modifications of the attributes of the one substance. But does Spinoza's claim that they are not substances mean that they are not real? There is much in Spinoza's work to suggest that he considers finite modes not to be real. They cannot be different parts of the one substance, because Spinoza argues that substance is indivisible, without any parts (*Ethics* I.13). Spinoza also says that our notions of time, measure, and number are merely aids to the imagination. Thus the world as it really is is a single individual—one that exists necessarily and timelessly and is indivisible and infinite. The universe is a single a priori system that expresses "God's nature." This suggests that the viewpoint of "the common order of nature," or our normal view of the world as consisting of finite and transitory things, is just an illusion.

On the other hand, Spinoza never explicitly says that finite modes are unreal, and he often talks about the individuality of bodies, which suggests that they are real. If finite modes are not real, how should we think of them?

There is here a question of interpretation. The notion of substance involves two elements: first that of independent as opposed to derivative existence; and second that of a subject as opposed to a characteristic or property. For Descartes, these two elements of the notion of substance coincide; all independent existents are also subjects, and all derivative existents are properties. If Spinoza's notion of substance follows that of Descartes, then for him, too, all dependent existents are properties.[25] In Spinoza's system, this means that the finite modes (what we normally take to be objects, such as chairs, mountains and trees) are, strictly speaking, only adjectival properties, and that they are not things at all. What we mistakenly call things (the finite modes) are really only properties of God.

We have now considered two features of the traditional interpretation of Spinoza: first, Spinoza holds that the concepts "independent existent" and "a subject of properties" coincide; and second, as a consequence, he holds that the finite modes are really properties of God. A third feature of the standard interpretation of Spinoza has led some commentators to challenge the entire interpretation. The third feature is that, for Spinoza, God is the subject of all propositions or statements.

Some commentators on Spinoza have argued that it is absurd to claim that God is the subject of all propositions. Such a claim, they contend, implies that contradictory properties must be predicated of God and also that all kinds of atrocities and immoral acts must be attributed to God. For instance, the claim seems to imply that God both is and is not 6 feet tall, because Bill is 6 feet tall and Arthur is not 6 feet tall and God is the real subject of the proposition "Bill is 6 feet tall" and "Arthur is not 6 feet tall."

Do these absurd consequences in fact follow from Spinoza's doctrines? There are two alternative ways of arguing that they do not:

1.   One alternative is to reject the standard interpretation of Spinoza that we have just considered. For example, Curley argues that, for Spinoza, the substance/mode distinction does not coincide with the distinction of subject/predicate.[26] He denies that, for Spinoza, God is the real subject of all propositions. This alternative reading of Spinoza implies that the modes are not merely adjectival properties of substance. It denies the standard interpretation according to which Spinoza thinks that modes are properties of God.

2.   The second alternative is to defend the standard interpretation, first by arguing that Spinoza really does think that God or substance is the subject of all properties, and second by denying that this has absurd or damaging implications. According to this second alternative, Spinoza is not committed to the absurd claim that God has contradictory properties, because God's properties are not the same as the properties that we normally attribute to finite modes. In other words, just because Bill is 6 feet tall, we do not have to say that God is 6 feet tall. Instead we should say that God has some property such that Bill is 6 feet tall. Similarly,

just because Jack the Ripper was a murderer, we do not have to conclude that the one substance is a murderer. Instead, we should say that God or the one substance has some property, such that Jack the Ripper was a murderer. In general, the properties that belong to God are not the same properties as those that we normally (and mistakenly) attribute to finite modes. Consequently, the standard interpretation does not have to impute to Spinoza the absurd claim that God has contradictory properties.[27]

Given the standard interpretation of Spinoza, how would Spinoza answer the question "What are finite modes?" He would claim that particular things are not really things or objects at all. They are properties of God, expressed in determinate ways. This book is an attribute of the one substance. It is the attribute called *extension*, modified in a determinate way. It is a property and not a thing.

Conclusion

It is difficult to assess Spinoza's thought, for one instructive reason: the strong interconnection among all the parts of his philosophy. Later propositions in the *Ethics* explain and amplify earlier ones, and the earlier propositions form the logical basis for those that come later. It is difficult to know where to break into this circle.

Spinoza's theory of substance hinges on his largely unspoken thoughts about explanation and justification. For Spinoza, anything that exists must have an ideally complete explanation that traces any belief about it to its source and makes explicit the reasons for it. Spinoza seems to assume that the mind somehow functions according to the procedures of ideal justification and explanation. Perhaps this working is subliminal or only ideal, but it means that we cannot properly conceive of something without at the same time conceiving of its justification. True knowledge of any event or fact must include knowledge of its rational cause. This means that we cannot conceive of anything in isolation. Moreover, since for Spinoza explanation and existence are very closely bound notions, nothing can exist in isolation, and all truths form a single deductive system.

These points are relevant to Spinoza's conclusions about substance because of the second part of his definition: substance is that which is conceived through itself. If conceiving of any object necessarily involves explaining that object, then substance, which is conceived through itself, must be its own explanation or must be self-caused.

Since substance is conceived through itself and cannot have a cause external to itself, there is an obvious difficulty in supposing that there might be more than one substance. If there were more than one substance, the substances could not causally interact and each substance would have to be completely self-contained— a universe unto itself. As a consequence of his views on explanation and causation, Spinoza is faced with two options. He must accept either that there is only one substance or that there are different substances that cannot interact.

The later Rationalist philosopher Leibniz accepts a similar line of argument. Having views of explanation and causation and a definition of substance that resemble Spinoza's, Leibniz also claims that there cannot be causal interaction between substances. Consequently, Leibniz is faced with the same two options: either there is only one substance or there are different substances that cannot causally interact. But, unlike Spinoza, Leibniz argues for the second of these two alternatives.

As we have seen, the essentials of Spinoza's metaphysics are rooted in his Rationalistic view of explanation and his definition of substance. These two points should be examined critically. First, Spinoza assumes that the conception of any thing must include its explanation, which implies that nothing can be properly conceived of or understood in isolation. Because he assimilates causation to logical implication, Spinoza implicitly holds that part of the concept of any thing is the concept of that thing's cause. Against Spinoza, we might argue that it is possible to conceive of and know something without knowing its cause. One way to substantiate this would be to claim that causation should be distinguished from logical implication. Another way to argue this would be to deny that ideally the concept of any thing must involve its cause.

Second, Spinoza defines substance as an independent existent; his Rationalism interprets the word *independent* so strongly that nothing but Nature as a whole counts as independent. We could argue against this by challenging Spinoza's definition of substance as something that is an independent existent. An alternative definition of substance could be this: substance is that which has properties but is not itself a property. This alternative definition does not imply that substances must be independent. According to this alternative definition, ordinary finite objects can count as substances, even though they are not independent.

Next, we must examine Spinoza's assumption that everything must have a complete explanation. This might be portrayed as a demand that we make of the world: we expect the world to behave rationally such that every event can be explained. But even if this demand or expectation is coherent, there is no guarantee that it will be met. There is no logical guarantee that the world will conform to this expectation. Moreover, Spinoza holds an especially strong form of the principle that everything must have a sufficient cause. For example, he claims that, if God does not exist, then there must be some cause for His nonexistence. He also insists that there be a reason for the existence of the totality of things. Many philosophers would argue that the latter question does not make sense—that, although it is legitimate to seek explanations for particular events and facts, it is not legitimate to try to explain everything in one fell swoop or as a totality.

Study Questions

1. Why does Spinoza lay out the *Ethics* as a deductive system in the style of Euclid?

2. Why does Spinoza say that substance must be conceived through itself?

3. How does Spinoza argue that existence belongs to the essence of substance?

4. How does Spinoza argue that there is only one substance?

5. Compare Spinoza's view of substance with Descartes's.

6. Does Spinoza think that finite modes are real?

Discussion Questions

1. Must there be a complete explanation for everything?

2. Is it correct to say that the universe as a whole is the only real thing?

C H A P T E R   5

Spinoza: The Nature of the Mind

Spinoza's substance has an infinite number of attributes, and each mode can be regarded under any of these attributes. However, for some reason that Spinoza never explains, we are acquainted with only two attributes, thought and extension. Before we examine Spinoza's philosophy of mind, we shall look at his view of science and how this relates to the attribute of extension.

God's Causality and Science

To characterize the relation between substance and modes, Spinoza says that God is the immanent cause of all things (*Ethics* I.18). He asserts that infinite things follow from God's nature in infinite ways, just as it follows from the nature of a triangle that its three angles are equal to two right angles. Spinoza is claiming that the causal relation between God and the modes is like logical necessity.

But how do the finite modes follow from the Divine Nature? Spinoza does not mean that the existence of any particular finite mode, like the Empire State Building, can be deduced directly from God's nature. For when he says that every individual finite thing must be conditioned by another finite thing ad infinitum (*Ethics* I.28), he means that any particular mode must be conditioned by an earlier state of the universe.

So where does the Divine Nature fit in? When Spinoza talks about the eternal essence of God, he is referring to divine attributes, one of which is extension. Physical extension is characterized by certain basic scientific laws; and when Spinoza refers to the Divine Nature, he often has in mind the basic laws of physics.

Given this point, we might argue for the following interpretation of Spinoza's view of scientific explanation. A particular mode or event, such as the throwing of a stone, cannot alone suffice to determine a further particular thing, like the breaking of glass. General causal laws are also needed to explain the broken glass. Any particular thing can be deduced from the laws of Nature, if and only if these causal laws are taken together with the appropriate antecedent conditions. In other words, antecedent conditions plus causal laws jointly entail a particular fact. Or in Spinoza's own terminology, particular finite modes and the Divine Nature—specifically, the nature of the attribute extension—together determine the existence of a finite mode.

Spinoza denies any transcendent cause of the world. God is not a mysterious super-being who caused a temporally datable first event. One infinite aspect of God's essence is constituted by the laws of Nature, and these laws are a necessary cause of what happens. In other words, rather than being the creator of the world, God is the immanent cause. Spinoza denies the traditional account of creation and attempts to replace it with a more scientific model.

This interpretation of Spinoza's view of scientific explanation implies that the attribute of extension is characterized by fundamental natural laws. These laws are axiomatic in that they are logically independent from each other and in that all other laws are capable of being deduced from them. One problem with this view of Spinoza is that he sometimes says that modes themselves follow directly and with necessity from the nature of God. This suggests, contrary to *Ethics* I.28, that particular finite modes can be deduced directly from God's nature.

Spinoza seems committed to the idea of a complete and unified physical science. According to Descartes (and other dualists), this is not possible, since some physical events, like the action of the pineal gland in the brain, are mentally caused and therefore cannot be explained by any closed or single system of physical causes. Spinoza thinks that any physical change is a completely determined effect within a closed set of physical causes and laws, and this implies the possibility of a complete and scientific physical explanation.

The Infinite and Eternal Modes

There are two types of infinite and eternal modes in Spinoza's metaphysics: immediate infinite modes and the mediate infinite modes. A mode, for Spinoza, is a dependent existent—something that is conceived through and exists in substance. Theoretically, each mode can be conceived through any of the infinite attributes of substance. With respect to extension, Spinoza mentions motion-and-rest as an immediate infinite mode (*Ethics* I.21 and I.22), which follows directly from the nature of the attribute. Motion-and-rest is the primary characteristic of physical extension, or Nature. The mediate infinite and eternal mode, with respect to extension, Spinoza calls "the face or aspect of the Universe as a whole." Although there is motion-and-rest and although the individual modes of Nature are continually changing, Nature as a whole remains constant.

Hampshire says that it is reasonable to translate Spinoza's terms *motion* and *rest* as "energy."[28] This is because Spinoza seems to regard rest as something positive, rather than as the mere absence of motion. Spinoza considers motion to be essential to the constitution of all extended things. Within the extended universe, the overall proportion of motion-and-rest is constant, since the extended world constitutes a single closed or self-contained system of causes. For Spinoza, the amount of movement or energy in Nature is intrinsic to Nature; there can be no question of an external cause or interference from outside. This is because God—or Nature—contains the prior and inherent cause of all things. Spinoza also holds that, in principle, all changes in the qualities of objects (such as a change of color) can be explained in purely quantitative terms, as measurable changes in the velocity and configuration of small particles. What Locke later called "the secondary qualities" are for Spinoza ultimately only changes in the motion-and-rest of elementary particles. In this respect, Spinoza's thought resembles Descartes's and Locke's.

In the note to *Ethics* II.13 where he discusses motion-and-rest, Spinoza says that simple bodies are distinguished from each other only by motion-and-rest, quickness, and slowness.[29] Otherwise, these simple particles are qualitatively identical. Compound bodies are composed of simple bodies that move together in unison. In fact, a body remains qualitatively the same so long as each of its parts remains in the same relation to the other parts, with respect to their motion-and-rest.

A complex body is defined by a fixed relation among the movements of its parts. Any more-or-less stable composition can be regarded as a single individual. Spinoza says that we can conceive of progressively greater and more complex wholes until we conceive of the whole of extended Nature as a single individual, the parts of which change in infinite ways while Nature itself remains one and the same. This individual is the mediate infinite and eternal mode that Spinoza calls "the face of the Universe."

Spinoza's theory of matter is in many ways similar to that of Descartes, and was influenced by it. However, the views of the two philosophers differ in some important respects. According to Spinoza, motion-and-rest is a primary characteristic of matter. For Spinoza, the physical or extended universe is a single closed system, and this implies that nothing exists outside the physical universe to cause movement. Thus, for Spinoza, motion-and-rest must be an intrinsic feature of the material world. On the other hand, for Descartes, the essence of matter is spatial extension, and the extended universe is not a closed system, because it is open to the outside influence of God and finite minds. Furthermore, for Descartes, matter is a substance; for Spinoza, it is a feature of the one substance as conceived through the attribute known as extension.

The Attributes

God is a substance with an infinite number of attributes. Spinoza defines an attribute as being that which the intellect perceives as the essence of substance.

The attributes do not follow from the nature of God; rather, they constitute that essence. Spinoza explains that the attributes are so-called because to conceive God intellectually is to attribute to Him such and such a nature; but as God is infinite, there are infinite ways of conceiving Him.

Spinoza claims that each attribute must be conceived through itself (*Ethics* I.10). He means that, for instance, when some physical event is to be explained, it must be done through the attribute of extension and its modes alone. The explanation should not involve a reference to the mental. But if each attribute is to be conceived through itself, what is the precise relation between the attributes and the underlying substance, which is also to be conceived through itself? Different interpreters of Spinoza have expressed different views on this point, but we shall confine ourselves to examining two, both of which relate to the discussion of finite modes in Chapter 4:

1.   One view is that God or substance is related to the attributes as subject is to predicate. The attributes are the essential properties of God. According to this traditional view, Spinoza has a Cartesian-type notion of substance, whereby a substance is both an independent existent and the subject of properties. Although each attribute is to be conceived through itself, it does not exist in itself, but rather "in" substance.[30] This view has the consequence that the modes, the modifications of the attributes, are adjectival. This was discussed in Chapter 4.

2.   An alternative view is that Spinoza does not have a Cartesian notion of substance and, consequently, that the attributes are not the properties of substance. According to this view,[31] substance is identical with the attributes themselves; that is, substance consists in the collection of the infinite attributes. In his note to *Ethics* I.29, Spinoza distinguishes between active and passive Nature. On the basis of this and other passages, Curley suggests that Spinoza's substance is not the whole of Nature, but rather only the active or primary elements in Nature. He suggests that the active element in Nature is simply the attributes. If Curley is right, it is inaccurate to present Spinoza as a pantheist, for God is not nature as a whole but simply the infinite attributes.

Although Curley's interpretation fits many passages, especially *Ethics* I.29, it also fails to explain adequately why Spinoza should think that substance is indivisible. If substance is the collection of the infinite attributes, why should Spinoza call extension an attribute of God rather than a part of God?

| Extension and Thought

At *Ethics* II.7, Spinoza says that the order and connection of ideas is the same as the order and connection of extended things. According to Spinoza, thought and extension are not two separate substances, but one substance comprehended through different attributes. More specifically, an extended mode and the idea of that mode are one and the same but are expressed through different attributes.

Spinoza's extended modes are determined by previous modes ad infinitum and by the physical laws that govern extended objects. Similarly, modes of thought on ideas are determined by previous modes of thought ad infinitum and by the laws that define the nature of the attribute thought. However, it is misleading to say that, according to Spinoza, the chain of physical and mental causes are parallel, if this suggests two distinct chains. There is only one chain of modes, but it can be viewed in different ways.

The relation between the human mind and body, for Spinoza, is simply a special case of the one order in Nature being viewed through different attributes. The mind is the same mode as the body, but it is comprehended through the attribute of thought rather than through the attribute of physical extension.

The Mind and the Body

Descartes's theory of the mind has two main features. First, he argues for substance dualism—that minds are substances distinct from matter and bodies. Second, he claims that the mind and the body interact causally with each other.

Spinoza's theory of mind can be understood in opposition to Descartes's. Spinoza thinks that there are problems inherent in a two-substance theory of mind/body. These are in large part the problems of consistently combining the tenets of Rationalism with any view other than monism, which were mentioned in Chapter 4. There are also problems more specific to the interaction between mind and body. A person is whole or a unity; and according to the dualist, the causal relation between the mind and body must be especially intimate. Yet the interaction required by dualism is deeply mysterious. The interaction is mysterious because Descartes's dualism implies that minds and matter are unlike each other. For Descartes, matter is essentially spatially extended, and minds are not; conversely minds are essentially conscious, and matter is not.

Spinoza rejects Descartes's substance dualism, but he asserts an attributive dualism, according to which thought and extension are two distinct attributes of the one substance. For Spinoza, particular minds and bodies are not distinct substances. Instead, they are the same particular mode conceived through the distinct attributes of thought and extension.

Spinoza also rejects interactionism and tries to account for the unity of the mind and body without it. He says that the mind and the body are one and the same mode, expressed in two ways. Since the mind and the body are the same mode, there can be no question of any interaction between them.[32]

Moreover, Spinoza contends that the two attributes must be conceived through themselves (*Ethics* I.10). Thus, we can view a human being through the attribute of extension as a material body, subject to and governed entirely by physical laws. Alternatively, we can conceive of a person through the attribute of thought as a mind or idea, subject to and governed entirely by the laws of thought. These two ways of conceiving the same finite mode are distinct and self-contained. There can be no interaction between the physical and the mental.

Similarly, the universe as a whole, when conceived through the attribute of extension, is a self-contained physical thing; whereas the universe as a whole, when conceived through the attribute of thought, is a self-contained infinite idea. These are two self-contained ways of conceiving of the one substance. There can be no physical explanations of the universe conceived through the attribute of thought, and there can be no mentalistic explanations of the universe conceived through the attribute of extension. Each attribute must be conceived through itself.

The Mind as the Idea of the Body

According to Spinoza, the mind and the body are the same individual, but the object of the mind is always the body itself. The mind is a complex idea, and the object of that idea is simply the body. This is because an idea (for instance, of a circle) and its object (the circle itself) are one and the same thing regarded under different attributes. It sounds strange to say that the object of the mind is always the body. Does this mean that I cannot perceive anything external to my body? Spinoza's answer would be that, for instance, in the case of my perceiving a tree, the object of my mind is not the tree itself, but my own body as it is modified or affected by the tree. At *Ethics* II.17, Spinoza discusses the difference between the idea of Peter's body that constitutes the essence of Peter's mind, on the one hand, and Paul's idea of Peter, on the other. Spinoza says that Paul's idea of Peter "indicates the disposition of Paul's body rather than the nature of Peter." While this disposition of Paul's body lasts, Paul's mind will perceive Peter, even if Peter no longer exists. In perception we are aware of our own body as it is affected by something else. This point has important consequences for Spinoza's theory of knowledge.

All Things Have Souls

Since the mind and the body are the same individual, every change in the body must involve a change in the mind; and just as the body is composed of individual parts, so the constitution of the mind is complex (*Ethics* II.15). For every part of the body, there is an idea. Indeed, one consequence of Spinoza's theory is that every extended mode must also be capable of being apprehended under the attribute of thought, as an idea. For every extended mode, there must be an idea, with which it is identical. Since Spinoza claims that the mind is the idea of the body, it may seem as if he is saying that all extended things have minds or souls. In fact, Spinoza does say that all things are to different degrees animated—and literally, *animated* means having a soul or animus (*Ethics* II.13).

However, Spinoza does not mean that all things have minds or souls, if the words *mind* and *soul* are taken in their normal sense. First, if being an extended individual is a matter of degree, and if the only real individual is the universe as a whole, then the same must apply to modes of thought. Being an individual mode of thought or mind must be a matter of degree, too. So the ideas that correspond (or are identical to) the most simple modes of extension should not be called "minds" in the usual sense. Second, we are unaware of many of the physical processes in our own bodies. Yet there must be an idea for every minute change in the body; and furthermore, such ideas form part of one complex idea—the mind. Clearly, we cannot equate having an idea in Spinoza's philosophy with being conscious. Spinoza could claim that only minds at least as complex as the human mind are conscious.

Materialism

Descartes is an ontological dualist. He thinks that there are at least two kinds of substances in the universe: minds and matter. Although Spinoza rejects ontological dualism, it would be a mistake to think of him as espousing a Materialist ontology. According to a Materialist ontology, there are no mental substances; only material substances exist. What we call "minds" are merely material things or substances, like brains. One reason why Spinoza is not an ontological Materialist is that he denies that material objects are substances. For Spinoza, there is only one substance. Furthermore, the one substance has both mental and material attributes, neither of which is reducible to the other. For Spinoza, thought is not reducible to extension, nor vice versa, thus, neither extension nor thought has primacy over the other. The two attributes, thought and extension, are different but equally valid ways of conceiving the one sub-stance. Consequently, according to Spinoza, just as every mental change is identical with a material change, so every material change is identical with a mental change. In Spinoza's terms, every extended mode is identical with a corresponding mode of thought. The ontological dualist asserts that two kinds of things exist—minds and matter. The ontological Materialist holds that only one kind of thing exists—material things. Spinoza denies both positions and asserts that the one substance can be conceived equally through the attribute of thought or through that of extension.

It is incorrect to think of Spinoza as a Materialist for another reason. Many Materialists hold that mental phenomena must be given physical explanations. Thoughts and feelings must be explained in purely physical terms. In holding that the attributes of extension and thought are distinct and self-contained, Spinoza denies the possibility of physical explanations of mental phenomena. All physical events must be explained in purely physical terms, and all mental events must be explained in purely mentalistic terms.

No Ownership of Ideas

In asserting the existence of only one substance, Spinoza denies that human minds are substances. For him, minds are modes of thought and are to be viewed, perhaps, as fragments of the Divine Understanding. According to Spinoza, the human mind does not have ideas; instead, it is an idea, albeit a complex one. We have seen that Spinoza follows Descartes in regarding individual material things as temporary forms of one homogeneous piece of matter. For Spinoza, the one substance, conceived through the attribute of extension, is the material universe as a whole. Similarly, the one substance, conceived through the attribute of thought, is a single thought of great complexity.

Descartes believes that thoughts or ideas are properties of mental substances; that is, minds have thoughts. For Spinoza, however, there are no finite mental substances to have thoughts or ideas. There is only the one substance, and thought is an attribute of it. Particular thoughts or ideas are merely modifications of that attribute. This implies that, for Spinoza, it is incorrect to claim that the human mind has thoughts; instead, we should assert that human minds are thoughts. Consequently, ideas exist unowned by finite minds.

The Reality of Finite Minds

In Chapter 4, we saw that Spinoza may be committed to the claim that individual finite modes are unreal. If we ask Spinoza what exists, he may deny that particular material objects—like computers, trees, and mountains—are real. He may instead claim that only the whole material universe exists as a substance conceived through the attribute of extension. According to this view, finite individual material objects do not exist as substances, but only as modes. Similarly, Spinoza may deny that finite individual minds are real. If we ask him what exists, as conceived through the attribute of thought, he may reply that particular finite ideas, such as minds, are not real. Instead only one idea, the Divine thought as a whole, exists as a substance conceived through the attribute of thought. Finite individual minds thus do not exist as substances, but only as modes. They are properties of the one substance, manifested in particular ways.

Study Questions

1. What does Spinoza mean by claiming that God is the immanent cause of all things?

2. What does Spinoza mean by "the face of the Universe as a whole"?

3. Explain how Spinoza distinguishes among modes, attributes, and substance.

4. How is Spinoza's view of matter different from Descartes's?

5. Is Spinoza a Materialist?

6. Why does Spinoza reject Descartes's dualist theory of mind?

7. Descartes thinks that the mind has ideas; Spinoza thinks that the mind is an idea. Why does Spinoza think this?

Discussion Questions

1. Spinoza rejects the claim that the mind is a substance. If individual finite modes are not real, this implies that the mind is not real, in much the same way as physical objects are not. Is Spinoza's view about the reality of the mind plausible?

2. Is Spinoza's theory of mind an improvement on Descartes's?

CHAPTER 6

Spinoza: Theory of Knowledge

Spinoza's theory of knowledge is an important link between his metaphysics and his ethics. Spinoza's theory of one substance with infinite attributes implies that there cannot be an extended thing without an idea, and vice versa. The order of ideas and the order of extended modes are one and the same. For Spinoza there is a hierarchy of things from the most simple finite and transitory modes up to the only real individual: the whole universe, or the infinite and eternal order of Nature. Much the same can be said of the attribute of thought. Ideas range from the most confused and inadequate to the most clear and adequate ideas. This hierarchy of ideas forms the basis of Spinoza's theory of knowledge and the link to his ethics. By attaining the more adequate ideas in the hierarchy we may achieve freedom.

Kinds of Knowledge

In note 2 of *Ethics* II.40, Spinoza sets out his three-fold classification of knowledge.

1. Imagination

Spinoza calls the first kind of knowledge "imagination," which he subdivides into knowledge from vague experience and knowledge from hearsay. Imagination includes knowledge from sense perception, but Spinoza argues that this is an inadequate form of knowledge (*Ethics* II.19 and II.24–II.28). His point is that the ideas of sense perception arise from interreaction between the human body and the external body concerned, and hence involve the nature of both these bodies. But knowledge of the external body involves knowledge of yet further things. The knowledge we have in sense perception is therefore incomplete and inadequate. Similarly, true knowledge of the human body involves knowledge of the parts of the body, and this is lacking in perception. Because of its incompleteness, Spinoza says that sense perception involves inadequate ideas. He calls it, aptly enough, "consequence without premises," reflecting his assimilation of the causal explanation to logical implication. Imagination involves ideas that correspond to the impact of external things on the body; and this is confused because the order of the ideas is not imposed from within according to any rational order, but rather is imposed from without. Since the idea involves something external to itself, it is incomplete.

Spinoza also includes in his definition of imagination the crude association of ideas from personal habit and from what happens to be observed. No form of imagination involves logical thought and order, and hence imagination always lacks the certainty of that which can be logically demonstrated. Spinoza shares Descartes's rationalistic view that sense experience is an inferior source of knowledge compared with reason, but unlike Descartes he does not use the argument from illusion, nor does he cite the deceptiveness of our senses to make this point. Like Descartes, Spinoza has a mathematical view of knowledge, which stresses the theoretical possibility of knowing all things a priori. Although Spinoza argues that what is learned through sense experience is radically incomplete and low-grade, he does regard knowledge gained through the senses as having some use; it can tell us about the existence of particular finite modes.

2. Reason

Spinoza's second form of knowledge, called "reason," consists of "common notions and adequate ideas of the properties of things." The common notions are the ideas that form the basis of all reasoning. This second form of knowledge consists of universal, timeless, necessary truths that follow from each other in a deductive system, as in mathematics and the physical sciences.

The knowledge of reason obviously conforms to Spinoza's model of knowledge. It is clear and distinct and follows a proper logical order, rather than obeying the laws of psychological association. In this sense, the second kind of knowledge is internally rather than externally determined. Spinoza says that the ideas of reason are "adequate." His use of the word *adequate* is special, resembling Descartes's earlier principle that clear and distinct ideas are true. An adequate idea is one that, considered in itself, has the intrinsic marks of a true idea: coherence, clarity, and distinctness.

3. Intuition

Although Spinoza regards reason as an adequate form of knowledge, intuition is yet more perfect. Spinoza discusses intuitive knowledge in Part V of the *Ethics,* but mostly in terms of its good effects on humanity. The precise nature of this third kind of knowledge is hazy. Intuitive knowledge has much in common with reason: it is eternal, necessarily true, internally determined in a logical order, and inferential. It is distinctive because the inferences involved in intuition are immediate, without reference to general rules, and because they give us detailed knowledge of how individual modes follow from the nature of the attributes. The crucial point is that Spinoza views this third type of knowledge as more potent than reason, for intuition gives us a love of God and personal freedom. Those who have this third type of knowledge naturally understand the way in which things follow from the nature of God and are less subject to evil passions.

Truth and Falsity

Given his views, Spinoza appears to have problems accounting for the possibility of false ideas or beliefs. According to his theory of attributes, every idea and its object or ideatum are one and the same thing, expressed differently. At axiom 6, in Part I of the *Ethics,* Spinoza states that a true idea must agree with its ideatum or object. Consequently, since every idea must have a corresponding extended mode, it seems impossible that an idea should not agree with its object. Each idea simply is its object.

How then is Spinoza to account for false ideas? One suggestion is that an idea is false for Spinoza when it is incomplete. Spinoza gives two examples of the privation of knowledge or false ideas. The first occurs when people judge themselves to be free because they are unaware of the causes of their actions. The second involves our looking at the sun and imagining it to be 200 feet away, because we are ignorant of the true distance and of the cause of our imagining (*Ethics* II.35). In both cases, inadequate and incomplete knowledge results in false ideas.

Just as the whole system of extended things is regarded as one individual universe in which each constituent represents a mere partial aspect of the whole, so too are ideas in relation to the attribute of thought. It is possible to read Spinoza as saying that there is really only one idea, which he calls "the infinite intellect of God." If this is correct, then no partial idea can be true in and of itself, but only in the context of the complete system of ideas.

Some commentators interpret Spinoza as claiming that there is only one truth, with all human ideas and beliefs constituting incomplete fragments of the one true idea, and that, because they lack completeness, those fragments must be false. But Spinoza never actually says this. Instead he claims that all truths relate as part of a deductive system. When he argues that false ideas are incomplete, he does not mean that one must be familiar with the complete system of true ideas before anything can be known. He means that it is necessary to know the basis of the deductive system—for instance, the fundamental laws of the attribute extension—and what he calls "the common notions" (*Ethics* II.38).

So when Spinoza accounts for the falsity of some ideas in terms of their incompleteness, this does not mean that all finite ideas are false and that only the infinite idea of God is true. Spinoza's model for incompleteness seems to be sense perception. When I look at the sun and judge it to be 200 feet away, my judgment is at least partly true (according to Spinoza) because the sun does indeed look as if it were 200 feet away. This type of example may have led Spinoza to believe that any false idea is partly true and that correcting error is simply a matter of adding new information.

Determinism and Free Will

Spinoza is a determinist. First, he believes that everything must have a sufficient reason, and he assimilates the causal relation to that of logical implication. Second, he says, at *Ethics* I.33, that things could not have been brought about by God in any manner or order different from that which obtains. Nothing in the universe is contingent, but all things are conditioned by the Divine Nature, which could not have been any other way. Spinoza seems to be claiming that this world is the only possible world. He says that all apparent contingency is the consequence of our ignorance of the order of causes.

The exact nature of Spinoza's determinism is not clear. Certainly he thinks that the nature of the attributes is determined logically; the laws of Nature are absolutely necessary truths. Less clear is the question of the infinite series of finite modes. Is the series of finite modes completely determined, so that every truth is absolutely necessary and the actual world is the only possible world? Or on the other hand, is each finite mode determined by previous modes and by the nature of the attributes, so that each particular fact is not absolutely but only relatively necessary? (That is to say, each is necessary relative to the previous finite modes, which are themselves necessary relative to the previous finite modes, and so on.) The answer to these questions depends on whether the finite modes can be directly deduced from the Divine Nature, the attributes. If they can be deduced from God's Nature, Spinoza's system is rigidly deterministic, and every truth is absolutely necessary and can be known a priori. If, on the other hand, the finite modes cannot be directly deduced from the Divine Nature, then some truths are only relatively necessary.

In either case, Spinoza clearly opposes the Cartesian notion of free will. He is against the idea that bodily movements are caused by mental acts of free choice. For Spinoza, there can be no mind-body interaction, since the mind and the body are one and the same. Moreover, all human behavior is part of the chain of natural causes, and as such it is determined. We only think we are free, because we are unconscious of the causes of our actions—although we are conscious of our desires. Spinoza likens our situation to that of a stone in flight: the stone wishes to be in motion and falsely believes that its free desire is the continuing cause of its motion. When we do what we want to do, we falsely believe that our desire is the free cause of our actions. But according to Spinoza, the action must be explained by some physical cause and not by attribution to any mental act or desire. The mental and the physical (or more accurately, the extended) do not form two distinct realms that can interact; rather they constitute two complete and exclusive ways of regarding Nature. For this reason, Spinoza says that the will is not a free cause and that there is no free will.

Despite his attack on the Cartesian notion of free will, and despite his determinism, Spinoza does have a positive theory of human freedom. This is the basis of his ethical system. Spinoza attempts to oppose freedom to constraint rather than to necessity. To act freely is not to act from an uncaused mental decision, but to act from the necessity of one's own nature. Human freedom resides in the power of reason to control the emotions, because reason is determined not by external causes but from within.

When Spinoza says that reason is determined from within and is consequently free, he means that reason, unlike imagination, follows a logical order in ideas. Reason allows us to understand how things follow by necessity from the Divine Nature. In particular it can liberate us from negative passions that are based on inadequate ideas. Insofar as a person grasps the necessity of things and sees reality as a whole, she is free; liberated by a clear understanding. In the grip of passions, we appear to be under the power of external forces; but as soon as we form a clear and distinct idea of a passion, it ceases to be one and we are freed. In this way, a clear understanding that all things are necessary gives the mind power over the passions (see the note to *Ethics* V.20). This understanding, which liberates us from the bondage of the passions, at the same time instills in us an intellectual love of God or Nature.

However, if the power of the mind over the emotions is defined by knowledge alone, there is a problem with Spinoza's ethics and his positive views of human freedom. As we acquire understanding and more adequate ideas, we inevitably become free of delusive passions and learn to love God. But since they are a part of Nature, our actions are causally determined; so in what sense, if any, are we free to become persons of understanding? In saying that we can actively become more perfect, Spinoza implies that we already have some freedom of choice, but this implication seems to contradict the deterministic nature of his metaphysics. Does how we think of things rest with us? In what sense am I, as a finite mode, responsible for my understanding (or lack of it) if my thoughts and actions are completely causally determined?

Study Questions

1. What are Spinoza's three kinds of knowledge? Why are the differences between them important to Spinoza?

2. Why does Spinoza call sense perception "conclusions without premises"?

3. Spinoza and Descartes both have some difficulties explaining how false beliefs are possible; but the difficulties are very different. What is this difference?

4. What does Spinoza mean by an "adequate idea"?

5. Why does Spinoza reject Descartes's notion of free will?

6. Why is Spinoza a determinist?

7. What is the relation between Spinoza's view of knowledge and his ethics?

Discussion Questions

1. Is there anything wrong with Spinoza's account of knowledge gained through sense perception?

2. Can a determinist like Spinoza have a theory of ethics?

Leibniz (1646-1716)

Born in Leipzig in 1646, near the close of the devastating Thirty Years War, Gottfried Wilhelm Leibniz appears to have been a conscientious character from childhood on. He claimed to have taught himself Latin, achieving fluency by the age of twelve, and began a lifelong habit of composing poems in Latin for occasions such as weddings and holidays. In 1661 Leibniz entered Leipzig University, where his father had been Professor of Moral Philosophy. There he studied rhetoric, mathematics, and Hebrew, as well as Greek and Latin. He also became familiar with modern thinkers such as Bacon, Hobbes, and Descartes.

Leibniz then spent three more years at Leipzig, studying law. In debt to relatives, he hoped to gain an income as a tutor of law, but was denied candidacy. Disappointed, Leibniz moved on to the University of Altdorf, near Nuremberg. His doctoral thesis was already prepared, and he was formally awarded the degree the following February (only five months after registering). His dissertation was an impressive discussion of cases in which valid legal grounds exist simultaneously for the opposing sides. He was promptly offered a professorship at Altdorf but evidently decided that he did not want an academic career.

In 1667 Leibniz took a post in the court of the Elector of Mainz, which was to involve him in various diplomatic missions. His first major task concerned the election of a king of Poland. Although the large treatise he produced on this subject had little effect on the election itself, it was admired by contemporary political scientists for its analytic power.

His next important plan was to distract Louis XIV of France away from his neighbors, to attack Egypt instead. Leibniz again used his powers of reasoning in writing the proposal, and was invited to Paris to present it to the king. By the time he arrived, England had already declared war on Holland, and France was about to do likewise, rendering the project redundant. Interestingly, though, it was very similar to the plan Napoleon actually carried out more than a century later. Leibniz remained in Paris for four years, reveling in the intellectual stimulation of the city. He became acquainted with the mathematician Christian Huygens and pursued his own mathematical studies vigorously. He developed a calculating machine that could add, subtract, multiply, and divide. While on another diplomatic mission in 1673, Leibniz exhibited his machine at the Royal Society in London. Back in Paris, besides studying with Huygens, Leibniz met Malebranche, Arnauld, and Tschirnhaus and became a member of the French Academy of Sciences, where he also exhibited a clock of his own invention. This intense activity culminated in his discovery of differential and integral calculus in 1676. It was not until 1684 that he published his findings, however, causing a mutually unflattering controversy with Newton (who had also written on and then not published the subject) over who deserved the credit for first discovering this branch of mathematics.

Late in 1676, Leibniz moved to Hanover to act as adviser and librarian to Duke Johann Friedrich. Although accepting this post meant intellectual isolation for him, he seemed, at least initially, to enjoy being free from the distractions of Paris. His secretary Eckhart was later to describe Leibniz as an optimist who made the best of everything. He continued to correspond with many of his learned contemporaries and to pursue his own studies. After Duke Johann Friedrich died, his successor Duke Ernst August gave Leibniz the daunting task of researching and compiling a detailed history of the House of Brunswick, beginning with the year 768. Destined never to be completed, this project burdened Leibniz for the rest of his life. From 1687 to 1690, Leibniz traveled in Germany, Austria, and Italy, investigating historical materials in libraries and archives.

In 1690 Leibniz returned to Hanover, where he spent most of his time from then on. His duties during these years were many and various: as well as writing the history, Leibniz administered the state mint and library and served as an adviser on legal and political questions. He evidently became very close to the Duchess Sophie and her daughter, Sophie Charlotte (later queen of Prussia). He had many philosophical discussions with Sophie Charlotte, who often requested that he write down his comments so that she could consider them at her leisure. These notes later resulted in his *Theodicy,* the only large philosophical work that Leibniz published during his lifetime.

Although his publications were few, he actually wrote a prodigious amount. For example, he maintained written correspondence at any given time with an average of 150 to 200 contemporaries on a variety of topics. By 1704, Leibniz had completed a commentary on Locke's *Essay Concerning Human Understanding,* but in view of Locke's death that same year, he felt it inappropriate to publish the critique, which eventually came out in 1765.

Apart from his paid positions and his mathematical and philosophical studies, Leibniz had many enthusiasms and schemes. At one stage, for example, he hoped to improve the German economy with silk production. In his own garden he experimented with silk worms feeding on mulberry trees, and he was granted production licenses in both Berlin and Dresden. In Berlin the silk industry eventually did become quite important. At other times Leibniz was consulted on engineering and architectural projects; between 1679 and 1686, he tried various experiments, designed windmills and pumps, and drafted extensive plans for draining the Harz silver mines. In 1700 Leibniz founded and became first president of the Berlin Academy of Sciences.

Leibniz also attempted to encourage an alliance first between the various Christian faiths and later between the Christian states. This was a long-term ambition; the treatise showing how Catholic and Protestant differences could be resolved is thought to have been in existence by 1686. Much later, in 1711, Leibniz approached Czar Peter the Great with his vision of a united Europe. Leibniz was an apparently tireless figure who enjoyed the patronage of many eminent contemporaries. In Hanover, however, he was not popular. His universalist approach to religion and politics had earned him the nickname "Lovenix," meaning "believer in nothing," and during his later years, when he could no longer travel much, he seems to have been a lonely figure. He remained a bachelor all his life. Leibniz died on November 14, 1716 and was buried quietly in the Neustadter Kirche.

CHAPTER 7

Leibniz: Truth and Reason

Despite the fact that Leibniz was a prolific writer, there is no long single systematic exposition of Leibniz's philosophy as a whole. The *Monadology* (1714), like the *Discourse on Metaphysics* (1686) and the *New System* (1695), is only a short summary of part of his thought, and the work is very condensed. In addition, Leibniz wrote much of his philosophy in letters and notes, and the emphases and details of his ideas changed as a result of his correspondence. Thus, the depth of Leibniz's thought cannot be understood by studying the *Monadology* in isolation.

One of the fundamental differences between Spinoza's philosophy and Leibniz's is that much of Leibniz's metaphysics is influenced by his theory of the proposition. Whereas Spinoza hardly discusses the nature of language, this is a central concern for Leibniz and forms an important underpinning for the claims of the *Monadology*.

Leibniz's theory of the proposition has two parts. First, he argues that the subject-predicate form of proposition is basic and that all other forms of proposition can be reduced to this form. In a subject-predicate proposition, a property is affirmed or denied for the subject of the proposition; for example, "Water is wet," or "Washington was the first president of the United States." As Leibniz is well aware, not all propositions are of this grammatical form; for example, hypothetical propositions take the form "If it is Friday, then we should go to the bank." Likewise, relational propositions, such as "the tree is to the left of the bush" are not of the subject-predicate form. Leibniz's point is that these types of propositions, which are not of the subject-predicate form, can be reduced to propositions that are of this form.

Leibniz is interested in this point mainly because it has metaphysical implications. The metaphysical counterparts of subject-predicate propositions are substances and their properties. If subject-predicate propositions are basic, the universe should be completely describable by means of this type of proposition. This would mean that the universe ultimately consists only of substances and their properties. Leibniz uses this last point to argue that spatio-temporal relations between substances are not an additional item in the universe, and hence that space and time are not real. These arguments are examined in Chapters 8 and 9.

The second part of Leibniz's theory of the proposition is his analysis of truth. What is it that makes a proposition true? Leibniz's surprising answer to this question profoundly influences his view of substance and is the topic of the present chapter.

Truth

According to Leibniz, a proposition is true if and only if the concept of the predicate of the proposition is contained in the concept of the subject. In a letter to Arnauld, Leibniz says: "In a true proposition, the notion of the predicate is in the notion of the subject."[33] The predicate of a proposition is contained in the subject when the former is entailed by the latter. For example, in the proposition "the hairless man is bald" the idea of the subject ("the hairless man") contains the predicate concept ("is bald"), obviously.

According to Leibniz, in all true propositions the concept of the subject contains the concept of predicate, even when this containment is not at all obvious. For example, the proposition "Washington is the first U.S. president" is true because the concept ("Washington") contains the predicate ("is the first U.S. president"), even though this containment is not at all obvious.

Finite and Infinite Analysis

Leibniz defines a "necessary truth" as a truth that cannot be denied without contradiction. He realizes that his view of truth as concept inclusion appears to have the consequence that all true propositions are necessary. If the concept "bachelor" contains the concept "is unmarried," then the proposition "All bachelors are unmarried" cannot be denied without contradiction. (In the later terminology of Kant, it is termed *analytic*). Similarly, if the concept "Washington" contains the predicate "is the first U.S. president," then the statement "Washington was the first U.S. president" also cannot be denied without contradiction. Leibniz was aware of this problem; he writes: "There is something which has perplexed me for a long time. I did not understand how the predicate could be in the subject, without the proposition thereby becoming necessary."

Leibniz tries to solve this problem by distinguishing between propositions that have a finite analysis and propositions that have an infinite analysis.

1. Finite Analysis

A proposition such as "A male is a male" is a self-evident statement of identity of the form "*A* is *A*." It cannot be denied without immediate self-contradiction. Other propositions, such as "The hairless man is bald," "My brother is a male," and "A triangle has three sides," can be shown to be statements of identity by a finite process of analysis. For instance, analysis of the concept of a triangle shows us that, by definition, a triangle is a two-dimensional figure with three sides; so the proposition "A triangle has three sides" can be shown by a finite process of analysis to be a statement of identity (namely, "A three-sided figure has three sides") and to be of the form "*AB* is *A*." Once the concept of a triangle is properly understood, it becomes self-evident that the proposition "A triangle has three sides" is a statement of identity of the form "*A* is *A*."

2. Infinite Analysis

Other true propositions, like "Washington is the first U.S. president," and "Julius Caesar died in 44 B.C." do not appear to be statements of identity. But they do not appear to be so only because we do not know their full analysis, which would show them to be of the form "*AB* is *A*." Despite their appearance, Leibniz claims that such propositions really are statements of identity and that, if the concept of Julius Caesar were completely understood, it would be self-evident that the proposition "Julius Caesar died in 44 B.C." is a statement of identity. The reason it does not appear so to us is that we are incapable of completing the analysis of the concept of Julius Caesar. The analysis of the complete concept of any individual is known only to God and is infinitely long.

Leibniz makes these points by distinguishing *the* concept of Caesar from *a* concept of Caesar. To have *the* concept of Caesar, we would need to have complete knowledge of him and every detail of his life; but such knowledge is only accessible to God. Finite minds like ours can only have *a* concept—partial and incomplete—of any individual like Caesar, and consequently we cannot see that true propositions like "Caesar died in 44 B.C." are indeed identical, or of the form "*AB* is *A*." Only God can see that the concept of Julius Caesar includes and entails every predicate that is true of the man.

In summary, Leibniz claims that in all true propositions the subject contains the predicate. Leibniz defends this claim by arguing that we should distinguish two kinds of propositions: those like "the triangle has three sides" whose analysis is finite and which constitute necessary truths; and those like "Caesar died in 44 B.C.," whose analysis is infinite and which constitute contingent truths.

Primitive Concepts

Leibniz's theory of truth as concept inclusion can be understood by reference to his idea of primitive concepts. Leibniz called the list of primitive concepts "the alphabet of human thoughts" and likened the formation of complex concepts from their primitive constituents to the formation of words from combinations of letters. For example, the concept "bachelor" is a combination of the concepts "man" and "unmarried"; the concept "man" is a combination of the concepts "male" and "human being," and so on.

Even though we are not aware of it, our normal concepts are simply combinations of primitive concepts. Our concept of the person Julius Caesar is such a combination. This is why we are not aware that the proposition "Caesar died in 44 B.C." is in reality a statement of identity. The concept of Caesar contains the predicate "died in 44 B.C.," because all the primitive concepts that constitute the concept of Julius Caesar include all the primitive concepts that make up the predicate. In effect, the complete concept of Julius Caesar is a combination of simple concepts that can be represented by a string of letters "*ABCDE* . . ." When we say that Caesar died on a particular day, we are saying something that is already included in the list and can be represented as "*ABCD* . . . is *A*."

Despite these explanations, two important points remain unclear. First, it remains unclear what positive argument Leibniz can give us for the claim that in propositions like "Caesar died in 44 B.C." the predicate concept is indeed contained in the subject concept. Leibniz thinks that *the* complete concept of Caesar—the concept as God has it—will contain all the predicates true of that man. But why should Leibniz think that? As we shall see, he argues that an individual substance can be completely individuated only by all of its properties.

Second, Leibniz's theory of truth as concept inclusion appears to imply that all truths are necessary. It appears to leave no room for the idea of contingent truths—truths that could be false. Despite this, Leibniz denies that all truths are necessary, partly to avoid the determinism inherent in Spinoza's view of the universe. Leibniz's distinction between necessary and contingent truths still needs to be explained.

Substances and Complete Concepts

Leibniz defines a "substance" as a subject to which many predicates can be attributed, but which cannot itself be made the predicate of any other subject. Leibniz believes that the individual soul is a substance, and this means that the soul is the subject of properties but is not itself the property or attribute of any subject. On the other hand, redness is not a substance, because it is the property or attribute of red things.

For Leibniz, the concept of every individual substance is completely determinate. The complete concept of the individual substance contains every fact about that substance, right down to the most minute detail. From the complete concept of any substance, it is possible to infer all the properties of that substance.

Leibniz holds that every predicate must be contained in the subject, because otherwise we would be unable to distinguish an individual from all other possible individuals. For instance, many possible individuals could have been called

"Adam" and could have led lives very similar to Adam's. But none of these possible individuals is Adam. Leibniz calls these possible individuals "several alternative possible Adams."[34] Suppose that Adam did in fact exist. According to Leibniz, the only description that would suffice to describe him as a completely unique individual, distinct from all other possible individuals, would be the description that specifies the complete notion of Adam—the sum total of all predicates true of Adam. So Leibniz's thesis that every predicate must be contained in the subject is based on his view about what individuates a substance. A substance is defined and individuated from all other possible individual substances by the sum total of its predicates. If any one of the predicates were different, the individual would be a different individual. According to Leibniz, if you were not now reading this page, but were doing something else instead, you would not be you: you would be a different person. In other words, Leibniz implies that all the properties of an individual substance are essential properties. This entails that every predicate be contained in the subject.

The Principle of Sufficient Reason

In sections 31 through 33 of the *Monadology*, Leibniz claims that all reasoning is based on two great principles: the Principle of Contradiction, which states that two contradictory propositions cannot both be true; and the Principle of Sufficient Reason, which states that "No fact can be real or existing and no statement true unless it has a sufficient reason why it is thus and not otherwise." Leibniz says that these two principles delineate two kinds of truths. Truths of reason are necessary, and their denial involves contradiction. Truths of fact are contingent, and their opposite is possible.

In section 36 of the *Monadology*, Leibniz says: "there must be a sufficient reason for contingent truths or truths of fact." Immediately after this, he says that the analysis of reasons for contingent facts can be continued without limit. In other words, the analysis of contingent truths is infinitely long.

The Principle of Sufficient Reason is a corollary of Leibniz's theory of truth. The principle states that for every fact there must be a sufficient reason why things are so and not otherwise. Leibniz says that everything must have a cause; but like Spinoza, by *cause* he means sufficient reason. Leibniz believes that the Principle of Sufficient Reason follows from his definition of truth. Stating a reason for the truth of any proposition consists in giving an a priori proof of that proposition. All propositions have an a priori proof, which is why Leibniz says that nothing happens without a cause. For Leibniz, giving the a priori proof of a proposition consists in revealing that the subject contains the predicate. In the case of contingent propositions, this proof is infinite and cannot be known by finite beings like us. Like Spinoza before him, Leibniz claims that a priori knowledge of every truth is possible, but only in principle.

Contingent Truths and Existence

As we have seen, Leibniz's view of truth seems to imply that all truths are necessary. The complete concept of any substance contains the sum total of its predicates; therefore, to deny that the substance has any one of those predicates is to state a contradiction. This seems to imply that all truths are necessary, and that no truths are contingent.

For Leibniz, the root of all contingency is existence and, ultimately, the free choice of God. His theory of truth is an account of what it means for a predicate to be truly attributed to a subject. However, this does not mean that the subject actually exists. According to Leibniz, propositions like "Eve is the first woman" are ambiguous. They—and the word *is*—can be understood in two ways: as essential or existential.

Normally we take such propositions to have existential import; that is, we say that "Eve is the first woman" is true if and only if there actually existed a person Eve who in fact was the first woman. Understood in this way, a proposition of the form "*A* is *B*" is equivalent to the proposition "*AB* is an existent thing."[35]

However, according to Leibniz, propositions like "Eve is the first woman" can lack existential import. If they do, their truth does not depend on the existence of individuals; in such a case, the proper focus is essential, not existential. Thus, for Leibniz, the proposition "Eve is the first woman" can be regarded as true even if Eve never existed. Understood in this way, a proposition of the form "*A* is *B*" is equivalent to the proposition "*AB* is a possibly existent thing."

To underline the point, we might compare singular propositions like "Eve is the first woman," understood in this nonexistential way, with universal propositions like "All unicorns are animals." Such universal propositions merely assert that certain concepts include other concepts, and their truth does not depend on the existence of individuals. Consequently, the proposition "All unicorns are animals" is true, even if no unicorns actually exist. For Leibniz, singular propositions such as "Eve is the first woman" may similiarly lack existential import.

If we understand singular propositions as lacking existential import, then, given Leibniz's definition of truth, propositions like "Eve is the first woman" are ultimately reducible to identical propositions. Given that they are true at all, they are necessary truths, and their truth does not depend on the existence of individuals. On the other hand, if they do have existential import, their truth will depend on the existence of the relevant individual, as specified by the complete concept of that individual, and they will be contingent.

Therefore, although it is a contradiction to deny the essential truth that Eve is (or was) the first woman, we can deny without contradiction that Eve ever existed. Propositions that assert actual existence are contingent. The one exception to this claim is the proposition that God exists, which is not contingent but absolutely necessary.

Contingency and God's Free Choice

For Leibniz, the contingent is what exists, because what exists depends on the free choice of God. Leibniz's position can be explained as follows. There are an indefinite number of possible Adams. Each one of those possible individuals is individuated by its complete concept—the list of all the predicates true of it. Because of Leibniz's view of truth, it is impossible for any one of those predicates to be false of that particular individual. However, only one of those possible Adams may exist. Which one exists is a contingent truth, dependent on the free choice of God. The nature of each possible individual is thus fixed logically by its complete concept. On the other hand, the actual existence of any individual is a contingent fact and depends on the free choice of God.[36]

Similarly, this actual world is only one among an infinite number of possible worlds. Possible worlds are individuated by the individuals each comprises. If any contingent fact were different, we would inhabit a different possible world. The nature of each possible world is fixed logically by the natures of the individuals which comprise that world. However, only one possible world can exist, the actual world. Which of the infinite number of possible worlds exists is a contingency, decided freely by God. Leibniz says that God freely chooses which of all possible worlds to make actual, and this choice is the source of contingency in Leibniz's system. He calls this "the principle of contingency or of the existence of things."

According to Leibniz, the internal nature of any individual substance is fixed logically, although it is a contingent matter whether that individual substance actually exists. In brief, Leibniz implies that all existential propositions (except those asserting the existence of God) are contingent, and furthermore, that only existential propositions are contingent.

The distinction between necessary and contingent truths is important for Leibniz, because without it he would be forced to deny the freedom of God. If all propositions were necessary, then the only possible world would be the actual world—this world. In which case, God would not have a free choice.

Contingency and Sufficient Reason

In the *Monadology*, Leibniz says that necessary truths are based on the Principle of Contradiction and that contingent truths are based on the Principle of Sufficient Reason. Both kinds of truth are capable of a priori proof. However, the proofs of contingent and necessary propositions differ.

Necessary propositions cannot be denied without contradiction. In sections 33 through 35 of the *Monadology*, Leibniz says that necessary truths are either explicitly identical, like "every circle is a circle," or they can be reduced to an explicitly identical proposition by means of a finite process of analysis. Leibniz believes that all necessary truths are provable a priori, for they either are explicitly identical or can be made explicitly identical by a finite process of analysis.

In sections 36 through 39 of the *Monadology,* Leibniz also implies that contingent existential propositions are provable a priori. According to the Principle of Sufficient Reason, there must be a sufficient reason for contingent truths. Leibniz claims that the reason for a contingent proposition entails an infinitely long analysis or proof. He also asserts that the ultimate reason for any series of contingencies must lie outside that sequence, in the existence of God. He implies that the difference between the necessary and the contingent is that the a priori proof of contingent existential propositions is infinitely long and ultimately involves a reference to the free will of God.

The Principle of the Best

According to Leibniz, all contingency in the world is due to the free will of God, because God freely chooses what exists. However, we can have a priori knowledge of God's choice, and this seems to undermine the claim that God's choice is free.

According to Leibniz, we can know a priori that God exists. It is a necessary truth that God exists. We also know a priori that God is perfect and that, being perfect, He chooses the best of all possible worlds. Thus, we can know a priori that the actual world is the best of all possible worlds.

In order for us to show that there is sufficient reason for any contingent fact, we must establish that the fact is necessarily part of the best of all possible worlds. Thus giving a proof of any contingent fact involves showing how the fact is part of a causal chain or series that produces the best of all possible worlds.

What Leibniz has in mind can be explained as follows. Any contingent existential fact can be deduced from an earlier state of the universe, given the laws of nature. However, the laws of nature are themselves contingent and subject to the will of God. Since we know a priori that God chooses the best, the laws of nature He chooses must be for the best. And so, for instance, the laws will be such as to realize the greatest variety of form at the least expense. The principle of the best can provide us with some limited a priori knowledge of the world.

However, the complete infinite proof of any contingent fact can be known only to God. Leibniz says that only God, Who can comprehend the one infinitely complex series of things, can understand the a priori reason for any contingent fact. Thus, Leibniz often compares the contingent to a surd (such as the square root of 2), which is an infinitely continuable fraction, while he compares the necessary to an integer, which consists of a finite number of prime factors. Because the a priori proofs of contingent propositions are infinitely long, humans have to learn these facts a posteriori, by experience.

Study Questions

1. What are the two parts of Leibniz's theory of the proposition, and how are they important for his metaphysics?

2. What is Leibniz's theory of truth?

3. How and why does Leibniz distinguish between different kinds of analytic propositions?

4. How would Leibniz argue for the claim that the complete concept of a substance contains all of its properties?

5. How does Leibniz try to account for contingent truths?

6. What is the relation between Leibniz's theory of truth and the Principle of Sufficient Reason?

Discussion Questions

1. Is a substance individuated by all of its properties?

2. Is Leibniz's theory of truth correct?

CHAPTER 8

Leibniz: Monads

Leibniz's theory of the proposition falls into two parts: his definition of truth, and his view that the subject-predicate form of proposition is basic. Since Leibniz defines a true proposition as one in which the subject concept contains the predicate concept, his definition of truth requires his view that all propositions are reducible to the subject-predicate form. If some propositions were not reducible to this form, Leibniz's definition of truth could not be applied to them.

Leibniz's view that all propositions are reducible to the subject-predicate form should not be confused with the view that all propositions actually are of that form. According to Leibniz, some propositions are not of the subject-predicate form, but he attempts to reduce them to that form. For example, hypothetical propositions, such as "If anything is dog, then it is an animal" are of the form "If A, then B." Leibniz says that such hypothetical propositions can be conceived of in a subject-predicate form. The proposition "If anything is a dog, then it is an animal" can be reduced to the subject-predicate proposition "The concept of a dog contains the concept of being an animal."[37]

Relations

Among the most important propositions not expressed in the subject-predicate form are relational propositions, like "Jesus was the son of Mary" or "*A* is longer than *B*." Propositions of this type seem to have two subjects and they suggest that there is a complex fact such that a certain relation holds between those two subjects. Relational propositions do not assert that a property belongs to a substance, although Leibniz believes that they must be reducible to such an assertion.

In his fifth paper to Clarke, Leibniz sets out three ways of conceiving of the relation of length between two lines L and M: as the ratio of L to M; as the ratio of M to L; and as a ratio between L and M abstracted from both lines. Leibniz considers that this last way of conceiving relations is mistaken. He says that it cannot be said of both L and M together that they are the subject of this relation; for instance, if L is twice as long as M, it cannot be said that both L and M are the subjects of the ratio two to one. Leibniz says that a ratio (and relation) considered in this way is a "mere ideal thing" or an "entity of reason." Leibniz means that a ratio of two to one is not a real thing but a mental construction, which has its basis in the nonrelational properties of substance.

Leibniz holds that "there are no purely extrinsic denominations." By this he means that relations are reducible to the properties of substances and that, when a proposition expressed by a relational sentence is true, it is true by virtue of the truth of some subject-predicate propositions. According to Leibniz, what is said by a relational proposition can be shown by purely subject-predicate propositions. If we assert that A has relation R to B, the same thing can be said by asserting that A has certain properties and that B has certain properties. Parkinson calls this Leibniz's weaker thesis about relations.

Leibniz also affirmed a much stronger thesis about the nature of relations. If substance A has relation R to B, then this can be reduced to subject-predicate propositions about A alone or to subject-predicate propositions about B alone. This stronger thesis is important for Leibniz's theory of monads, and we shall examine it later in this chapter.

Leibniz's stronger thesis depends on the weaker one, although the reverse is not true. Thus, if the weaker thesis can be shown to be false, the stronger thesis must be false, too. Can all relational propositions be reduced to the subject-predicate form? In other words, is Leibniz's weaker thesis about relations true? We must distinguish here between a symmetrical and an asymmetrical relation. The phrase "is similar to" stands for a symmetrical relation because, if A is similar to B, then B is similar to A. Leibniz held that the proposition "A is similar to B" can be reduced to the two subject-predicate propositions "A has property F now" and "B has property F now." But how is Leibniz to reduce asymmetrical relations to the subject-predicate form? Leibniz claims that the proposition "Paris is the lover of Helen" can be reduced to the proposition "Paris loves, and by that very fact Helen is loved." There are two weaknesses in this analysis. First, the phrase "by that very fact," which is obviously essential to the analysis, may itself be relational. Second, the terms occurring in the analysis are themselves relational. As another example, consider "John is the father of James." According to Leibniz's analysis, this nonsubject predicate proposition must reduce to the proposition "John is a father, and by that very fact James is a son." But the terms *father* and *son* are already relational terms; therefore, the analysis does not support Leibniz's contention that relations can be reduced to simple predicates or intrinsic denominations.

Substance

Leibniz accepts the traditional Aristotelian definition of an individual substance as the subject of predicates that is not itself the predicate of any other subject. However, Leibniz believes that an individual substance has a complete concept that is necessary and sufficient to distinguish that individual from all other possible individuals. Leibniz thinks that every substance must have a complete concept. The concept of a substance is complete because whatever can be truly said of that substance must be contained in the concept of it. Leibniz claims that the complete concept of a substance is both necessary and sufficient to identify that individual substance and to distinguish it from all other possible individuals. Because the complete concept of a substance is both necessary and sufficient to distinguish it from all other possible individuals, no two individuals share the same complete concept. This means that no two individuals can be exactly alike. This result, called the Principle of the Identity of Indiscernibles, follows from Leibniz's view that each substance must have a complete concept.

The Principle of the Identity of Indiscernibles

This principle states that numerically different individuals must be qualitatively dissimilar. In section 9 of the *Monadology*, Leibniz says "there are never in nature two beings which are exactly alike." Since there cannot be two substances with the same complete concept, there cannot be two substances that are exactly alike. So stated, the principle putatively expresses a necessary truth: it is self-contradictory to suppose that there might be two qualitatively identical individuals. Indeed, the Principle of the Identity of Indiscernibles is a necessary truth for Leibniz because it follows from his view that each substance must have a complete concept, and Leibniz regards this as a necessary truth. However, in his fifth letter to Clarke, Leibniz suggests that the Principle of the Identity of Indiscernibles is contingent. In the letter he argues that it is not absolutely necessary to suppose that there cannot be two exactly similar individuals; however, such duplication is contrary to the will of God. We can be certain of this because everything must have a sufficient reason, and God could not have a sufficient reason for creating two identical individuals. Suppose, for example, that there are two qualitatively identical individual bodies A and B, and God fills one space with A and another space with B. Leibniz argues against Clarke that which body fills which space is arbitrary, or without reason. Therefore, since everything must have a reason, there cannot be two such bodies. In this way, Leibniz connects the Principle of the Identity of Indiscernibles with the Principle of Sufficient Reason. This is important for Leibniz's view on space.

Sometimes Leibniz appeals to the empirical claim that one will always be able to find qualitative differences between two individuals, however much alike they may seem to be at first sight. But once again, this suggests that the Principle of the Identity of Indiscernibles is contingent.

Is the Principle of the Identity of Indiscernibles true? Could two individuals with identical properties possibly exist? Arguably the principle is true if we allow spatial and temporal relations to count toward the properties of a substance, and if we assume that two things cannot be in the same place at the same time. Suppose that we have two billiard balls, which are exactly alike with respect to shape, size, color, and texture. Since they cannot occupy the same place at the same time, they must have different spatial and temporal relations or positions. If we include these relations and positions among their respective properties, the two objects must have different properties.

Leibniz, however, argues that spatial objects are not substances, and this is a point we shall return to later. Furthermore, Leibniz claims that all relations can be reduced to qualitative predicates, or intrinsic denominations. For this reason, he cannot include spatial and temporal relations among the properties of a substance. Thus, according to Leibniz, two substances cannot differ solely with respect to their spatio-temporal relations and positions. If they do differ in this way, it must be because they differ with respect to their intrinsic properties.

Monads

While Spinoza affirms that there can be only one substance, of which finite objects are only modes, Leibniz holds that there are infinitely many substances. He argues that these substances are simple, and for this reason he calls them "monads" (from the Greek word *monas*, which means "unity" or "that which is one"). On April 30, 1687, Leibniz wrote to Arnauld: "what is not truly *one* being is not truly one *being*."[38] In section 1 of the *Monadology*, Leibniz says "the monad . . . is nothing else than a simple substance." The claim that substances are simple has, for Leibniz, two radical implications: first, it means that material objects are not real; and second, it implies that the basic elements of reality—the monads— are like minds and that they lack spatial extension.

On the basis that substances are simple, Leibniz argues that spatially extended physical objects are not substances. By definition, a simple substance or monad must be indivisible. But spatially extended bodies are, on the contrary, infinitely divisible; consequently, substances cannot be spatially extended. Since, by definition, substances are what ultimately exist, this means that physical objects in space are not real.

What, then, is real? According to Leibniz, reality consists solely of an infinity of extensionless monads and their mental states. This reality merely appears to consist of spatial physical objects. To illustrate this point, Leibniz uses the analogy of a rainbow, in which colorless particles of water are seen as colored. Similarly, an aggregate of individual unextended substances are perceived as extended. Reality is so perceived by the monads themselves. So, physical spatial bodies are merely the appearances of and for mindlike monads.

Given that all substances must be indivisible, and given that extended matter cannot be a substance, it is easy to see why Leibniz concludes that substances must be mindlike entities with mental states. If they are not extended, what else could they be? If the only candidate attributes are extension and consciousness, and if extension cannot be an attribute of substances, the only remaining option is consciousness. And insofar as reality appears to be extended, it must appear so to some mind.

As we have seen, the basis of Leibniz's views lies in his claim that substances are simple. Leibniz can support the conclusion that substances are simple with seemingly innocuous premises. First, in section 2 of the *Monadology*, he asserts that any compound (that is, anything that has parts) is ultimately only a collection of simples (that is, things without parts). In other words, compounds require simples; they would not exist but for the simples on which they depend. If created substances do not depend on anything else, except God, it follows that such substances are simples, without parts.

We can summarize this argument as follows:

1. A compound is nothing but a collection of simples.

2. Anything with parts depends for its reality on those parts.

---

3. Therefore, any compound depends for its reality on simples.

4. Substances do not depend for their reality on anything else (except God).

---

5. Therefore, anything with parts is not a substance.

The conclusion of this argument is that all substances must be simples; they cannot have parts. Leibniz uses this conclusion to argue further that matter cannot be a substance and that substances must be nonspatial monads.

There are at least two ways to resist the above argument: by denying premise 1, and by denying premise 4. One alternative to accepting premise 1 is to claim that there can be compounds without simples, in which case reality would be infinitely divisible without having any ultimate building blocks. Leibniz rejects this alternative as absurd. He claims that there cannot be an infinite regress of dependency; such a regress must end somewhere. And if it must end, there must be simples.

Leibniz does not seem to think that premise 4 is true by definition.[39] As we have seen, he defines substance as the subject of predicates that is not itself the predicate of any other subject. Nevertheless, Leibniz appears to be committed to premise 4, because he claims that an aggregation is only a state of being of its constituents, and he takes this to imply that aggregates are not truly substances.[40]

Monads and Causality

Leibniz says that "each substance is like a world apart, independent of everything but God." He means that no created substance can interact with any other created substance. In section 7 of the *Monadology*, Leibniz characterizes monads as "windowless" because they can neither receive nor impart any causal influence. In section 51, he says: "the influence which one monad has upon another is only ideal." Substances cannot interact, because the proposition "*A* acts on *B*" is relational and reduces to a simple subject-predicate proposition about the properties of *A* and *B*, respectively. Furthermore, Leibniz argues that interaction between substances is impossible because each substance has its own complete concept, and this predetermines all its predicates at all times. Each individual substance has a predetermined and self-contained history that unfolds with the necessity of a mathematical series in accordance with its own individual nature and without any outside influence except that of God. Each substance develops alone in accordance with its predetermined individual nature. In section 11 of the *Monadology*, Leibniz says of substance, "an external cause can have no influence upon its inner being."

Thus, like Spinoza before him, Leibniz denies the possibility of causal relations between substances. Yet this denial is apparently incompatible with Leibniz's assertion that monads require the causal influence of God in order to continue to exist (see section 51 of the *Monadology*). If causality is impossible between created substances, how is it possible between God and created substances?

Leibniz also argues that there must be an infinity of substances. Because of the principle that God wills the best of all possible worlds, there must be as much variety in the world as is possible, and, therefore, God has created an infinite number of monads (see sections 57 and 58 of the *Monadology*). This is important because it links Leibniz's two definitions of contingency. As we saw in the previous chapter, Leibniz defines a contingent proposition as one that is true in virtue of the principle of the best, and he also defines a contingent truth as one that requires an infinitely long proof. These two definitions are linked because God, in creating the best universe, creates an infinite number of substances; but since all substances are connected, the task of explaining any single contingent fact is infinitely complex.

Monads and Mirrors

Leibniz says that all things are connected; that is, any individual substance stands in relation to all other substances (section 56). Consequently, for Leibniz, the complete concept of a substance *A* contains relations to all other things at all times. In this sense, any individual substance expresses the whole universe. Leibniz means that, from the predicates of any substance *A* alone, it is possible to infer all the predicates of all other substances. Because of this, Leibniz says in section 56 of the *Monadology*, "every simple substance has relations which express all the others, and it is consequently a perpetual living mirror of the universe" (see section 61).

Clearly, Leibniz's view that relations are reducible to the properties of substances is important here. Leibniz's stronger thesis about relations is that the relations between A and B can be inferred from the properties of A alone or from the properties of B alone. Given that all substances stand in relation to each other, this view of relations is equivalent to the claim that each substance expresses the whole universe. So, if that thesis about relations is to be rejected, the view that monads reflect the universe must also be rejected. Earlier in this chapter, it was suggested that Leibniz's stronger thesis about relations ought to be rejected because it is based on his weaker thesis about relations, which is itself inadequate.

Points of View

Each monad reflects the universe from its own point of view. The point of view of each monad is characterized by the relative confusion of its perceptions (section 60). Because of the principle of the identity of indiscernibles, no two monads can have the same perceptions. In a way, however, the perceptions of each monad are the same as those of any other monad, because these perceptions are in each case simply a reflection of the whole universe—that is, of all the monads. Nevertheless, the perceptions of monads differ with respect to their state of confusion. What each monad perceives more or less clearly defines its own unique point of view. This accounts for the phenomenon of perspective. It also explains how monads appear to stand in different spatial relations to each other when spatial relations are merely an appearance in the mind and when reality is nonspatial (see section 61 of the *Monadology*).

Leibniz's thesis that the perceptions of monads are, in varying distributions, confused allows him to talk about each monad's having a point of view. Because the perceptions of monads are confused to varying degrees, there is also a hierarchy of monads. There are three kinds of monads: bare monads, animal souls, and rational souls. Bare monads have a completely unconscious perception and have no memory (sections 20 and 21). An infinite aggregate of these monads forms the unextended basis of what appears to be extended physical objects. Animal souls have some degree of memory and discrimination in their perceptions (section 27). Rational spirits alone have self-consciousness or apperception; they can reason, and they have knowledge of good and evil; these are the souls of humans and angels (sections 28 through 30 of the *Monadology*).

Preestablished Harmony

The mirroring by each monad of all others underlies the appearance that there is a universal causal interaction between monads. But since there are in fact no such causal relations between monads, this mirroring cannot be explained causally. Each monad develops spontaneously and in isolation, in accordance with its predetermined nature. How, then, can there be correspondence and correlation between the unfolding, self-contained history of all the monads? How can a change in any one monad be reflected in the changing state of any other monad, given that there is no causality between them? Leibniz rejects the occasionalist view that God constantly intervenes in the course of the world. Instead, he advances the doctrine of preestablished harmony (section 78 of the *Monadology*). According to this doctrine, God created each monad and its dispositions in such a way that at each instant the perceptions of every monad correspond in every detail. God determines the nature of each monad so that its state is coordinated in a preestablished harmony, without the need for interference (section 51).

Study Questions

1. Why does Leibniz think that relations are not real?

2. What is the Principle of the Identity of Indiscernibles, and what role does it play in Leibniz's metaphysics?

3. How does Leibniz argue for the claim that reality cannot be spatially extended?

4. What is a monad?

5. Why does Leibniz think that it is impossible for two substances to interact causally with each other?

6. What is Leibniz's doctrine of preestablished harmony, and how does he argue for it?

Discussion Questions

1. Is the Principle of the Identity of Indiscernibles true?

2. Must the universe consist of simples?

3. Spinoza asserts that there is only one substance, and Leibniz claims that there are an infinite number of substances. How should we account for this difference in their views?

4. What are the similarities between Leibniz's monads and Descartes's view of the mind? Leibniz claims that monads have unconscious perceptions; how would Descartes react to this claim, and why?

Leibniz: God and Space

The Ontological Argument

Leibniz's first argument for the existence of God is the ontological argument, of which he gives two formulations. The first formulation follows that of Descartes and Anselm, according to which God is defined as a being that contains all perfections. The argument here is: existence is a perfection and, therefore, God must exist. Leibniz's second formulation of the ontological argument is derived from Spinoza. This formulation begins with a definition of a "necessary being" as one whose essence includes existence. By definition such a being must exist, and God is such a being.

However, Leibniz supplements these formulations with an argument to show that God is possible. Descartes's version of the ontological argument is incomplete, says Leibniz, because it merely assumes and does not prove that God is possible. Leibniz tries to rectify this defect by showing that the concept of God does not contain a contradiction—that it does not contain incompatible predicates. He tries to do this as follows. Leibniz says that God is a being whose essence involves all perfections and that, by definition, all perfections are simple unanalyzable qualities. Leibniz then argues that there cannot be a contradiction in attributing to the same thing any conjunction of simple qualities; such qualities must be compatible by virtue of their being simple. Since such qualities are not self-evidently incompatible, their incompatibility (if it existed) would have to be demonstrated. However, Leinbiz says, there cannot be any demonstrable incompatibility between simple unanalyzable qualities, because demonstrating incompatibility requires analysis.

The weakness of Leibniz's argument is that he gives no indication of what simple perfections are. Furthermore, the argument certainly does not show that the traditional perfections of God are compatible, because the traditional perfections of God—like perfect wisdom, goodness, knowledge, and power—are complex qualities that can be analyzed. Therefore, Leibniz's attempted proof of the possibility of God is empty; it has no application to what is usually called "God."

The Cosmological Argument

Unlike the ontological argument, which is a priori and based solely on the nature of the concept of God, the cosmological argument is a posteriori and is based on the existence of contingent things. Here, there must be a sufficient reason for every contingent fact and event. Even if each event can be adequately explained by previous events and so on ad infinitum, questions remain about how to explain the series of events as a whole. We still require answers to questions such as, "Why does the series as a whole exist at all?" and "Why does it proceed as it does?" These questions must have answers, because of the Principle of Sufficient Reason; and according to Leibniz, these answers must be found outside the series of events as a whole, in the existence of a necessary being. The system of nature as a whole depends on the existence of God. Because contingent things do exist, there must also exist a necessary being.

It might seem that the cosmological argument depends on the assumption that there was a first event. Since the first event cannot be explained by earlier events, it would require an alternative explanation, arguably in terms of the existence of God. However, Leibniz's version of the cosmological argument does not require the assumption of a first event; it is unaffected even if events stretch infinitely into the past. According to Leibniz, explaining each event by previous events ad infinitum does not supply a complete reason for any event, because unanswered questions remain as to why there is a world at all and why it should be as it is. The point is crucial and contentious. If each single event in an infinite series of events can be explained by prior events, does any question remain about how to explain the series as a whole? In his *Dialogues on Natural Religion,* Hume argues against Leibniz that the cause of the whole series of events is simply the sum total of the causes of each of the members. Since one can give an explanation of any single event, there does not remain a further question about the series of events as a whole. Furthermore, Kant argues that it is illegitimate to ask questions about the cause of the series of events as a whole, because the series as a whole is not an object of possible experience, and the notion of a cause has application only to objects of possible experience.

In the cosmological argument, Leibniz asserts that, because contingent things exist, there is also a necessary existent. But he has not yet shown that the necessary existent is God. As a first step, Leibniz needs to show that there is only one necessary being. He tries to do this by arguing that, because all contingent things are connected, a complete reason for any one of them is enough for all of them. In effect, Leibniz is trying to show that the existence of only one necessary being suffices to explain nature as a whole. To this it may be replied that such a sufficiency does not prove the existence of only one necessary being.

To establish that this single necessary being is God, Leibniz tries to show that the necessary being is a voluntary agent who chose to create the world by making actual one of the possible worlds. Leibniz thinks that the contingency of the actual world shows that the world was freely chosen, since God's choice could have been different without contradiction. Even if we accept this point, however, Leibniz faces a difficult question: could God really have chosen a possible world other than this one? The difficulty is that, according to Leibniz, God must have all perfections, and this seems to imply that God must choose the best of all possible worlds. If God could choose otherwise, He would be less than perfect. On the other hand, if God could not have chosen otherwise, His choice was not free. Leibniz's answer to this point is to say that motives for action "incline without necessitating."[41] Thus, God necessarily chooses as He does, but His choices are nevertheless free. This answer is important, because ultimately the source of contingency in Leibniz's metaphysics is the choice of God. If God's choice of which possible world to make actual is not a free choice, then Leibniz's system is completely deterministic.

The Argument from Preestablished Harmony

Monads appear to be engaged in universal interaction; but if in fact they are causally independent of each other, Leibniz has to account for the appearance of universal interaction in terms of a preestablished harmony. Leibniz argues that this preestablished harmony between an infinity of monads requires the existence of God, who can contemplate and coordinate an infinity of states. In fact, this argument for God is a version of the argument from design, according to which a certain feature of the universe—for instance, its orderliness—can only be accounted for as the work of God. The particular weakness of Leibniz's own special form of this argument is the premise on which it is based: the denial of causal relations between substances.

Existence

As we saw in Chapter 2, Kant criticizes the ontological argument for treating existence as a property, and this criticism also applies to Leibniz's version of that argument. In addition, Leibniz faces further, more general problems regarding existence and his theory of truth. Leibniz claims that all propositions are reducible to the subject-predicate form and that their truth is attributable to the fact that the subject concept necessarily contains the predicate concept. If this theory of truth applies to existential propositions like "Caesar exists," it implies that all existential truths are necessary truths and that Caesar is a necessary being. If the theory of truth does not apply to such existential propositions, Leibniz's theory of the proposition has an important and undermining exception.

Furthermore, Leibniz has claimed that all existential propositions (except those concerning God) are contingent; he has also claimed that only existential propositions are contingent. We must remember that, for Leibniz, truths like "Caesar crossed the Rubicon" are not contingent if they do not presuppose that Caesar actually exists. In such a case, they lack existential import and instead merely fix the content of the concept "Caesar"; thus, they are true whether the man exists or not. In this respect, existential truths like "Caesar exists" are fundamentally different from nonexistential truths like "Caesar crossed the Rubicon," which are necessary. This difference, which is so important to Leibniz's analysis of contingency, is undermined by his implicit treatment of existence as a predicate in the ontological argument.

In summary, Leibniz faces a dilemma. Are existential propositions like "Caesar existed" reducible to the subject-predicate form? If they are, their truth consists in the subject containing the predicate, and they are necessary propositions—exactly as propositions like "Caesar died in 44 B.C." are necessary. If, on the other hand, existential propositions are not reducible to the subject-predicate form, then Leibniz's theory of the proposition is false. In short, Leibniz cannot give a satisfactory answer to the question "Is existence a predicate?"

Extension

In the 1630s Descartes not only articulated many basic principles of modern science, he also effectively laid down a program for the development of physics. This program was based on his idea that all the properties of matter were geometrical. According to Descartes, the essence of matter is to be spatially extended, and all properties of matter can be reduced to modes of extension or ways of being extended.

Although Descartes's physics was accepted and taught in universities throughout Europe by the 1660s, the publication in 1687 of Newton's *Principia* saw the gradual replacement of Cartesian physics by the more comprehensive Newtonian system. Leibniz disagreed with both the Cartesians and the Newtonians. He challenged Descartes's views on matter, but he also argued vigorously against the Newtonian view of space and time.

Leibniz disagrees with Descartes in at least three ways. First, whereas Descartes views spatial extension as simple or unanalyzable, Leibniz contends that extension is analyzable in terms of plurality, continuity, and coexistence. Spatial extension consists of a continuous repetition of that which is coexistent. Second, Leibniz denies that all the properties of matter can be reduced to spatial extension. Matter must have some nongeometrical properties; it cannot consist solely of extension, because there must be something to be extended (or simultaneously and continuously repeated). According to Leibniz, the nongeometrical property of matter, which fills out space by being continuously repeated, is the force of resistance. In other words, whereas Descartes asserts that extension is the fundamental feature of matter, Leibniz contends the contrary: that the essence of matter consists in forces of resistance and not in spatial extension, and that extension itself arises because the forces of resistance are repeated in a continuous way. Third, Leibniz argues that Descartes is mistaken in regarding matter as a substance at all. All substances must be simple and indivisible; and therefore, something extended cannot be a substance at all. Because he claims that substances must be unextended monads, Leibniz tries to account for the nature of matter in terms of the states of these nonspatial entities.

Matter

For Leibniz, matter primarily consists of certain passive forces of resistance: impenetrability and inertia. Matter is impenetrable in that no two bodies can occupy the same place at the same time. This applies to liquids and gases as well as to solids. Matter has inertia because it cannot be moved and kept moving without the application of force. In other words, matter is resistant to bodies and to motion.

These qualities of resistance, which Leibniz calls "materia prima," form the qualities by virtue of which bodies occupy space. The qualities of resistance are uniform in all matter and constitute the nongeometrical properties of matter that are repeated continuously and simultaneously to make matter spatially extended.

Since, according to Leibniz, nonspatial monads and their states of perception and appetition (or desire) are all that really exist, they must be the real foundation of the material universe, which is only an appearance. What appears as extended matter must consist of an infinite collection of indivisible monads. Therefore the passive force of matter—its inertia and impenetrability—has its real basis in the confused perceptions of the monads. Passive force or materia prima is simply an abstraction based on the confusion of monads and their perceptions.

As well as having passive force, matter has an active force, which Leibniz calls "materia secunda." This active force is required by the nature of motion. Over periods of time, matter in motion can be distinguished from matter at rest by its change of position. But matter in motion must also be distinguishable from matter at rest at each instant of time. At each instant of time, a moving body is indistinguishable from a body at rest, except with respect to the presence of active force in the former, which is not present in the latter. It is by virtue of this active force that bodies move and that moving bodies can produce effects on other bodies.

Like passive force, the active force of moving bodies is simply an abstraction whose real foundation lies in the states of the monads. Active force is based on the state of appetition of monads. Thus, Leibniz's physical theory has its basis in the states of monads; and both active and passive force are founded on the states of monads. Spatial extension is a logical construction derived from the spatial relations of apparently extended bodies.

Space and Time

Leibniz developed his theory of space and time in his letters to Clarke.[42] In these letters, Leibniz advocates a relational theory of space and time that is diametrically opposed to the Newtonian absolute theory put forward by Clarke.

According to the Newtonian theory, space is logically prior to the matter that may or may not occupy it. Space is an unlimited whole, and any region of space is part of this infinite whole. Bodies occupy parts of space; and although bodies have volume, space is not a property of bodies. Because (according to the absolute theory) space is prior to the bodies that happen to occupy it, it is meaningful to suppose that a finite material universe could have been differently situated in absolute space—say, 10 meters to the left of where it actually is located. Similar statements apply to time. In particular, the universe could have been created earlier or later than it in fact was, with respect to absolute time. Absolute motion is motion with respect to absolute space for a period of absolute time. Thus, for Newton's theory, it is meaningful to suppose that the whole finite material universe might move with respect to absolute space.

Leibniz's own theory of space and time has two aspects. First, he denies the existence of absolute space and time. For him, space is not a container that exists logically prior to and independent of physical bodies. Instead, the existence of matter logically precedes the existence of space: physical objects or forces happen to be ordered spatially, and space is nothing over and above these spatial relations. It is merely a system of relations.

This relational view of space has several consequences. First it implies that to suggest that the universe could have been created in a different position or that the universe can change position in space is meaningless. For Leibniz, there is no absolute space, so an object can change position only relative to another object. Space is nothing over and above the spatial relations between objects; consequently, it is meaningless to suppose that all objects could have been differently situated while maintaining their positions relative to each other. Similarly for time: according to the relational theory, it is meaningless to suppose that the universe could have been created earlier or later, because time is nothing over and above the temporal relations between events. God creates time by creating temporally related events. And since there is no absolute time, there can have been no time before the creation of events.

Because he rejects the concepts of absolute space and absolute time, Leibniz also rejects the idea of absolute motion. For Leibniz's theory, there can be no such thing as motion against the background of unmoving absolute space. The motion of any physical body must occur relative to the motion of other physical bodies.

This leads to a second implication of Leibniz's relational theory. The theory implies that there can be no vacuum or void. Leibniz denies the existence of empty space, not because he thinks space must be full, but because he rejects the very idea of space as a container whose parts can be full or empty. He rejects the concept of a vacuum because it presupposes the idea that space is absolute.

Leibniz argues for the relational theory by claiming that Newton's view contravenes the Principle of Sufficient Reason. Leibniz says that God could have no possible reason for creating the universe in a different region of space or at a different period of time. Since everything must have a sufficient reason, it cannot make sense to say that the universe could have been created earlier or elsewhere in space; these cannot be genuine alternatives, contrary to the claims of the absolute theory.

Leibniz also argues that Newton's theory violates the Principle of the Identity of Indiscernibles. Points and empty regions of absolute space are clearly qualitatively similar in all respects (that is, they are indiscernible), and yet the absolute theory maintains that they are numerically distinct.

Leibniz also challenges Newton's view on theological grounds. He claims that the Newtonian idea of space and time as absolute, infinite entities contradicts the uniqueness of God. If God is the only infinite individual, space and time cannot be absolute and infinite.

The second aspect of Leibniz's own view is more positive. As we saw in Chapter 8, he argues that reality consists only of substances and their properties, and he asserts that these substances are monads, which lack spatial extension. These claims have the dramatic implication that material objects in space are not real. Given this theory of space and time, Leibniz can offer a different argument for the same conclusion. As we have seen, he argues that relations are ideal—that is, not real. This point, together with the relational theory of space and time, implies that space and time are unreal or ideal. In other words:

1. All relations are ideal.

2. Space and time are nothing but relations.

   ———————————————————————————————

3. Therefore, space and time are ideal.

This argument supports the contention that reality consists of nonspatial monads, and this contention is the basis of Leibniz's positive explanation of what space and time are. Space and time are appearances that have their real basis in the points of view of monads.

Leibniz often stresses the dynamic nature of the monads; their perceptions change continuously, and the basis of this change is their appetition—their striving toward the future. Such statements strongly suggest that time is real and that monads are temporal. Yet Leibniz's own arguments commit him to the claim that time, like space, is merely an appearance, and that monads are nontemporal.

Study Questions

1. Why and how does Leibniz argue for the existence of God?

2. What are the differences between Descartes's and Leibniz's views of matter?

3. What are the differences between a relational and an absolute theory of time?

4. Why does Leibniz reject the absolute theory of space?

5. How does Leibniz argue that it is meaningless to suppose that the universe could have been created ten minutes earlier than it in fact was?

6. Explain how Leibniz's relational theory of space supports his views on the nature of monads.

7. How does Leibniz use the Principle of Sufficient Reason and the Principle of the Identity of Indiscernibles to support his view of space?

Discussion Questions

1. How do Spinoza and Leibniz define substance? Should we accept their definition?

2. Could the universe have been created ten minutes earlier than it was?

Rationalism

Rationalism is the view that reason, without the aid of sense perception, can give us knowledge of the world. The three Rationalists—Descartes, Spinoza, and Leibniz—contend that at least some knowledge of reality can be discovered by reasoning alone, without sense experience. Reason can discover self-evident principles, and other knowledge can be rationally deduced from these. The most important of these principles is the Principle of Sufficient Reason, which states that nothing happens without a reason.

In its mildest form, the Principle of Sufficient Reason merely asserts that every event must have cause. However, because of the way in which they understand the idea of cause, the Rationalists accept a stronger version of the principle—one that goes beyond claiming merely that every event must have cause.

First, the Rationalists tend to understand the Principle of Sufficient Reason as implying that there must be a complete explanation of everything that happens. For example, Spinoza believes that all purely physical movement can be explained entirely in terms of the laws of nature, and that these laws of nature amount to the principles of mechanics. Moreover, the principles of mechanics themselves must have an explanation; there must be some reason why these laws are as they are and not some other way. These laws must be seen as following from other more basic principles. Ultimately, all physical laws must be derivable, by logical deduction, from a few fundamental principles that constitute self-evident and necessary truths.

Second, the Rationalists tend to think of causation on the model of logical deduction. Given the totality of causes, the effect must be as it is. Given the causes, the effect follows with logical necessity, much as the conclusion of a valid argument follows logically from its premises.

Consequences of the Principle

Rationalism has four central features that result from the Principle of Sufficient Reason, when this principle is understood as a demand for a complete and logical explanation for everything.

First, the Rationalists tend to regard the ideal of knowledge as a deductive system of truths, analogous to a mathematical system. For the Rationalists, mathematics supplies us with the paradigm for knowledge. Mathematics provides us with clarity, certainty, and order by building on self-evident and undeniable principles with step-by-step logical deductions. Rationalists tend to assume or argue that this model can and should be followed in other branches of knowledge.

The Rationalists are inclined to regard sense experience and observation as an inferior form of reasoning. Spinoza calls sense perception "conclusions without premises," emphasizing that the cause remains unknown. In addition, sense perception does not reveal the causal and deductive connection between things, unlike knowledge gained through reasoning. And like Leibniz and Descartes, Spinoza considers the ideas of perception to be confused and unclear.

The Rationalists also tend to view all truths as knowable a priori. Since they do not distinguish a priori claims from analytic truths, as Kant later does, they tend to regard all truths as truths of reason. As a consequence, they imply that truths of reason can give us knowledge of the world, contrary to the later argument of the Empiricist Hume, who claims that truths of reason can only tell us about the relations between our ideas and not about what exists in the world.

Because of their tendency to treat all truths as necessary, Rationalists cannot easily admit contingency in their systems. Consequently, they either affirm determinism, as in the case of Spinoza, or have difficulties in trying to give an adequate explanation of contingency, as in the case of Leibniz.

Some Differences Among Descartes, Spinoza, and Leibniz

The preceding model of Rationalism is obviously simplified, and it does not take into account important differences among the three philosophers. Descartes was the first philosopher in the modern period to overtly espouse the mathematical/geometrical view of knowledge, which is a distinguishing mark of Rationalism. Nonetheless, in some respects, Descartes's philosophy fits less neatly into the preceding model of Rationalism than do those of Spinoza and Leibniz. Although Descartes is often regarded as the founding father of modern Rationalism, he also greatly influenced Locke and, through him, the other Empiricists.

Despite his geometrical view of knowledge, Descartes claims that particular truths have to be known by sense experience and cannot be known by reason alone. Descartes states that particular truths are known a posteriori and not a priori, even though he also argues that the evidence of the senses in general needs to be vindicated and corrected by reason. In claiming that knowledge of particulars is achieved a posteriori, Descartes resembles the later Empiricists more than Spinoza and Leibniz do.

Descartes affirms that the will is free and is quite unlike matter, which is completely determined by mechanical laws. Because Descartes claims that the will is free, he does not have the problems accounting for contingency that we find in the philosophies of Leibniz and Spinoza. He is not committed to the determinism which Spinoza embraces and Leibniz tries to avoid.

There are some other less obvious differences between the philosophy of Descartes, on the one hand, and the philosophies of Spinoza and Leibniz, on the other. Descartes is more explicitly concerned with establishing the foundations of knowledge than are Spinoza and (especially) Leibniz. In this respect, Descartes's philosophy is close to that of Locke, who also accepts a foundational view of knowledge and whose definition of knowledge was influenced by Descartes's epistemology. Spinoza and Leibniz are not so overtly or centrally motivated by epistemological questions.

Furthermore, for Descartes, the claim that we can only perceive our own ideas is an important postulate. It is one of the explicit assumptions of his scepticism and one of the reasons why he claims that we need to build a bridge between experience and reality. While the claim that we can only perceive our own ideas is also a central thesis of the Empiricists, it does not play such an important or explicit role in the works of Spinoza and Leibniz.

Descartes also shares with the Empiricists a similar view of the mind, which again distinguishes him from both Spinoza and Leibniz. Like the Empiricists, Descartes tends to treat mental states as both self-evident and incorrigible. This means that I cannot have a mental state without knowing that I have it, that I cannot be ignorant of my current mental states, and that I cannot be mistaken about them. Descartes often characterizes the mind in terms of the transparency of consciousness—an approach quite unlike that of Spinoza or Leibniz. For Spinoza, ideas are the mental counterpart of physical objects. According to Spinoza, objects and their corresponding ideas are the same thing viewed under two different attributes of the one substance. Indeed, there is an idea corresponding to every minute part of my body, even though I am not aware of such ideas. For Spinoza, ideas do not have to be known. Leibniz's monads also have unconscious perceptions. In different ways, Spinoza and Leibniz admit that the mind has nontransparent features; and in this respect, they differ from Descartes and the Empiricists.

We have briefly seen some of the ways in which Descartes's philosophy differs from the more traditional model of a Rationalist and from the views of Spinoza and Leibniz, which conform more closely to that model. We have also seen some ways in which Descartes's philosophical position resembles that of the Empiricists, whom he influenced. However, perhaps the most striking difference between the philosophy of Descartes and that of Spinoza and Leibniz is that Descartes is a dualist. He claims that there are two different *kinds* of substances in the universe—mind and matter—distinguished by the fact that minds are essentially conscious and matter is essentially spatially extended. Spinoza and Leibniz reject dualism; both argue that there is only one kind or type of substance in the universe. Spinoza is a monist, arguing that mind and matter are only two attributes of the one substance. Leibniz is a pluralist, arguing that there is only one *kind* of substance, mindlike monads, of which there are an infinite number. Thus, Spinoza's rejection of dualism leads to monism, while Leibniz's rejection of dualism leads to pluralism.

T W O

The Empiricists

The growth of science in seventeenth- and eighteenth-century Europe depended on the development of two methods for acquiring knowledge: mathematical reasoning and observation. Galileo and later (and more explicitly) Descartes stressed the importance of mathematics and mechanical explanation in science. On the other hand, Bacon emphasized science's experimental and observational aspects and its role in making useful predictions. These differences of emphasis were important at a time when the nature and limits of knowledge had become live concerns because of the waning influence of the Church and of appeals to authority.

In his search for certainty, Descartes argued that knowledge based on sense experience was unreliable and had to be guaranteed by the intercession of reason. Descartes saw mathematics—and in particular, geometry—as a model for human knowledge, because of its certainty and clarity. He and later Rationalists claimed that knowledge could be gained through reason alone; rational thought and deduction could reveal the rational order in the universe.

On the British Isles, the philosophical emphasis was different. While the Rationalists stressed the importance of deduction in the new science, Francis Bacon emphasized the importance of systematic observation and induction. Bacon was the forerunner of the Empiricists. Locke, Berkeley, and Hume are called Empiricists because they share common philosophical concerns and general assumptions—not because they follow a defined school of philosophy.

To put the point crudely, the core of Empiricism is that all knowledge is empirical. This means that all knowledge must come from experience. All of our concepts and complex ideas are built from the simple ideas we receive from experience. Consequently, there are no innate ideas, and words that seem to stand for ideas not acquired from experience are either confused or vacuous.

A second point of common emphasis follows from the first. Empiricists tend to deny the importance of reason as a source of knowledge about the world. Deductive reasoning can only reveal the logical connections between our ideas; it never yields knowledge of what actually exists. On its own, a priori reasoning never increases our knowledge of what exists; it only results in claims like "All triangles have three sides." Consequently, Empiricists tend not to regard mathematics as a model of knowledge. Furthermore, they tend to reject the a priori claims of traditional metaphysics.

Third, the Empiricists of the Modern period claim that we can only perceive our own ideas. We are immediately aware of our own ideas with certainty, as a given in experience. This claim, in conjunction with the Empiricist view of knowledge, seems to place a veil of ideas between the perceiver and the world. It suggests that Empiricists ought to be committed either to scepticism regarding the external world or to the task of avoiding that scepticism.

These very broad generalizations about the emphases of the Empiricists should not be taken to indicate uniformity in their views, even when their views are contrasted to those of the Rationalists. There are important differences in the views of the three Empiricists; none of the three conforms to the simple generalizations about Empiricism given above; and sometimes the similarities between an Empiricist and a Rationalist are just as important as the similarities between two Rationalists. For example, as we shall see, there are many deep similarities between the philosophies of Locke and of Descartes. Thus, Locke endorses a mathematical view of knowledge that in some ways resembles Descartes's, and some readers of Locke have identified Rationalistic tendencies in Locke's view of science and causation. Furthermore, Descartes, like Locke, claims that we can only perceive our own ideas.

Again, although Locke and Berkeley are called Empiricists and Leibniz is called a Rationalist, the similarities between the philosophies of Berkeley and Leibniz are probably more striking than those between Locke and Berkeley. Berkeley and Leibniz both argue for the thesis that the universe contains no material substances. According to Berkeley and Leibniz, the universe consists of active minds. Furthermore, they both abhor what they see as atheistic tendencies in Locke's philosophy. Consequently, it would be misleading to contend that, because he is an Empiricist, Berkeley eschews metaphysics in comparison to Leibniz. Nonetheless, we shall see Empiricist principles at work in the arguments of Berkeley.

Of the three philosophers considered here, the broad generalizations of Empiricism best fit Hume. Locke and Berkeley appear to think that the ideas of cause and substance can be derived from experience, and they sometimes rely on principles like "Everything must have a cause." Hume, on the other hand, does not; and for this reason, he is often viewed as being more consistent in his Empiricism than the earlier two philosophers.

John Locke (1632–1704)

John Locke was born on August 29, 1632, in England's west country. His father was a lawyer, and Locke was educated at home up until the age of 14, when he went to Westminster School. In 1652 he went on to Christ Church, Oxford, where he studied Aristotelianism. Although no doubt influenced by it in a general way, he revolted against the medieval scholasticism of the Oxford curriculum and was apparently more attracted to the "new science" or "natural philosophy" introduced by Sir Robert Boyle, who ultimately founded the Royal Society. The emphasis on practical research and experiment in those days was innovative and exciting; previously, even knowledge of human physiology had been absorbed only from books, as part of the classical Greek tradition. Locke spent many years studying medicine and did not really develop his interest in philosophy until the 1660s, when he is believed to have been stimulated by his independent reading of the works of Descartes.

In 1659 Locke was elected to a Senior Studentship—tenable for life—at Christ Church. The following year he became a lecturer in Greek and later a Reader in Rhetoric, as well as, for a time, Censor of Moral Philosophy. In 1674 he finally received his license to practice as a medical doctor. Although he did practice medicine intermittently, it never became Locke's regular profession. In fact he had a rather varied career—indicative, perhaps, of the turbulent times he lived in. The Civil War had broken out when Locke was only 10 years old, and his father fought in the Parliamentary army. On the January morning in 1649 when the king was to be executed, Locke and his fellow pupils at Westminster school were in close proximity, although most likely prevented by their Royalist headmaster from joining the gathering crowd. Later in life, Locke was to become more dangerously implicated in politics.

In 1665 he acted as secretary on a diplomatic mission to the Elector of Brandenburg. The two-month-long mission failed to secure either the Elector's alliance or a promise of neutrality in the Dutch war; and on his return to England, Locke resumed his Oxford studies rather than pursuing further diplomatic activities. During the following summer, however, Locke met Lord Ashley, later a prominent figure in the political world of Charles II. Locke's connection with him was to be a fateful one.

In 1667 he became Ashley's secretary and physician, but their relationship seems to have been friendly as well as professional, and Locke loyally performed a variety of duties in Ashley's service. It is said that Locke once performed a chest operation that saved Ashley's life. He also tutored Ashley's son and assisted with various political tasks, including the drafting of a new constitution for the Carolina colony. When Ashley became the first Earl of Shaftesbury and Lord Chancellor of England in 1672, Locke was also rewarded with a new post. He became secretary in charge of the Lord Chancellor's ecclesiastical business and, later, secretary to the council of trade and plantations. Within a year of his appointment as Chancellor, however, Shaftesbury had alienated the king, and soon thereafter he lost his job. Locke went back to Christ Church and his studies, free from official duties but better off financially than he had ever been before.

Toward the end of 1675, Locke left England for several years. Poor health initially prompted him to go to France, where he met some of the leading medical men. He divided his time in France between Montpellier, where he was able to take the cure, and Paris, where he could absorb the intellectual atmosphere of the period. He met Cartesians and anti-Cartesians and became friendly with a pupil of the scientific philosopher Gassendi, whose work was to influence him significantly.

During Locke's time abroad, Shaftesbury's misfortunes at home had resulted in a year's imprisonment in the Tower of London. By the time Locke returned, his friend was free and soon engaged once more in rather dangerous activities in support of the Duke of Monmouth, a natural son of Charles II and a Protestant aspirant to the throne of England whom the king had banished to Holland. Shaftesbury organized clubs in support of Monmouth and tried to arouse opposition to the legitimate successor to the throne. Locke's involvement in all this is uncertain. He based himself in Oxford, but while there he was said by a fellow college member to live "a very cunning and unintelligible life . . . no one knows where he goes or when he goes or when he returns."

In July 1681, Shaftesbury was arrested on a charge of high treason and spent another few months in the Tower before being acquitted. When Monmouth was arrested about a year later, Shaftesbury went into hiding and escaped to Holland, where he died in 1683. Later that year Locke also fled to Holland. Because of Locke's long association with Shaftesbury, the king ordered his expulsion from the studentship at Christ Church. After Charles II's death and Monmouth's rebellion, Locke's name surfaced again as one of Monmouth's supporters, and the Dutch government was asked to extradite him. For a time, Locke went into hiding under an assumed name: Dr. van den Linden. He refused a subsequent offer of a pardon from the king, saying that, "having been guilty of no crime," he had "no occasion for a pardon."

Locke did not return to England until 1689, after James II had been removed and William of Orange enthroned. King William offered him an ambassadorial post, but Locke preferred the humbler office of Commissioner of Appeals, which afforded him time to pursue his philosophical studies.

During his five years of exile in Holland, Locke consolidated his written work, and in 1688 a French abstract of the famous *Essay Concerning Human Understanding* was published. A year later the Latin version of *A Letter Concerning Toleration* was published anonymously; the topic was controversial, and Locke only admitted his authorship of the letter in his will. In 1690 he published a second letter and the *Two Treatises on Civil Government*, as well as the *Essay Concerning Human Understanding*.

Between 1691 and the year of his death, 1704, Locke spent most of his time in the household of Sir Francis Masham, at Oates in Essex. While he remained active as Commissioner of Trade and Plantations, he spent part of each year in London meetings, but for the most part his last years were spent in philosophical study and controversy. Among his many visitors at Oates was Isaac Newton, with whom Locke probably discussed not only science, but also biblical criticism, in which both were interested. As well as working on a second draft of the *Essay* during this period, Locke published many replies to his critics. Another controversial piece of Locke's appeared anonymously in 1695: the *Reasonableness of Christianity*.

Locke was a modest, cautious man who deliberately kept emotion and enthusiasm out of his academic writing. His private correspondence, however, and the testimonies of his many friends reveal a surprisingly warm character who loved children and frequently went to enormous trouble on their account. "To live," he once wrote to Esther Masham, "is to be where and with whom one likes."

CHAPTER 10

Locke: Ideas and Qualities

Locke conceived the idea of writing the *Essay Concerning Human Understanding* after discussing "the principles of morality and revealed religion" with friends. The discussions must have been inconclusive, because they prompted Locke to investigate the nature of knowledge itself and the ability of humans to know the truth. Locke's *Essay* is intended to "inquire into the original, certainty and extent of human knowledge together with the grounds and degrees of belief, opinion and assent" (I.I.2). Locke is primarily concerned with the nature and limits of knowledge. He undertakes his examination of the understanding to discourage needless speculation about matters beyond our capacity, since in his view such speculation ultimately encourages scepticism. By exploring the capacity and limits of the understanding, Locke seeks to avoid the extremes of groundless speculation and universal scepticism and to clarify the prospects of science.

A member of the Royal Academy of Science in England and friend of Boyle and Newton, Locke wrote at a time when the new science was growing in confidence. He describes himself in the *Essay* as "an under-labourer clearing the ground a little and removing some of the rubbish" in the path of science (I.I.2). Evidently, Locke wrote the *Essay* partly to clarify and articulate the basis of the new science—perhaps to separate it from the pseudo-science of alchemy—and also to show what its implications might be for knowledge. Indeed part of Locke's aim may have been to amend common sense in order to unite it with the newly flourishing science of his time.

Locke has been traditionally dubbed the founding father of Empiricism. This is primarily because he stresses that all our ideas originate in experience. The traditional view is not strictly accurate, however, because Hobbes argued for

Empiricist principles before Locke, and important Rationalist themes run through Locke's work. In opposition to the traditional view, some recent commentators have emphasized the Rationalistic elements in Locke's philosophy—for instance, in his definition of knowledge and in his view of science.[43] However, these questions need not detain us if we bear in mind that the question of whether Locke was more of an Empiricist than a Rationalist is somewhat anachronistic, since the categories of Empiricism and Rationalism did not exist during Locke's time. Of more importance is the question of whether the Empiricist and Rationalist elements in Locke's philosophy conflict.

When Locke describes the origin of certain ideas, his inquiry seems to belong to armchair empirical psychology, because it involves the casual observation of the mind. Although the distinction between philosophy and psychology did not exist in the seventeenth century, Locke's primary aim is to inquire into the justification and limits of knowledge.

The Role of Ideas

Locke calls his philosophical approach "the new way of ideas" (I.II.8). The term *idea* plays a crucial role in his work. Unfortunately, Locke inherits from Descartes a wide and ambiguous use of this term. Locke defines an idea as "whatsoever is the object of the understanding when a man thinks" (I.II.8). Like Descartes before him, Locke claims that ideas can only have the properties that the mind perceives them to have. Having ideas is thus both evident and incorrigible (see Chapter 1). And like Descartes, Locke takes all ideas to be in the mind and to be the immediate objects of perception and reflection. This implies that we do not directly perceive external objects, and it raises at once the problem of how we can know anything about the nature of the external world, given that we are only ever directly acquainted with our own ideas. How can we get beyond the direct knowledge we have of our own ideas to gain knowledge of the external world? We shall consider Locke's approach to this problem later.

In using the word *idea* loosely, Locke ignores some important distinctions. For example, an idea could be the content of sense perception, which is nowadays called sense data. Alternatively, an idea could be a concept, or it could be a mental image. Clearly, the experience of seeing something is quite different from the phenomenon of having a concept. But Locke seems to lump these phenomena together under the term *idea*, which encourages him to treat both concepts and sense data as mental images.

Innate Ideas

Book I of the *Essay* is dedicated to an attack on the doctrine of innate ideas and serves as an introduction to Locke's theory that all ideas are derived from experience.

Locke says that at birth our minds are like "white paper, void of all characters, without any ideas" (II.I.2). The main argument in favor of innate ideas or principles is that certain principles are universally held to be true. Against this argument, Locke says that the universal acceptance of a principle does not show that it is innate, unless it can also be shown that the principle could not be known in any other way. Locke claims that, in any case, there are no universally accepted principles.

In reply to these points, it might be suggested that certain principles are in the mind at birth, but that we only come to know them at a later stage of mental development. Locke says that this reply could mean two things. First, it could mean that we have innate capacities for learning certain truths. Locke agrees with this claim, but he points out that on these grounds almost every true principle could be counted as innate. Second, the reply could mean that the principles lie innate in the mind. To this, Locke objects that the only evidence that an idea or proposition is in the mind is that it is perceived or understood, and that a principle could not be innate unless it was understood at birth.

Locke does not deny that the mind has innate capacities for learning, and his arguments against innate ideas and principles are directed against crude versions of the theory of innate ideas. Since the doctrine of innate ideas was popular in Locke's time, it is unclear to what extent Locke's specific target is Descartes, especially considering Descartes's view that innate ideas are not like pictures hanging in a gallery.

Locke's main attack against the doctrine of innate ideas, however, is his own positive account of the origin of ideas—his view that all our ideas are acquired from experience. This forms the basis of Locke's Empiricism and shows that postulating innate ideas is unnecessary.

In his *New Essays on Human Understanding,* his commentary on Locke's work, Leibniz replies to Locke's attack on the theory of innate ideas by developing the theme of innate capacities.[44] He argues that the mind is innately determined to believe certain principles rather than others. Leibniz argues against Locke that necessary truths are universally true and cannot be learned by sense perception, since sense perception can only give us knowledge of particulars. Leibniz argues that induction from sense experience can never establish necessary truths as such, because necessary truths are universally true. Consequently Leibniz sees a need for innateness to account for our knowing necessary truths. According to Leibniz, we are innately disposed to believe certain principles.

The Origin of Ideas

Locke is called the founder of Empiricism because of his view that the materials of knowledge are all given in experience. In Book II of the *Essay,* he claims that there are two fountains of knowledge from which all our ideas spring: sensation and reflection. Through sensation, the mind receives simple ideas of sensible qualities (like those of yellow, hot, cold, hard, sweet, and bitter) from external objects. By reflecting on how the mind reacts to these ideas of sense, we acquire psychological ideas (like those of perceiving and thinking).

Locke defines reflection as the "perception of the operations of our own minds within us" (II.I.4). By reflection, we acquire psychological ideas. The understanding actively performs three basic operations on the simple ideas acquired through sensation: combination, comparison, and abstraction. By observing its own performance of these operations, the understanding furnishes itself with ideas of its own acts, such as doubting, believing, and willing.

Simple and Complex Ideas

In Book II, Locke attempts to classify ideas, and he first distinguishes between simple and complex ideas. Complex ideas are compounded out of simple ideas, which are not themselves compounded out of further ideas. Complex ideas arise from the operations of the mind, which has the power to repeat, compare, and unite simple ideas in an indefinite number of ways, thereby producing complex ideas. Whereas the mind actively constructs complex ideas, it passively receives simple ideas in experience. Simple ideas form the material from which complex ideas are constructed. Locke argues that the mind is incapable of inventing new simple ideas and is restricted to those it passively receives in experience. It is just as impossible for the mind to construct or invent new simple ideas as it is for a blind man to have ideas of color. The mind "cannot invent or frame one new simple idea" (II.II.2).

In Book II, Chapter I, Section 25, Locke says that simple ideas are passively received. He also says that simple ideas are the smallest unit of experience; a simple idea cannot be dissected into different ideas. Both of these features of simple ideas are important parts of the Empiricist theory of perception, and both are later challenged by Kant. Briefly, Kant argues that experience cannot consist of passively received ideas of sense, because experience also requires a conceptual element that implies activity—for instance, the activities of classification and judgment. Kant also argues that experience requires a certain unity and, therefore, cannot consist of discrete or atomic elements.

Locke divides simple ideas into four kinds, depending on their origin:

1. Those received through one sense only, such as smell and color

2. Those received through more than one sense, such as spatial extension, shape, and motion, which may be acquired through both sight and touch simultaneously

3. Those received through reflection, which Locke subdivides into the categories of thinking and volition (Locke calls the power to think "the understanding," and the power of volition "the will")

4. Those received through both reflection and sensation, such as pain, pleasure, and the ideas of power, existence, unity, and succession.

Primary and Secondary Qualities

Like Descartes, Locke distinguishes between primary and secondary qualities. Locke's discussion of this distinction is contained in Book II, Chapter 8, as part of his discussion of simple ideas. This discussion is commonly held to be one of the most important parts of the *Essay*. It raises the question of whether we can truly say that material objects are colored. More generally, it raises the question: what are material objects really like? Locke, like the chemist Boyle and the physicist Newton, accepts a corpuscular theory of matter and tries to identify the philosophical implications of that theory. Locke's discussion of primary and secondary qualities also raises questions about the nature of sense perception. As we shall see (in Chapter 13), Locke's distinction is later challenged by Berkeley.

Locke also comments on the difference between ideas and qualities. Ideas in the mind are the immediate objects of perception and thought. Qualities, on the other hand, belong to external objects, and Locke defines them initially as the powers in an object to produce ideas in the mind. He says that primary qualities of bodies are "those which are utterly inseparable from the body in what state soever it be" (II.VII.9). These properties—which all material things have in themselves, whether they are perceived or not—include solidity, shape, extension, motion, and number. No subdivision of a body can deprive it of these properties. Locke also holds that the ideas we have of such primary qualities really resemble the qualities themselves.

Colors, tastes, sounds, and so on are the ideas of secondary qualities. Locke says that secondary qualities themselves are nothing in the objects but "the power to produce the various sensations in us by their primary qualities" (II.VII.10). The ideas of secondary qualities are produced in us "by the operation of insensible particles on our senses" (II.VII.13). Locke advances the theory that the physical world is corpuscular—that objects consist of many tiny particles. It is in terms of these tiny particles and their primary qualities that we should explain our perception of the ideas of secondary qualities. In more contemporary terminology, our perception of colors is caused by the operation of light waves on the retina, and our perception of sounds is due to the wave motion of air molecules on the ear. Locke says that the ideas of secondary qualities do not resemble the secondary qualities themselves.

Locke's distinction between primary and secondary qualities has two parts. First, primary qualities are the intrinsic properties of all material things. But secondary qualities are simply the power of objects to produce certain ideas in us; and the real foundations of these secondary qualities, or powers, are the primary qualities of the minute particles. Color in a material object is simply the arrangement of certain particles and their primary qualities, and this is the basis of the power of that object to cause in us the idea or sensation of color.

The second part of Locke's distinction is what may be called the resemblance thesis. The ideas of primary qualities resemble primary qualities themselves, but the ideas of secondary qualities resemble nothing in the object. Thus, our ideas of colors, sounds, and the like do not resemble secondary qualities, which are merely the powers to produce such ideas of these qualities in us; nor do such ideas resemble the grounds of these powers, which are the primary qualities of minute particles.

In two ways, Locke's exposition of the primary/secondary quality distinction in Book II Chapter VIII of the *Essay,* can be misleading. First, although Locke sometimes defines a quality as a power, he usually does not treat primary qualities as powers; instead, he regards them as the intrinsic properties of things and as the grounds for certain powers.[45] On the other hand, secondary qualities are powers—the powers of objects to produce certain ideas in us. Second, when Locke says that primary qualities are primary because they exist in objects, whether these are perceived or not, this may invite the erroneous corollary that secondary qualities do not exist in objects.

Arguments for the Distinction

In Chapter VIII of Book II, Locke advances several arguments for the primary/secondary quality distinction. First, he argues that dividing objects into parts does not take away their primary qualities, which shows that primary qualities are utterly inseparable from objects. Locke presumably thinks that the minute particles of matter do not have secondary qualities. He concludes that primary qualities are intrinsic features of all material objects. This argument does not, however, establish the second part of his distinction—that primary-quality ideas resemble their qualities and that secondary-quality ideas do not.

Second, to argue that nothing like our ideas of secondary qualities exists in the objects, Locke draws an analogy between the ideas of secondary qualities and feelings of pain and nausea. There is nothing equivalent to the feeling of pain within objects that cause us pain. The same goes for secondary-quality ideas. It should be noted that this argument does not give us a reason to suppose that anything resembling our experience of primary-quality ideas exists within objects.

Third, in section 21, Locke points to perceptual illusions. A bowl of lukewarm water may feel cold to one hand and hot to another, yet the water itself cannot be both hot and cold at the same time. Locke uses this point partly to show that our ideas of secondary qualities are not in the object. He also uses it to show that his own theory can explain such perceptual illusions. Locke's comments suggested to Berkeley something rather different—namely, that Locke was arguing that secondary qualities can produce illusory effects, but that primary qualities cannot. To this, Berkeley retorts that we are also subject to illusions regarding primary qualities.

Perhaps Locke's best argument for the distinction is that the corpuscular theory of science is sufficient to explain the causal mechanisms of perception and that this theory gives us no reason for believing that our ideas of colors, sounds, and other secondary qualities resemble qualities in objects. Locke notes that things evidently have no color in the dark. To explain this, it is enough to suppose that the structure of surfaces reflect light differently and that this causes in us ideas of color. It is not necessary to suppose that anything in the object resembles those ideas of color.

Some Famous Criticisms of the Resemblance Thesis

In order to assess Locke's distinction, it is necessary to answer two related questions. First, what is the exact nature of the supposed resemblances between primary-quality ideas and primary qualities? Second, does Locke's distinction rest on an adequate theory of perception? We shall examine the second question in the next section, and the first in this one.

Berkeley criticizes Locke's distinction by arguing that the resemblance thesis is inconsistent with Locke's own view of perception. Berkeley agrees with Locke that the immediate objects of perception are ideas in the mind and that "the mind perceives nothing but its own ideas." Berkeley, however, thinks that it is inconsistent to maintain concurrently (as Locke does) the resemblance thesis—that our ideas of primary qualities resemble the primary qualities themselves.

First, following Berkeley, we should ask how we could ever *know* that the resemblance thesis is true, given that we can only perceive our own ideas. Since we can only ever be acquainted with our own ideas, how is it possible to know anything about the external world? In particular, how is it ever possible to know that the ideas of primary qualities resemble the qualities in the external world?

Second, Berkeley argues that the resemblance thesis does not even make sense. The very idea of resemblance only makes sense if two things that are said to resemble each other can in principle be compared. Berkeley claims that we should not talk of resemblance between mental ideas and material qualities, given that only the former can be perceived. The resemblance thesis requires us to compare ideas directly with the qualities of external objects and to ask whether they resemble one another. Berkeley insists that we cannot do this, since we cannot preceive the qualities of external objects. According to Berkeley, resemblance requires the possibility of comparison, which is lacking in this case.

Third, Berkeley claims that Locke has no reason for distinguishing between our ideas of secondary qualities and our ideas of primary qualities. Both are equally ideas in the mind, and both are equally subject to illusions; consequently, there is no reason to think that one type rather than the other fundamentally resembles the qualities of material objects. We shall return to Berkeley's criticisms of Locke's resemblance thesis in Chapter 13.

One problem with trying to assess Locke's resemblance thesis (and Berkeley's criticisms of it) is that Locke does not state clearly whether he intends the thesis to apply to particular primary qualities (such as being the shape of a particular cube) or to general primary qualities (such as having a shape). The more favorable interpretation of Locke is that the term "primary qualities" refers to general primary qualities. This interpretation would allow us to claim that Locke's resemblance thesis simply means that, with respect to the primary qualities, things look or appear as they really are. Material objects not only appear shaped, but they also really do have a shape. On the other hand, with respect to the secondary qualities, like color, things do not appear as they are; material objects appear colored, but really they are not colored.[46] If this is what Locke means, then the resemblance thesis appears to be more plausible, even though we still may question whether it is right to claim that objects are not colored.

The resemblance thesis is only one part of Locke's distinction between primary and secondary qualities. He also tries to distinguish between them on the grounds that primary qualities are inherent properties of material objects, whereas secondary qualities are simply powers. This second part of Locke's distinction appears to be less controversial than the first. It does not require him to claim that objects are not really colored. The claim that objects are not colored is controversial in itself, but it is also unclear what Locke should say about it; remember, Locke does claim that secondary qualities are powers of objects to cause ideas in us.

The second part of Locke's distinction merely requires the thesis that color and other secondary qualities are not inherent properties of objects, whereas shape and other primary qualities are. We can explain Locke's claim in two ways. First, the general primary qualities are essential to the idea of a material object: all material objects must have a shape, a size, and so on but they need not have a color or a smell, for example. Second, we should explain the secondary qualities of objects in terms of primary qualities, and not the other way around.

Locke's Theory of Perception

To finish our assessment of Locke's distinction between primary and secondary qualities, we need to ask whether it relies on an adequate theory of perception. Most commentators believe that Locke holds a representationalist theory of perception, according to which the ideas we perceive represent external objects. He says that ideas in the mind are the immediate objects of perception and that the mind perceives nothing but its own ideas. Locke also claims that our ideas are caused by external objects and that they represent the properties of these objects. He says that the mind can know external objects "by the intervention of the ideas it has of them" (IV.IV.3). In other words, we can know external objects only indirectly, by directly experiencing the ideas that represent them.

Locke's representational theory should be contrasted with the theories of direct realism and phenomenalism. The direct realist holds that the immediate objects of perception are physical objects that exist independently of our perceiving them; according to most interpretations, Kant holds such a theory. The phenomenalist holds that physical objects are simply logical constructions out of sense experience and that, when we describe physical objects, we are only making hypothetical statements about what we would perceive under certain conditions. Locke's theory of perception is different from both of these views, because for him physical objects exist independently of our perceptions of them, but they are not the immediate objects of perception.

As noted earlier, Locke's representational theory faces the problem of explaining how we can ever know anything about external objects, given that our perceptions are limited to our own ideas. Descartes faced a similar problem. In fact, Locke himself states this objection to his theory of perception. He asks, "How shall the mind, when it perceives nothing but its own ideas, know that they agree with things themselves?" Unlike Descartes, Locke does not feel forced by this question into scepticism. He answers "it seems not to want difficulty."

Locke's response to the sceptical problem he himself raises is twofold. First, he explains how ideas of sense provide us with evidence for the existence and nature of external things, despite the fact that we cannot directly perceive them. Since such ideas are not under the direct control of our will, we must explain how they are produced (IV.XI.5). Our ideas of sense are caused by external objects, so we can infer the existence of such objects from our ideas. Furthermore, the different senses corroborate one another; together they testify to the existence of external things (IV.XI.7). Despite all this Locke admits that "we know not the manner in which they (our ideas) are produced" (IV.XI.1).

Locke's second response to scepticism is to dismiss it. The evidence of our senses is all the evidence we need and can expect for the existence of externals (despite the fact that we cannot directly perceive them). In opposition to Descartes, Locke calls it folly to expect logical demonstration and complete certainty with regard to such matters. We can infer that objects cause our ideas, and this is all the evidence we require for practical concerns or the "ordinary affairs of life" (IV.XI.10). Locke attacks the sceptical frame of mind, dismissing it as impractical. He contents himself with the thought that a true sceptic could never disagree with him, since such a person could not even claim to know what Locke's views are (IV.XI.1).

If we accept that Locke holds a representationalist theory of perception, we must focus on two relevant questions:

1. Does his distinction between primary and secondary qualities depend on the representationalist theory?

2. Is the representationalist theory of perception adequate, and (in particular) what should a representationalist say about the sceptical problems we have discussed?

Representations and Scepticism

The representational theory of perception implies that we can only perceive our own ideas; in the next section, we shall examine some of the implications of this claim for the notion of an idea.

The representational theory also entails that we cannot directly perceive external objects. The impossibility of directly perceiving the external world appears to imply scepticism, especially when combined with an empiricist view of knowledge. If knowledge is based entirely on sense perception and if it is impossible to perceive exernal objects, how can we ever have knowledge of the external world? Descartes accepts the thesis that we can only perceive our own ideas, but ultimately he tries to escape from the scepticism inherent in this thesis by relying on a priori knowledge of God, which he acquires through reasoning. In other words, Descartes attempts to avoid scepticism through his rationalist view of knowledge. This escape route is not available to the Empiricist Locke, who claims that all knowledge is based on experience. As we have seen, Locke tries to escape scepticism about the external world by arguing that such scepticism is not really an implication of his theory of perception and by dismissing scepticism as impractical.

Of course, someone who thinks that we can only perceive our own ideas could argue in favor of scepticism and deny that it is possible to have knowledge of the external world. But such a person could not maintain consistently that ideas are representations of external objects, having no basis for claiming to know that ideas are representations of external objects.

It seems that someone holding a representational theory of perception must argue against scepticism and must argue that the theory does not really entail scepticism about the external world. Does Locke succeed in avoiding the apparent sceptical implications of this theory of perception? There are two potential problems at issue here: one concerning meaning, and the other concerning justification.[47]

The first problem is whether phrases such as "real things outside us" and "the unperceivable causes of our ideas" can have any genuine meaning, given that we can only perceive our own ideas. If material objects are in principle unperceivable, can the term "material objects" be meaningful? This question is answered in the negative by Berkeley in his attack on the notion of material substance. Whether such phrases should be judged meaningful, given a representationalist theory of perception, depends on the nature of meaning itself.

According to a broadly verificationist approach to meaning, sentences can only be meaningful if there is in principle some way of verifying or refuting them. A sentence that purports to describe an essentially unverifiable state of affairs is not meaningful and is neither true nor false, according to such a theory of meaning. A broadly verificationist interpretation of meaning would hold that sentences like "unperceivable objects cause our ideas" cannot be meaningful, given that we can only perceive our own ideas.

On the other hand, a nonverificationist or realist approach to meaning holds that the question of whether sentences are meaningful and can truly or falsely describe a state of affairs is independent from the issue of whether they can be verified. According to this account of meaning, sentences such as "unperceivable objects cause our ideas" can be meaningful even if we cannot perceive such objects.

Given that Locke embraces a representational theory of perception, if he is to maintain that phrases like "material objects" and "the unperceivable cause of our perceptions" are meaningful, he ought to accept some nonverificationist view of meaning. It is not clear whether Locke would have done so, however. For Locke, all meaning is tied to what we can experience: all meaningful words stand for ideas, and all ideas must be derived from experience.

Now let us assume that Locke can give a positive answer to the problem of meaning. It still remains to be shown that we can justifiably believe that the external world exists, given that we can only experience our own ideas. Following Locke, one might claim that the existence of the external world is an explanatory hypothesis; the simplest way of explaining our perceptual experiences is to postulate material objects as their cause.

In opposition to this, other philosophers, notably Kant, argue that we do not need to infer the existence of physical objects if in fact we directly perceive them. Philosophers such as Kant and Wittgenstein argue that our belief in the existence of an objective world is not akin to our belief in a scientific theory. Such philosophers assert that the existence of an objective world is an indispensible condition for either language or experience; therefore, it is unthinkable that the objective world should not exist, given that we have a language or have experiences (see Chapter 20).

Representations and Qualities

The representational theory of perception implies that we can only perceive our own ideas. This has implications for how we should think of ideas. The theory implies that we must think of ideas as things or as mental items. In other words, it requires that we reify sense data or treat the ideas of sensation as mental objects. Locke, like Descartes before him and Berkeley and Hume after him, tends to reify sense data, regarding perception as a special relation between people and these mental items. This is why Locke sometimes compares ideas with pictures.

We may doubt whether it is correct to think of ideas or sense data as mental items or objects. An alternative view, which we shall examine in more detail in Chapter 13, is that ideas are not mental things but are the way in which we perceive. In other words, the phrase "a red idea" should not be taken literally to refer to a red thing in the mind, but is rather a shorthand means of expressing the manner in which a person perceives. Instead of taking the statement "John has a red idea" as indicating a relation between John and an idea, the statement may be thought of as a nonrelational statement about the manner in which John is perceiving. According to this view, talking about sense data or ideas is a shortcut for describing the way in which a person perceives. This alternative view implies that it is a mistake to claim that we see ideas, or to say that ideas are the objects of perception. According to this alternative view, it would be more accurate to assert that the idea is the perceiving.[48]

Does Locke's resemblance thesis require a reification of ideas or sense data? It does seem to require a comparison between ideas and external objects. But ideas can only be compared with external objects if ideas are things or mental objects. If it is wrong to treat ideas as things it is also a mistake to ask whether our ideas of both primary and secondary qualities resemble the qualities of objects themselves.

Summary

Locke's ultimate concern is to show what the human understanding can and cannot do. In this way, he hopes to reveal its limitations, thereby preventing pointless speculation about matters beyond our grasp, which only encourages scepticism.

The mind can only use ideas to think, perceive, and understand. Consequently, Locke tries to explain how we acquire our ideas. He argues against innate ideas; and more positively, he claims that all ideas are derived from experience. According to Locke, all ideas are either simple or complex. Simple ideas are derived from sensation or reflection. Among the simple ideas acquired through sensation are our ideas of primary and secondary qualities. Having discussed Locke's treatment of simple ideas, we shall in the next chapter examine his account of complex ideas.

Study Questions

1. Why and how does Locke argue against the existence of innate ideas?

2. How does Locke distinguish between primary and secondary qualities?

3. What arguments does Locke offer for distinguishing between primary and secondary qualities?

4. Is Locke a direct realist?

5. How does Locke's view of perception compare with Descartes's?

6. How does Locke's use of the term *idea* compare with Descartes's?

Discussion Questions

1. Does Locke establish that objects are not colored?

2. How would Descartes react to Locke's views on scepticism regarding the external world?

3. Is Locke right to dismiss scepticism regarding the external world?

CHAPTER 11

Locke: The Formation of Complex Ideas

In the first edition of Book II, Chapter 12 of the *Essay,* Locke divides complex ideas into three categories: ideas of modes, ideas of substances, and ideas of relations.

Whereas Locke thinks that the mind is entirely passive with respect to simple ideas, he claims that the mind actively forms complex ideas from simple ideas. Three activities are involved: combination, by which the mind unites various simple ideas into a single complex idea; abstraction, by which the mind separates common elements among various simple ideas (for example, we see many red things and, by abstraction, ignore their differences and form a general idea of redness); and comparison, by which the mind takes two ideas and compares them without uniting them into a single idea (according to Locke, this is how we form the complex ideas of relations).

Locke tries to explain the origin of our complex ideas in order to justify his Empiricist principles. He tries to show in detail how the three types of complex ideas can be derived from our experience of simple ideas. By attempting to show how complex ideas are derived from experience, Locke also reinforces his attack on innate ideas. As we shall see, a questionable dichotomy underlies Locke's strategy: the assumption that either ideas are ultimately acquired from experience or they must be innate.

Modes

The idea of a mode does not contain the supposition that modes can exist by themselves. Modes depend on the existence of substances. On the other hand, the ideas of substances are combinations of simple ideas that are taken to represent distinct particular things that can exist by themselves.

Locke subdivides modes into simple and mixed modes. Simple modes are various combinations of the same idea. Such modes come from the operations of enlarging and combining simple ideas of the same kind. Among the simple modes Locke includes our ideas of space, time, number, and infinity. For example, the idea of infinite space is built up from the extensions we meet in experience. Similarly with our ideas of numbers. Our ideas of mixed modes originate in the combination of simple ideas of different kinds; examples of such mixed modes are triumph, murder, and drunkenness.

Substance in General

In effect, Locke defines an individual substance as that which has properties but is not itself a property of something else. In his discussions of the idea of substance, Locke distinguishes three types of ideas:

1. The idea of particular substances or objects (like the idea of the sun or of a particular rose)

2. The idea of different kinds of substances (like the ideas of gold, lead, or oxygen)

3. The more abstract idea of substance in general

Given his overall Empiricist aims, Locke must explain how these ideas of substance can be derived from the simple ideas of reflection and sensation. In fact, Locke's discussion tends to concentrate on the more abstract notion of substance in general. He explains the origin of this general idea as follows (II.XXIII.1). First, through reflection on the regularities in the ideas of sensation, we notice that certain simple ideas constantly go together, which we unite to form a complex idea. For example, the ideas of the sensible qualities of a cherry come into the mind by perception, and we notice that these qualities go together. Next, we presume that this combination of qualities must have an unknown core, or that the qualities must have a substratum in which they subsist. In this way we form our idea of a particular substance. Such an idea results from our idea of a substratum and from the combination of simple ideas that go together. Finally, by abstraction from many such cases, we acquire the general notion of a substratum—the idea of pure substance in general.

The general idea of pure substance requires us to assume that all the properties of a thing have a support. In other words, since it is impossible for properties to exist by themselves, we must infer that there exists a substratum in which they subsist and which itself supports the qualities. Locke introduces the notion of substance in general in order to answer the question, "What is it that supports qualities and unites them into individual things?" Substance, so conceived, is distinct from all properties because it is the support for all of an object's properties. It is the substratum that underlies all of an object's properties. Being distinct from all properties, substance so conceived is propertyless. It has no nature except that of supporting its inherent properties; and because it has no positive nature, it is not to be identified with any particular kind of substance. Consequently, the idea of pure substance in general must be distinguished from the ideas of particular kinds of substances, such as silver, gold, or oxygen.

Locke's reasoning to show the need for the concept of substance in general can be summarized as follows. Take an individual object such as a cup. The cup has many properties or qualities. Because these qualities are universals while the cup itself is a particular, the cup must be distinct from each of its properties. Being distinct from each of them, it must be distinct from all of them. However, properties cannot exist on their own; they must inhere in something. For this reason, we require the notion of a substratum in which the properties inhere and which is itself distinct from all the properties. The chain of reasoning is as follows:

1. Any object is something distinct from each of its properties.

2. Therefore, an object is something distinct from all its properties.

3. Properties cannot exist on their own and must inhere in a substance.

---

4. Therefore, any object is a substance distinct from all of its properties.

Any particular object consists of pure substance or a substratum in which its properties inhere. Pure substance, so conceived, is not identical with any properties and has no positive essential nature. Different kinds of objects or substances must be distinguished by their properties. The idea that there are different kinds of substances is to be explained in terms of different sets of properties inhering in this pure substratum, which may be called "pure substance in general."

Substance and Empiricism

The notion of pure substance in general appears to be an anomaly in Locke's usually Empiricist philosophy. It is difficult to see how such a concept could be acquired from experience, as Locke's Empiricism asserts that all ideas must be. Yet Locke apparently argues that we need such a concept. Thus, logic and reason seem to require such a concept, while experience appears to deny it. There is clearly a conflict between Locke's Empiricism and what he takes to be a demand of reason.

Locke is aware of this tension. He says that we cannot have such an idea by sensation or reflection. He also calls the idea confused,[49] and he claims that if any idea had to be innate, it would be this one. Apparently, Locke admits that the notion of pure substance in general is inconsistent with his Empiricist views on the origin of ideas. How then, does he resolve the conflict?

Different commentators on Locke argue for different responses to this question. Some commentators argue that he rejects the idea of substance in general. They claim that, when Locke discusses the notion of substance in general, he is simply referring to a philosophical position inherent in common speech, without endorsing that position. The main evidence for such an interpretation of Locke is that he seems to admit that the notion of a substratum is inconsistent with his theory of the origin of ideas.

Other readers of Locke, including Berkeley, have argued that Locke does accept this notion of the pure substratum. [50] According to this more traditional interpretation, Locke, despite his comments to the contrary, really thinks that the idea of substance in general can be derived from experience. The mind experiences ideas of different qualities not in isolation but together in groups, and this togetherness is the basis in experience of the idea of substance. One difficulty with this interpretation of Locke is that it does not solve the problem: experiencing different qualities together is not the same as experiencing substance or pure substratum.[51]

Despite the textual evidence against this more traditional interpretation of Locke, other evidence seems to support it. In a letter to Stillingfleet, Locke briefly outlines the argument given earlier for the introduction of pure substratum or substance in general, and he adds "which I think is a true reason." It is not possible to decide on this controversial issue here. We shall return to it briefly in the next chapter, after we have examined Locke's theory of real and nominal essence and related this theory to his views on substance types.

A Problem with the Notion of Pure Substratum

Granting that the concept of a substratum conflicts with Locke's Empiricism, we might ask whether the reasoning that leads to its introduction is valid. Do we need such a concept?

One problem with the earlier argument for substance in general involves the step from premise 1 to premise 2. This step commits the fallacy of composition: the fact that an object is distinct from each of its properties taken singly does not prove that it must be distinct from all of them taken together.

There may be a deeper problem with the whole argument. The argument presents a twofold choice: either an object is nothing but all of its properties or it is something distinct from them. The argument tries to persuade us that, of these two alternatives, we should choose the latter. But this twofold choice itself seems problematic. If the idea of properties without a substance is absurd, then the idea of pure substance without properties should be equally absurd.

Locke's original argument seems to rest on an invalid contrast between an object and all of its properties, and this leads to the introduction of the concept of a pure substance or substratum, which is the notion of a thing that is not any kind or type of thing. If the contrast is invalid, it must then be incorrect to say that a cup is "something" distinct from all of its properties *or* to conclude that a cup is nothing but a composite of those properties. Both alternatives hinge on the contrast of a thing with all of its properties, and both depend on a mischaracterization of the difference between substances and properties. Every substance must be a particular type or kind of substance and, therefore, must have some properties. It is a mistake to ask, "Is that substance distinct from or identical to those properties?" This question is ill-formed if properties are neither identical to nor distinct from the substances that possess them.

Relations: Causality

As we have seen, Locke divides complex ideas into three kinds. Our ideas of relations form the third kind, and they arise from the mental act of comparing other ideas. Words like *daughter, whiter, smaller* all stand for relational ideas. To maintain his Empiricist view of the origin of our ideas, Locke argues that all ideas of relations can ultimately be explained as arising from simple ideas (II.XXV.9). To argue this, Locke examines the relational ideas of cause and identity.

There are a couple of reasons for being especially interested in what Locke has to say about the idea of cause. As he himself notes, causality is "the most comprehensive relation." Locke uses the notion often in his own account of ideas. For example, when he speaks of secondary qualities as causal powers and when he asserts that qualities cause ideas in us, he employs the notion of causation. Second, as we shall see in Chapter 16, Hume argues that the idea of cause cannot be derived from experience according to Empiricist principles. This leads Hume to a sceptical conclusion about the idea of causation. Locke, on the other hand, argues that the concept of a cause can be derived from experience.

Locke defines a cause as "that which makes any thing . . . begin to be" (II.XXVI.2). In terms of this definition, the dispute between Locke and Hume is over the crucial word *makes*. According to Hume, we do not actually observe one event causing or making another. We only perceive sequences of ideas and events, or one idea being followed by another. Hume claims that we do not perceive one event producing another, but only regularities in our simple ideas.

Locke, writing some 50 years before Hume, was aware of this problem, although not as sharply as Hume, and was committed to solve it. He suggests that the complex idea of causation is not derived from sense experience alone, but also from introspection or reflection. By reflection, we discover that we can move our arms (or other parts of our bodies) merely by willing them to move. Locke thinks we derive the idea of active causal power from the experience of our own will, from the simple ideas of reflection.

Identity and Diversity

In Chapter XXVII, Locke turns to the question of what it means for something to be identical to or different from something else at another time. He says that identity and diversity are special kinds of relations because the conditions for identity vary according to the nature of the thing in question (II.XXVII.7). In contemporary terms, identity criteria are relative to the relevant sortal terms, which indicate the kind of thing under consideration. The criteria for identifying the same horse differ from those for identifying the same piece of rock.

Locke begins by discussing the identity of material bodies. Each body can be uniquely described and identified on the basis of its spatial position at any time, because two bodies cannot simultaneously occupy the same place. In the case of compound bodies, like a cube of sugar composed of crystals, our criteria for identity relate to the particles out of which the body is compounded. For the compound body to be identical over a period of time, all its compound parts should be the same over that period, although they may be arranged differently. This implies that, if one atom is lost or added, the compound body will not be the same.

In the case of a living creature, identity does not depend on its possessing the same constituent particles, but on its partaking "of the same life." This depends not on which individual particles actually constitute the organism but on the arrangement and organization of the particles necessary and sufficient for life. According to Locke, this is because organisms are not mere parcels of matter but are particular complex organizations of parts that determine a common life. Hence, the identity of an oak tree is not changed because it grows; its identity over time consists in its having the same life over that time period.

Personal Identity

Locke distinguishes between the concepts of a human being and of a person, and he claims that the conditions of identity for these two concepts differ. The criteria of identity for a human being are similar to those for the identity of an organism, because a human being is an animal of a certain form. But to know the conditions for the identity of persons—for personal identity—we must ask what the word *person* stands for. Locke says "a person is a thinking, intelligent being which has reason and can consider itself as itself" (II.XXVII.9).

According to Locke, what makes a person the same through time is the individual's continuity of consciousness, since it is by consciousness that our different sensations and thoughts at any time belong to the same person. The identity of persons is to be found in the identity of consciousness through time. Locke says that personal identity reaches as far back as consciousness can be extended backward to any past action or thought. He thus attempts to account for personal identity in terms of memory. Although Locke himself does not express his point in this way, self X is the same person as an earlier self Y when X's present consciousness of the past is the result of Y's past consciousness of what was at that time present. I am the same person as I was ten years ago, because my present memories of ten years ago are the result of my experiences then.

Locke's Rejection of Other Theories

Locke argues against two opposing views of personal identity. First, in denying that the concept of a person is the same as that of a human being, Locke claims that the continuity of body is not a criterion for the identity of persons. Second, Locke says that the identity of persons is not to be found in the identity of mental substance or soul.

Locke is agnostic in relation to the mind/body problem. He does not argue for dualism or for materialism. He does not deny that there are mental substances, but neither does he deny that the mind might be a configuration of matter or that matter thinks.

Locke's view is that the identity of persons cannot depend on the identity of soul or mental substances, even if there are such things. Suppose that the soul of Socrates were reincarnated as the present Mayor of Queenborough. Even so, the Mayor of Queenborough would not be the same person as Socrates, unless the mayor had direct consciousness "from the inside" of the experiences of Socrates. If the same soul has two alternating and distinct sets of conscious thoughts and experiences, then in effect two alternating persons share the same soul.

Here Locke is using certain puzzle cases to show that the identity of a soul substance is irrelevant to the identity of persons; the same person could have two souls, and conversely two persons could have the same soul. Locke employs the same method to argue that the identity of bodies is irrelevant to the identity of persons or consciousness. According to Locke, we could suppose that two distinct incommunicable persons or consciousnesses might inhabit the same body—one by day, and the other by night. Conversely we could imagine the same consciousness acting in two distinct bodies, which would amount to the same person having two bodies. Moreover, the same consciousness might be passed from body to body; thus, the consciousness and memories of a prince might enter the body of a cobbler, and vice versa.

Locke admits that, ordinarily, the same person is also the same human being. But this does not imply that the concepts are the same, nor that the respective criteria for identity are the same. Locke uses puzzle cases to show that the concepts of a human being and a person and their conditions for identity are not the same. He also says that *person*, unlike *man*, is a "forensic term" carrying implications of responsibility for actions. If A is the same person as B, then B is responsible for the actions of A. A person is responsible for and imputes to itself past actions insofar as it is conscious of them on the same ground as it is conscious at present.

Some Well-known Criticisms of Locke

The main problem with Locke's account of personal identity is that we cannot remember all of our individual pasts. Locke's account seems to imply that only what can be remembered can belong to the same consciousness. Locke notices this problem himself: "Suppose that I wholly lose the memory of some parts of my life . . . yet am I not the same person that did those actions?" Locke answers that he is not the same person as he who did the forgotten actions, although he is the same human being. That is, Locke accepts the consequence of his account that personal identity extends only as far as memory. This has the further implication that moral responsibility extends only as far as memory.

Butler argues that Locke presupposes personal identity, rather than accounting for it. If so, consciousness of personal identity cannot constitute that identity, because it presupposes it. However, Locke is not saying that personal identity is constituted by consciousness of that identity. Locke's point is that a certain way of remembering an experience or action makes it mine. This may be doubted. Locke rules out as impossible that I might remember someone else's experience as though it were my own. If I remember an action or experience in this way, then Locke considers that it must have happened to me. If memory transference from person to person is possible—if it is possible for me to remember someone else's experiences from the inside, as though they were mine—the criteria for personal identity would have to differ from Locke's account.

Summary and Conclusion

In this chapter we have examined Locke's treatment of the three types of complex ideas: the ideas of modes; the ideas of substance; and the ideas of relations, like cause and identity. To maintain his empiricist theory, Locke must argue that all complex ideas can be derived from simple ideas. This he does case by case.

As we have seen, especially with the notions of substance and cause, there is room for reasonable doubt as to whether Locke actually succeeds in establishing his Empiricist principle that all complex ideas can be derived from the experience of simple ideas. Let us suppose that he does not succeed in his attempt, and that some ideas are not derived from experience. Does this mean that some complex ideas must be innate? Given the general framework of the debate between Empiricism and Rationalism, it does: if some of our ideas are not derived from experience, then those ideas must be innate.

However, we cannot conclude from this that some ideas really are innate, because we may question the underlying assumption that ideas are either innate or else acquired from experience in the ways Locke describes. Kant provides a framework that enables us to question this underlying assumption. He tries to distance himself from the use of the word *idea* common to Descartes and Locke, and he distinguishes between sense impressions and concepts, arguing that both are required for experience. This implies that an experience consisting exclusively of simple sense data is impossible (see Chapter 19).

Moreover, Kant argues that concepts and sense data differ in kind, rather than only in degree. Instead of regarding concepts as faint images, as Locke, Berkeley, and Hume tend to, Kant treats concepts as practical capacities. For Kant, to have the concept of a dog is to be able to make certain judgments and classifications. Although Kant does not explicitly make this point, his treatment of concepts as practical capacities enables us to question the assumption that concepts must either be innate or acquired from experience by abstraction. It also opens up a third possibility—that conceptual abilities are learned.

Study Questions

1. How and why does Locke distinguish between simple and complex ideas?

2. How does Locke's distinction between modes and substance compare with Spinoza's?

3. Why does Locke apparently think that there is an idea of substance in general?

4. Why is there a problem in reconciling the idea of substance in general with Locke's Empiricism?

5. How does Locke think that we acquire the idea of cause?

6. Why and how does Locke distinguish between a human being and a person?

7. Explain two views of personal identity that Locke rejects, and explain why Locke rejects them.

8. How does Locke's account of personal identity compare with Leibniz's views on what individuates substances?

Discussion Questions

1. Must all ideas be derived from experience?

2. Can personal identity be defined in terms of bodily criteria?

CHAPTER 12

Locke: Language and Knowledge

Locke's Theory of Language

In Book III of the *Essay,* Locke investigates the relations between words and ideas. He says that it is impossible to understand knowledge without first considering the nature of language, since knowledge "consists in propositions" (II.XXXIII.19). Locke thinks that it is easy to misuse words and become confused by them in the search for knowledge. In particular, Locke wishes to repudiate the idea that we can attain knowledge simply by working from carefully constructed definitions. Many Medieval scholastic thinkers thought that the essence of natural things and kinds could be revealed simply by disputation and reasoning. Locke argues that this view is based on a misunderstanding of how language works. The primary function of language is to communicate our ideas; and since our complex ideas are formed by the mind, they do not necessarily correspond to the essence of things in the world. For Locke, the purpose of definitions is not to obtain knowledge of the essences of natural things but rather to clarify exactly what ideas in our minds the words actually stand for, so that communication can be clearer.

According to Locke, meaningful words are sounds that stand as marks for ideas in the mind of the person who uses them. There is a difference between a mathematician, who uses the word *six* meaningfully, and a parrot, who repeats the sound *six* without at all understanding it. According to Locke, this difference is that the parrot does not have the idea of six in its mind when it utters the sound, whereas the mathematician does. Therefore, to use words meaningfully, we must have the corresponding ideas in our minds (III.I.2).

Locke usually insists that words stand directly for ideas rather than for the qualities or properties of things, because the only things we know directly are our own ideas. Locke says it is an abuse of words to try to use them to refer to anything but our own ideas. "A man cannot make his words and signs either of qualities in things, or of the conceptions in the mind of another."

According to Locke, the meaning of words is arbitrary. Each person could make any word stand for any preferred idea. However, Locke says that certain words have become associated with particular ideas "by long and familiar use," and that a regular connection between them has been established. In this way, particular words have come to stand for particular ideas (III.I.8).

For Locke, the main purpose of language is to communicate our own ideas to another person. Since ideas are "invisible" (III.II.1), we need some external signs to make our ideas known to others. He says that one person understands another when the ideas that the first person has while uttering the words excite in the other person the same ideas. The word *red* stands for an idea in my mind, and you understand my use of this word if it excites in you the same idea. Locke explains meaning in terms of having ideas; he explains understanding in the same way.

Some Popular Criticisms

Several questions have been asked about Locke's view of language. If the words you use stand for ideas in your mind, then how can I ever understand you? How is it possible, in Locke's account, for one person to know what another's words mean? Locke's thought contains two strands that make these questions pertinent. First, there is his theory of ideas and perception. Locke asserts that all I can ever perceive is my own ideas and that knowledge is based on experience. This invites scepticism not only regarding knowledge of external objects, but also regarding knowledge of other minds. As we saw in Chapter 3, Descartes has similar problems concerning other minds: how can I ever know what ideas other people are having (or even if they have ideas at all), given that I can only perceive my own ideas? The sceptical problem regarding other minds seems even worse than that involving external objects. Second, there is Locke's claim that the meaning of words should be explained in terms of the ideas speakers and hearers have in their minds.

Several contemporary commentators on Locke have argued directly against his attempt to explain meaning in terms of ideas.[52] They claim that it is not necessary to have ideas in one's mind in order to use a word meaningfully. For example, when I meaningfully utter the words "this is blue," I do not need to have an idea of blueness in my mind. All that is necessary is that I use the words intentionally and in accordance with the conventions of the English language. Furthermore, they argue that, given his views on ideas, Locke's account of language makes all meaning essentially private. It implies that I can only know what a word means for me—that is, what idea in my mind the word stands for. Some contemporary philosophers, following Wittgenstein, claim that any attempt (like Locke's) to explain meaning in purely private terms must fail, because language requires essentially public and shared rules of meaning. Without such rules, there can be no criteria for assessing when linguistic expressions are being used correctly or incorrectly. According to this view, the marks *lion* have no meaning except against a background of common usage that implicitly determines what is to count as a correct or incorrect use of them.

Locke also represents understanding as the having of certain ideas; I understand a word because it causes me to have an idea. However, we may question whether understanding can be explained in these terms. Some words might cause me to have ideas that have nothing to do with the meaning of the word; for example, the word *sea* might cause me to have an idea of summer holidays or of boats, and such associations could not be used to explain the meaning of the word *sea*.

A final point: Locke seeks to explain the meaning of words, presumably because he takes these to be the basic units of meaning. However, according to many contemporary theories of language, the basic units of meaning are sentences rather than words, because only with sentences (and not individual words) can we say anything. We should therefore treat sentence meaning as primary and seek to explain how the meaning of words contributes to the meaning of sentences. Sentences are not mere combinations of words, because sentences have structure. In Book III, Chapter VIII, Locke briefly discusses the idea of sentence structure and particle words like *is* and *but,* which he says do not stand for ideas.

General Words: A Problem

In Book III, Chapter III, Locke says that we need general words; it is impossible for us to give every particular thing a distinct name, and such names would be useless to anyone not acquainted with the particular in question. A language without general terms could provide no way of making comparisons and generalizations and, therefore, would be of little use in enlarging knowledge.

We need general words, but Locke asks: how are they possible, or how do they have meaning? The problem can be initially characterized as follows: some words are names that stand for particular things, but then what do general words stand for? It seems that general words must name universal entities. For example, it appears that the word *green* must name a universal thing, greenness. However, Locke rejects the claim that there are such universal entities. He says that only particulars exist. How, then, do general words have significance?

In claiming that only particulars exist, Locke rejects a strong realist view of universals. Some realists, like Plato, regard universals as real immaterial entities that exist outside space and time and are manifest in particular things. What all round things have in common is that they manifest the universal roundness. According to Plato, our ability to make generalizations can be attributed to our reason's acquaintance with the realm of universals (or forms) such as roundness. The claim that universal entities exist and that we know them through reason is incompatible with Locke's Empiricism.

In replying to the realists, Locke indicates that he can explain how general words have meaning, without postulating the existence of metaphysical entities like forms. Locke claims that words become general by being the signs of general ideas and that ideas become general by abstraction. In other words, general words like *red* name general ideas in our minds, rather than naming universal entities like Platonic forms.

Abstraction is an activity or function of the mind by which we acquire general ideas from the particular ideas given to us in sensation. For instance, by attending selectively to the quality that a group of round things have in common and ignoring their other properties, we acquire the general notion of roundness. Similarly, by attending to the color common to chalk, snow, and milk, we acquire the general concept or idea of whiteness. In this way, Locke tries to provide an Empiricist account of how general ideas are formed.

Another Problem: Classification

Locke has another reason for rejecting the Platonic picture: it assumes that there are essential natures common to all things of one kind. It thus implies that, for every general word, there must be some essential feature that divides natural things into kinds. This means that there is no indeterminacy or arbitrariness in classification and that the way we classify things reflects real and essential divisions in the world. Locke rejects such claims.

According to Locke, the mind selectively attends to certain similarities and not to others, and by abstracting from these comes to form general concepts. By picking out certain similarities and ignoring others, the mind forms general ideas that are capable of representing more than one individual. Because our classifications depend on the selections made by our attention, there is some arbitrariness in those classifications. For this reason, Locke says that general ideas are the inventions and creatures of the understanding.

On the other hand, Locke admits that things really do resemble one another and that our classifications have some basis in the real resemblances between things. In other words, the mind does not invent the objective similarities between things, and consequently our classifications are not entirely arbitrary. Locke further explains his views on classification by distinguishing between real and nominal essence.

Real and Nominal Essence

The nominal essence of a substance type or kind, such as gold, is a complex abstract idea of something having certain characteristics. We can recognize and classify an object as a piece of gold because of its yellow shining color, its weight, its malleability, and so on. We associate this complex idea with the name *gold*. The complex idea is formed by abstraction—by selective attention to the ideas and their corresponding qualities, which are common to the type in question.

Locke contrasts the nominal essence of gold with its real essence. The real essence of gold is its internal constitution, which is generally unknown. The observable characteristics of gold, which define its nominal essence, causally depend on the real essence of gold. These observable properties flow from the real essence, which consists of certain arrangements of the primary qualities of the minute particles of that substance type. The real essence of each substance provides a scientific basis for explaining why all substances of that kind share common observable properties. We can then explain scientifically why such properties and their ideas cluster in us and are not mere random associations.

According to Locke, since the real essence of things is unknown, it does not constitute the actual basis of our classification of things into kinds; instead, the nominal essence constitutes this basis. Since the nominal essence is an abstract idea of the mind, there may be a conventional element in such a classification; because people may classify differently, the nominal essence of gold may differ from person to person. No substance has a nominal essence until the mind refers that substance to a general idea. Although Locke is keen to emphasize the conventional element in such a classification of substances, he is not keen to overemphasize it. Although the nominal essences of substances are made by the mind, when the mind forms such complex ideas, it is guided by similarities that really are there in nature. In other words, our classification is developed according to nominal essence, but the nominal essence of substances is founded on their real essence, which remains unknown. According to Locke, we should expect broad, though not universal, agreement in classification according to nominal essence.

Definition

Locke says that a failure to distinguish between real essence and nominal essence leads to a false view of classification. Some of Locke's predecessors, the scholastic Medieval philosophers, believed that all natural things have fixed and eternal essences that divide them into species, and that these fixed essences can be discovered through a priori definition and reasoning alone. In contrast, Locke thinks that disputing the definitions of things is a fruitless method of inquiry, since such definitions only determine the nominal essences (which are relative) and not the real essences of things. In opposing the scholastics, Locke denies that we can have a priori knowledge of the world.

Locke gives his own positive account of the purpose and importance of definition. The function of words is to communicate our ideas; for two people to understand each other, the speaker and listener must have the same ideas. And since people may have formed a complex idea differently and still use the same word to stand for that idea, the primary purpose of definition is to make as clear as possible exactly what idea a particular word stands for. Locke warns us against abusing words by making them stand for unclear ideas or for several distinct ideas at once. Clear definitions are one remedy for these abuses.

For Locke, the purpose of definition is to make communication clearer. We should not suppose that definitions give us a priori knowledge of real essences.

Natural Kinds

Locke says that we sometimes use substance-type terms, such as *gold*, as if we were referring to the real essence of gold. It is worth briefly comparing Locke's views with those of the twentieth-century philosopher Kripke on natural kinds.[53]

Locke is highly critical of our intention to use words to refer to the real essence of things. Real essences are not known, and Locke tends toward the view that words can only signify ideas with which we are directly acquainted. On the other hand, Kripke argues that we do use natural-kind terms such as *gold* to refer to a substance with a certain internal constitution (or real essence). Suppose that the real essence of gold is in fact its atomic number 79. Kripke makes the following claims:

1. It is possible for a substance to be gold, even though it has observable properties that are quite different from those normally associated with gold, so long as that substance has atomic number 79.

2. It is possible for a substance with all the observable properties usually associated with gold to be something other than gold, so long as it does not have atomic number 79.

In this way, Kripke argues that if gold does have atomic number 79, it is not possible for gold to have a different atomic number, although it is possible for a particular piece of gold to have different observable properties than it does now.

However, Kripke does not claim that having atomic number 79 is a part of the meaning of the word *gold*. A person can understand the meaning of the term *gold* without knowing its atomic number and even without comprehending the concept of atomic number. The atomic number of gold has to be discovered empirically; it is not determined by the meaning of the term *gold*.

The comparison of Locke and Kripke highlights a problem with Locke's account. He attaches the meaning of the word *gold* to its nominal essence. But if *gold* meant a yellow, shiny malleable, heavy substance, as Locke suggests, it would be impossible to call gold *gold* when, for instance, at high temperatures it becomes a gas. Trying to define *gold* by its nominal essence is like trying to define the word for a disease by the usual symptoms of that disease; it then becomes impossible to say that someone with that disease might lack those symptoms.

Real Essence and Substance in General

We now return briefly to some of the issues raised in the previous chapter—namely, the notion of pure substance in general and the question of whether Locke endorses that notion. A superficial reading of Locke might lead us to think that he equates the notion of substance in general with that of real essence. Locke says that the idea of substance in general is an idea of we know not what; he also says that real essence is unknown. In addition, he calls both substance in general and real essence supports for a substance's qualities. These points might be taken to imply that the concepts of substance in general and real essence are identical for Locke.

However, the notions of specific real essences and of substance in general are distinct. The arguments for introducing the two notions are different, and so are the purposes they serve in Locke's philosophy. According to Locke, substance in general is the substratum of all an object's properties; but real essence consists in the primary qualities of the minute particles and is, therefore, the substratum of an object's secondary qualities. Furthermore, substance in general is essentially unknowable, but real essence is only generally unknown and could be known if our powers of perception were different.

The two notions differ, but does Locke separate them? M. Ayers argues that he does; he asserts further that, for Locke, the notion of substance in general is simply the notion of the determinable of which specific real essences are particular determinations, rather than being an entity distinct from all its properties.[54] According to Ayers, Locke does not accept the notion of pure substratum and the fallacious argument for its introduction. Instead, by "substance in general" Locke means simply "real essence in general"; he does not mean pure substratum. Ayers's interpretation of Locke is attractive, because it appears to solve the anomalies in Locke's position mentioned in the previous chapter. However, it also appears to be inconsistent with Locke's comment to Stillingfleet mentioned earlier.

Knowledge: Some Preliminaries

In Book II of the *Essay,* Locke attempts to explain the origin of our ideas, which form the material for knowledge. It is only in Book IV that he discusses knowledge itself. Like Descartes, Locke distinguishes between having an idea and knowing (see Chapter 2). Knowledge and belief entail making judgments; they do not consist in merely having ideas. Merely having an idea is not the same as judging that idea to be true or false. Locke says: "our ideas are not capable any of them of being false, till the mind passes some judgment on them" (II.XXXII.3).

Locke uses the term *knowledge* in a strict sense. According to Locke, for a belief to qualify as knowledge, we must be certain of it and we must be justified in our certainty. Given this strict use of the term, it follows that many propositions we might ordinarily claim to know should not actually count as knowledge. Locke declines to count beliefs that are merely probable as knowledge. He says "the highest probability amounts not to certainty" (IV.III.14).

Given that Locke claims that knowledge requires justified certainty, we might expect Locke to limit knowledge to fields like mathematics, where demonstrative certainty appears possible. For the same reason, we might expect Locke to question the possibility of empirical knowledge of the world based on the senses, for which certainty does not seem possible.

There is another reason for such expectations. Locke defines knowledge as the perception of certain relations of agreement and disagreement between our ideas (IV.I.1). This entails, as he points out at IV.III.1, that knowledge be confined to ideas. But if our knowledge is restricted to our ideas, knowledge of external objects and their qualities is impossible. Consequently, Locke ought, at the very least, to be sceptical of empirical knowledge of the world.

As a consequence of the two most basic features of Locke's definition of knowledge, we might logically expect him to have a view of knowledge similar to Descartes's, according to which the prime examples of knowledge involve knowing the logical relations between ideas. We might also expect Locke to be sceptical about the possibility of empirical knowledge of the world, since this does not fit his definition.

These expectations have led some readers of Locke to assert that he has a Rationalist definition of knowledge. However, Locke does not always fulfill such expectations. For instance, he argues that a limited amount of empirical knowledge is possible, and (as we saw in Chapter 10) he rejects scepticism.

Locke and Descartes

Even if Locke has a view of knowledge in some ways similar to Descartes's, this does not make him a Rationalist. First of all, in Books I and II, Locke argues that all our ideas are derived from experience. This means that all the materials for knowledge come from experience. In contrast, Descartes thinks that all clear and distinct ideas are innate and are supplied by reason itself, not by the senses. Even if Locke's formal definition of knowledge is similar to Descartes's, the two philosophers have very different views about the ideas that form the materials for knowledge; consequently, they have different views about the nonformal nature of knowledge. Briefly, for Locke, knowledge requires the senses; for Descartes, it requires reason.

Second, to some extent, the similarities between Descartes and Locke are superficial. They agree that "knowledge" requires certainty, but they disagree about the significance of this point. For Descartes, it is important to attain certainty, and the fact that certainty cannot be reached through sense experience means that we should set aside the prejudices of the senses and rely instead on reason. For Locke, on the other hand, certainty seems less important. He thinks that it is difficult to attain certainty in our empirical investigation of nature, but his attitude toward this difficulty is pragmatic. If we cannot have true knowledge of nature through sense experience, we should be satisfied with probable belief. And we should still carry on with our carefully controlled empirical investigations of nature, even though they do not lead us to certainty.

The Agreement Between Our Ideas

In Chapter I of Book IV, Locke defines knowledge as the perception of certain relations of agreement and disagreement between our ideas. He lists four sorts of agreement and disagreement: identity and diversity; relation; coexistence or necessary connection; and real existence. In discussing these relations, we shall find that the first two clearly fit Locke's definition of knowledge and that the final two are more problematic.

1. Identity and Diversity

This type of knowledge is expressed by "trifling propositions" such as "Red is red" and "Red is not blue," which merely require the judgment that an idea is what it is and is not another.

2. Logical Relations

This kind of knowledge is obtained by judging the logical relations between ideas. It is expressed with propositions like "The angles of a triangle equal 180 degrees." Locke thinks that this kind of knowledge can also be found in ethics, politics, and religion (IV.III.18), and he considers it the most extensive kind of knowledge.

3. Coexistence

Not all relations between ideas are logical. There are also regularities in our ideas when, for example, one idea is regularly accompanied by another. Often, our ideas come in clusters. This is what Locke means by the relation of coexistence between ideas. He says that our knowledge of substances or physical objects consists in the judgment that the ideas of certain qualities accompany each other or belong together. For example, according to Locke, our knowledge of gold consists in the judgment that the ideas of yellowness, weight, and certain powers always accompany each other.

Locke contends that knowledge of substances through coexistence of ideas is very limited. This is because experience is restricted to the secondary qualities, and we have no ideas of the primary qualities of the atoms on which the secondary qualities causally depend. Moreover, says Locke, we are ignorant of the causal relations themselves. Locke is reiterating here our ignorance of real essences.

Despite Locke's avowed pessimism regarding this third kind of knowledge, we might ask whether it is even possible. If knowing consists in perceiving relations between ideas, is knowledge of substances and their qualities possible?

4. Real Existence

At IV.I.7, Locke says that the fourth relation is "that of the actual real existence agreeing to any idea." Again, we should ask: if knowing consists in perceiving relations between ideas, is this fourth relation possible (since it is a relation between ideas and real things)?

Degrees of Knowledge

In Chapter II of Book IV, Locke describes three different kinds of knowledge claims, or different degrees of knowledge. Locke's classification is similar to Spinoza's (see Chapter 6).

Intuitive knowledge is an immediate perception of agreement between ideas, which, according to Locke, leaves no room for doubt. As an example Locke cites "Three is more than two." Like Descartes, Locke thinks that we have intuitive knowledge of our own existence and of certain principles, like "Every event has a cause."

Demonstrative knowledge is not immediate but requires intervening ideas and steps, as in a mathematical or logical proof. Because of these intervening steps, demonstrative knowledge is less certain than intuitive knowledge.

Sensitive knowledge is even less certain than demonstrative knowledge (IV.II.14). It is the knowledge we have of particular external objects when they are actually present to our senses (IV.III.1). This third degree of knowledge, which Locke calls the present testimony of the senses, is the basis for our knowledge of coexistence and the real existence of objects (though Locke claims that we have intuitive knowledge of our own existence and demonstrative knowledge of God's existence).

The Extent of Knowledge

In the previous four sections we have uncovered some problems for Locke's theory of knowledge. These problems amount to the question: does Locke's theory exclude sensitive knowledge of external objects? Locke thinks that we have such knowledge, and his reasons were discussed in Chapter 10.

Although Locke thinks that sensitive knowledge is possible, his definition of knowledge casts a pessimisic shadow on the hope that science will enlarge our knowledge of nature. At IV.XII.9 and 10, after arguing that we can only know nominal and not real essences, he claims that the new experimental method "will reach very little general knowledge concerning the species of bodies." He does not doubt that scientific progress will be useful, but he contends that we should be content with probable belief and opinion rather than insisting on true knowledge, since "our faculties are not fitted to penetrate into the internal fabric and real essences of bodies" (IV.XII.11).

Locke sharply contrasts the gloomy prospects for scientific knowledge with those for morality. Locke argues that moral knowledge can be demonstrated and therefore can be known with certainty. He says: "our proper employment lies in those enquiries and in that sort of knowledge, which is most suited to our natural capacities, and carries with it our greatest interest . . . Hence I think I may conclude that morality is the proper science and business of mankind in general"(IV.XII.11).

Study Questions

1. Why does Locke think that words must stand for ideas?

2. According to Locke, how do ideas become general?

3. What problems is Locke's account of general words supposed to solve?

4. How and why does Locke distinguish between real and nominal essence?

5. How does Locke's notion of real essence compare with his concept of substance in general?

6. What is Locke's definition of knowledge?

Discussion Questions

1. Do words have meaning by standing for ideas in our minds?

2. Does Locke establish the extent and limits of human knowledge?

George Berkeley (1685–1753)

George Berkeley was born in 1685 near Kilkenny, Ireland. He entered Trinity College, Dublin, when he was only fifteen and took his B.A. in 1704 at the age of nineteen. His studies included Latin, Greek, Hebrew, mathematics, and the works of Newton and Locke. In 1707 he published a work on mathematics and was made a fellow at Trinity. As was required by the Trinity fellowship, he also took holy orders in the Anglican Church.

He now began to fill the notebooks that would later be known as the *Philosophical Commentaries*. His *Essay Towards a New Theory of Vision* appeared in 1709, and the following year he published *A Treatise Concerning the Principles of Human Knowledge*. Three years later, the *Three Dialogues Between Hylas and Philonous* were published, mostly to justify and expand on ideas expressed in the *Treatise*. Berkeley was now only 28 years old, but these were to remain his best-known works. Despite dubbing himself a defender of common sense, Berkeley claimed that only minds and their ideas are real. Dr. Johnson thought he could refute Berkeley's thesis merely by kicking a stone; others declared that Berkeley was insane. As for himself, Berkeley admitted to being "young . . . an upstart . . . vain"; but "one thing, I know, I am not guilty of. I do not pin my faith on the sleeve of any great man. I act not out of prejudice and prepossession. I do not adhere to any opinion because it is an old one, a receiv'd one, a fashionable one, or one that I have spent much time in the study and cultivation of."

In 1713 Berkeley went to London, where he was befriended by many members of the country's intellectual elite, including Pope, Swift, Addison, and Steele. Pope was to attribute to Berkeley "ev'ry virtue under heav'n"; indeed, he made many friends who admired him greatly. During this early visit to London, however, he was not happy. He had hoped for recognition of his philosophy, but found that it was ignored and that people were reluctant even to discuss his views with him. When the opportunity arose for him to act as chaplain to Lord Peterborough, Berkeley took it. After another couple of years in London, he went to Italy in 1716 for a prolonged tour, toward the end of which he wrote a treatise in Latin on mechanics. *De Motu* was published on his return to England.

In 1721 Berkeley received the degree of Doctor of Divinity in Dublin. He also published *An Essay Towards Preventing the Ruin of Great Britain*. As this title suggests, he felt society to be corrupt. A sincerely religious man, Berkeley turned his thoughts away from the decadence of London and Dublin and toward the idea of creating a college in Bermuda. He stated that its purpose would be "the reformation of manners among the English in our western plantations and the propagation of the Gospel." In 1724, although he had been named Dean of Derry, Berkeley went to London to solicit support for the Bermuda proposal. He received promises both from private donors and from Parliament, as well as a charter for the college from King George I.

In 1728 Berkeley sailed for America with his new wife Anne, and bought 100 acres of land near Newport, Rhode Island. He had a house built there and named it Whitehall. He made good contacts at Yale College and was to correspond regularly with Samuel Johnson, a missionary and American philosopher. At this time Berkeley also wrote *Alciphron,* a philosophical defense of Christianity against freethinkers. In 1732, the anticipated funds from England were still not forthcoming. Arrangements were made for the numerous books intended for the Bermuda college to be donated instead to Yale; and Berkeley, disappointed, returned to London.

In 1734 he was appointed Bishop of Cloyne and returned to Ireland to live in his diocese. He served as Biship of Cloyne for 18 years, continuing to work and write in various ways to promote the enhancement of human welfare. In 1744 he published *Siris (A chain of Philosophical Reflexions and Inquiries concerning the Virtues of Tarwater, and divers other subjects connected together and arising one from another)*. Tarwater, which Berkeley had first encountered in America, was made by boiling in water the tar from the bark of pine or fir trees. Berkeley is said to have administered the remedy to the local population in Ireland for the successful treatment of such diverse ailments as smallpox, consumption, indigestion, asthma, and ulcers. In his treatise, Berkeley describes specifically the manufacture and virtues of tarwater and goes on to a more general discussion of the nature of the universe and God. *Siris* caused quite a stir, but more for its suggestion of tarwater as a cureall than for the philosophical ideas in the latter part of the paper.

In 1752 he went to Oxford to supervise the education of his second son. (He had seven children, three of whom died in infancy, and his eldest son survived only to age fourteen.) Berkeley himself died suddenly in 1753 while listening to his wife read from the Bible. He was buried in Christ Church College Chapel.

CHAPTER 13

Berkeley: The Denial of Matter

Berkeley's philosophy, as expounded in *A Treatise Concerning the Principles of Human Knowledge* and the *Three Dialogues between Hylas and Philonous*, is fundamentally anti-Lockean. Berkeley sees Locke's philosophy as sceptical and atheistic. (Locke in fact does argue for the existence of God, but God plays no important role in his system.) Berkeley overcomes these two faults, dramatically, by denying material substance. Minds and their ideas are all that exist. Our ideas of sense perception are not caused by material objects that lie behind a veil of perception, but directly by God. What we call objects are simply our ideas of sense, which exist only in the mind. Thus, there is no place for scepticism about their existence.

Berkeley defends his strange view with persuasive arguments, which raise problems for Locke. Berkeley's first attack on Locke focuses on the theory of abstract ideas and is contained in the introduction to the *Principles of Human Knowledge*.[55]

Abstract Ideas

That words can stand for particulars is not problematic for Locke. What is problematic and requires explanation is how they can stand for more than one thing—that is, how they can be general. Locke's answer is that words become general by standing for general ideas, while ideas become general by abstraction. The word *apple* is connected with apples by the general idea of an apple.

Berkeley attacks Locke's theory of abstract general ideas; he argues that there can be no such thing as an abstract idea. For example, it is impossible to have an idea of color that is not any particular color. Berkeley quotes Locke saying that the general idea of a triangle is the idea of a triangle that is not equilateral, isosceles, nor scalene, but "all and none of these at once." But of course, as Berkeley points out, no triangle can be all and none of these at once. Since such a triangle is impossible, there can be no idea of such a triangle, and thus Berkeley concludes that there can be no abstract ideas.

Berkeley argues as follows:

1. It is impossible that there be any bare motion—that is, motion that is neither swift nor slow, neither curvilinear nor rectilinear.

2. The abstract idea of motion is the idea of bare motion.

   ───

3. Therefore, the abstract idea of motion is an idea of something impossible.

4. There can be no idea of X, if X is logically impossible.

   ───

5. Therefore, there can be no abstract idea of motion.

As well as arguing that abstract ideas are impossible, Berkeley says that they are unnecessary. Berkeley denies some aspects of Locke's theory of language. He denies that general words are meaningful because they stand for general ideas. He says that a word can be used meaningfully even when the speaker does not have an idea in mind when speaking. Instead, Berkeley stresses that words have to be used in a certain way in order to be used meaningfully. Berkeley comes close to saying that understanding the meaning of a word amounts to knowing how to use it. The relevance of all this to general ideas is as follows: Berkeley denies general ideas; for him all ideas are particular. But a particular idea or image can be used to represent in a general way, just as a diagram of a particular triangle can be used to represent all triangles. General abstract ideas are unnecessary because a particular idea can be used to represent all the particulars of its kind. In other words, all ideas are particular, but we may put these particular ideas to a general representative use.

It has been claimed that Berkeley's attack on abstract ideas is valid only on the assumption that all ideas are images.[56] Obviously no triangle can have all possible proportions at once, and therefore there can be no image of such a triangle. But as Kant later argued, concepts are not images. Berkeley's argument seems to assume that they are and to attribute the same assumption to Locke. It is unclear whether Locke accepts that concepts are images, because of his vague use of the term *idea*.

In the preceding argument against abstract ideas, Berkeley's crucial premise is his second one:

2. The abstract idea of motion is the idea of bare motion.

Locke could deny this premise by saying that the abstract idea of motion is not the idea of motion (which is neither swift nor slow, etc.) but is the idea of what is common to all types of motion. Berkeley assumes that, because the abstract idea of motion contains no representation of the motion's being slow or fast, it is the idea of motion that is neither slow nor fast. He assumes that, if an idea of X lacks specification of whether X is F, it must be an idea of X that lacks F. But the idea of a flower that contains no specification of petal color is not the idea of a flower whose petals have no color.

Ideas of Sense

Following Locke, Berkeley maintains that we only perceive our own ideas. Furthermore, all ideas are necessarily mind-dependent; an idea can only exist in the mind that perceives it. For this reason, Berkeley says that the existence of ideas consists in their being perceived—that their *"esse is percipi."*

In the first dialogue, Philonous (who represents the views of Berkeley) tries to support these assumptions and eventually uses them to show that matter cannot exist. Philonous argues as follows:

1. In sense perception, we perceive nothing but certain sensible qualities.

2. All sensible qualities are nothing but ideas.

    _____

3. Therefore, we only perceive ideas.

Hylas, arguing against Philonous, challenges premise 2 by attempting to maintain that sensible qualities such as heat and sound are more than ideas and can exist independently of the mind.

Berkeley, through Philonous, tries to support premise 2 with various arguments. First, Philonous argues that intense heat is only an idea in the mind, because pain is only a sensation in the mind and intense heat is a pain.[57] But since all degrees of heat are equally real, it follows that all degrees of heat are ideas. This argument rests on the assumption that the pain one feels and the heat one feels are one sensation, since sometimes we cannot distinguish between them.

Second, Philonous repeatedly uses the so-called argument from illusion to show that various sensible qualities are nothing but ideas.[58] He employs this method of argument with respect to heat and cold, taste, smell, color, size, shape, motion, and solidity.

The Argument from Illusion

Berkeley uses this argument to show that the only thing we ever perceive is our own ideas. More precisely, he uses it to show that all sensible qualities are nothing but ideas—his linchpin premise 2 of his earlier argument. The argument from illusion has a vital role in Berkeley's attack on the existence of matter. It has also been influential in the thought of such early twentieth-century empiricists as A. J. Ayer and Bertrand Russell. For these reasons, the argument needs to be carefully considered. It can be summarized in three steps:

1. First Step

1. The real properties of an external object cannot change without the occurrence of a change in the object itself.

2. The colors I perceive can change without the occurrence of a change in the object itself.

   _____

3. Therefore, the colors I perceive are not the real properties of an external object.

The function of the first premise here is to set a criterion or standard that the real properties of an external object must meet. If those properties change, there must be a corresponding change in the object itself. The second premise tells us that the colors we perceive fail that test or criterion. Perceived color can change without the occurrence of any change in the external object; for instance, it can change if we wear colored glasses, or if the surrounding lighting is altered. (Similarly, sound may be distorted by distance or by use of a microphone.)

2. Second Step

4. Either the colors I perceive are real properties of external objects or they are only ideas.

5. The colors I perceive are not real properties of external objects. (This premise merely repeats statement 3, the conclusion of the previous step.)

   _____

6. Therefore, the colors I perceive are only ideas.

This second step is simple but important. Premise 4 presents us with two exclusive options and claims that they are exhaustive: either perceived colors actually exist in the external world or they are mental items—ideas. Since the first step already rules out the first of these two alternatives, we should conclude that the colors we perceive are ideas.

3. Third Step

The argument applied to perceived colors can be generalized to apply to all the sensible qualities we perceive. The sounds we hear, the tastes and smells we perceive and even sensations of touch are all subject to illusion. They can change without the occurrence of any actual change in the external object. Berkeley claims that the same point can be made about Locke's so-called primary qualities: the shapes and sizes we see and the weights we feel can also change without the occurrence of any change in the object. He concludes that they cannot be real properties of external objects and that they can only be ideas.

In this third step, we should substitute the phrase "all the sensible qualities I perceive" for the words "the colors I perceive" in premises 2, 3, 4, 5, and 6. According to Berkeley, we should generalize the argument from illusion and apply it to all the sensible qualities. This implies that all sensible qualities we perceive are only ideas—or in other words, that we only perceive our own ideas.

How Berkeley Uses This Argument

The final conclusion of the argument from illusion is that we can only perceive our own ideas. Berkeley uses this conclusion to present us with a dilemma. Prior to philosophical reflection, most of us would assent to the following two pronouncements: objects like tables and trees exist in the external world, and they possess in themselves properties like shape, size, and color; we perceive objects like tables and trees, and we perceive their shape, size, and color.

According to the argument from illusion, these two assertions are inconsistent and cannot both be true. If we want to insist that tables and trees are really part of the external world, the argument from illusion implies that we must admit that we never perceive them (because we perceive only our own ideas). If, on the other hand, we want to insist that we do perceive tables and trees, the argument from illusion tells us that they are not out there in the external world, because if we perceive them then they must be merely ideas.

Either tables and chairs are only ideas or they are never seen and perceived: this is the implication of the claim that we can only perceive our own ideas. Of these two alternatives, Berkeley chooses the first. He says that it would be contrary to common sense to assert that tables, chairs, and all other sensible objects are never perceived, and he unhesitatingly draws the conclusion that they are merely ideas.

Another Argument

At first glance the argument from illusion looks sound, despite the dramatic and counterintuitive nature of its implications. However, the argument has a weakness: it begs the question, assuming from the outset what it intends to prove.

The flaw is elusive and is best uncovered by considering a structurally similar argument. Imagine a person in the complete darkness of a sensory-deprivation tank who claims to see a castle. Alternatively, imagine a person in an empty desert who sees the mirage of an oasis. Such persons could reason as follows:

7.   I am seeing something.

8.   I am not seeing an external object.

9.   Given that I am seeing something, either I am seeing an external object or I am seeing my own ideas.

---

10.   Therefore, I am seeing my own ideas.

By understanding what is wrong with this argument regarding hallucinations, we can find a problem with Berkeley's argument from illusion. The problem here is that premise 7 begs the question. The premise assumes that there must be some *thing* that a person sees when experiencing a hallucination. It is only on the basis of this assumption that we reach the conclusion that the thing being seen cannot be a material object and therefore must be some mental idea.

Obviously a person having a hallucination is seeing, and their experience has a content. But we should not assume that this implies that they must be seeing some *thing*. We cannot assume that the experiential content of a person's seeing is the object of their experience or a thing that they are seeing. To make that assumption is effectively to assume that ideas exist as mental entities.

The alternative to making this assumption would be to argue that a person who is having a hallucination is not seeing any thing. This alternative would admit that a person experiencing a hallucination is seeing and that their seeing has an experiential content, but it would deny that that content is an object of their experience. In other words, the alternative would be to reject the claim implicit in premise 7 that the content of experience is a mental object. We could argue that the experiential content of the seeing is simply a way of seeing, and we could treat experience adverbially rather than as an object.

To be more precise, to avoid begging the question, we should replace premise 7 with the following statement:

7*.   I am having a visual experience.

If we replace premise 7 in the original argument with the non-question-begging premise 7*, the argument becomes invalid, since the conclusion no longer follows logically from the new set of premises. Without some new independent argument for the claims that premise 7 is true and that statement 7* is false, the argument from hallucination begs the question.

A Criticism of the Argument from Illusion

This criticism of the argument from hallucination can be used in critically assessing the argument from illusion, since the two arguments are similar. Premise 2 of the original argument from illusion was as follows:

2. The colors I perceive can change without the occurrence of a change in the object itself.

This premise, like premise 7, begs the question. Premise 2 effectively assumes that the colors I perceive are mental objects or ideas. It assumes that what can change (without there being any alteration in the external object) is some *thing*, which I perceive. Against this second premise, we could argue that what can change (without any alteration in the external object) is not some *thing* but the way we perceive or the phenomenological content of our perceiving. For instance, the way in which I perceive a white wall will change when the color of the light changes. Against this second premise, we could also insist that what I perceive is the color of an external object and that this objective color cannot change without any alteration in the object itself. To be more precise, we could replace premise 2 with the following statement:

2*. The way I perceive color can change without the occurrence of a change in the object itself.

Once we replace premise 2 with statement 2*, the original argument is no longer valid. Without some new independent argument for the claim that premise 2 is true and statement 2* is false, the argument from illusion begs the question.

An Alternative View of Perception: Direct Realism

At most, the comments of the previous section show that Berkeley's argument from illusion does not establish the conclusion that we can only perceive our own ideas. Of course, this does not imply that the conclusion itself is false. Even if the argument from illusion is inconclusive, the conclusion (namely, that we only perceive our own ideas) could still be true.

Instead of arguing that the conclusion "We can only perceive our own ideas" is false, it would be better to show what an alternative view would be like. The alternative view, which we can call direct realism, holds that we can directly perceive external objects and that the objects of perception are not ideas in the mind. Developing direct realism is important, because the claim that we can only perceive our own ideas is a central pillar in the philosophies of Descartes, Locke, Berkeley, and Hume. Kant, on the other hand, is a direct realist.

Phrases like "I see something" and "what I see" are ambiguous. They could refer to the content of the seeing—the experiential nature of the visual experience itself. Alternatively, they could refer to the thing actually seen—an external object that exists independently of the act of seeing. According to the direct realist, we should sharply distinguish the content of seeing from the thing seen. The experiential content of my seeing is not an object over and above the act of seeing; it is merely the way or manner in which I see. The independent object of my seeing—the thing I actually see, such as a tree or chair—is something quite distinct from my act of seeing; it exists whether I look at it or not.

According to the direct realist, a person suffering from a hallucination does not see an external object. While our tendency is to say that such a person is seeing something, what we mean by this is only that the person is seeing in a particular manner, or that the person's visual experience has a content. The direct realist asserts that it is tempting, but misleading, to claim that there exists a mental thing that such a person perceives. It is misleading because it implies that there exists some *thing*—some actual mental object—that the person perceives.

The English language is not conducive to making a clear distinction between the content of seeing and that which is seen. For example, when we ask someone "What are you seeing?" we could be asking them to describe their experience, or we could be asking them to describe an external object they are seeing.

According to the direct realist, failing to distinguish the content of experience from the independent object experienced can cause enormous confusion. It can lead us to reify the experiential content of the experience and treat it as if it were the thing seen or experienced. Descartes, Locke, and Berkeley use the word *idea* to refer to the content of experiences, but they tend to treat this content as if it were a mental item or a picture in the mind. In other words, they treat this content as if it were the thing perceived. The direct realist claims that they have failed to recognize that ideas are *not* an object over and above the act of seeing itself. Ideas are not the objects of perception; they are the way or manner in which we see. For this reason, the direct realist will argue that Locke, Berkeley, and Descartes are mistaken when they claim that we perceive our own ideas. Ideas are not objects we see, because ideas are not objects at all. According to the direct realist, ideas are merely the act or experience of seeing in a particular way.

To make the point clear, we might compare ideas to moods.[59] The direct realist claims that moods are not mental items. Although in English we refer to moods as *what* we feel, the direct realist does not think of a mood as an object. A mood is nothing over and above feeling a certain way. The direct realist contends that rather than asking a person "*What* do you feel?" as if the person were feeling a thing, it would be more accurate to ask "*How* do you feel?" A direct realist might compare ideas with moods: just as moods are the way we feel, ideas are simply the way we perceive. According to the direct realist, we should not be misled by the English language into treating the content of perception as a thing. Ideas are not what we perceive; they are the way we perceive.

Of course, none of the above constitutes an argument for direct realism. Nor does it constitute an argument against the claim that we can only perceive our own ideas. It merely indicates how some philosophers have tried to develop a direct realist view.[60]

Primary and Secondary Qualities

In his attempt to defend the view that some sensible qualities are not ideas but are really properties of objects that exist independently of perception, Hylas distinguishes between primary and secondary qualities. In the *Three Dialogues,* Philonous, arguing on behalf of Berkeley, attacks the distinction.

First, Hylas tries to distinguish between, for example, sound as it is perceived by us and sound as it is in itself (which is a vibration in the air). Philonous says that such a distinction leads to absurdities. It leads to the conclusion that real sounds (which are motions) can be felt or seen but never heard, and to the conclusion that motions in the air can be sweet, loud, soft, and so on.

Second, Hylas makes the general distinction between primary and secondary qualities. To this, Philonous repeats the argument from illusion, or the argument from the relativity of perception. He points out that the argument applies to the so-called primary qualities as well as to the secondary ones. Shape, size, speed of motion, and solidity all vary according to the conditions of perception, without requiring any change in the object, and therefore cannot be properties of objects themselves. Instead, they are simply ideas in the mind.

Third, Berkeley argues against Locke's claim that primary qualities resemble our ideas of sense, contending that "an idea can be like nothing but another idea." What Berkeley has in mind is that we only compare two things if it is possible to perceive them both. Because ideas are all that we can ever perceive, it is impossible to compare an idea with a primary quality of an unperceivable object; it is possible only to compare two ideas. Berkeley claims that it does not make sense to talk of resemblance when there is no possibility of comparison, and he argues that there is no possibility of comparing an idea and a quality.

Berkeley points toward a tension between the resemblance thesis and Locke's representative theory of perception—that is, between the following claims:

a. Primary qualities resemble their ideas.

b. We can only perceive our own ideas.

Berkeley argues that these two propositions are inconsistent, given two further claims that are both true:

c. We do not perceive primary qualities.

d. In order to be able to assert that two things resemble each other, we must in principle be able to compare them.

Claim c follows directly from claim b. Given that claims b, c, and d are all true, claim a (the resemblance thesis) must be false.

Some points need to be made about Berkeley's discussion of Locke's distinction:

1. Berkeley often talks as if Locke's point is that primary qualities really inhere in objects but that secondary qualities are simply ideas in the mind. Berkeley attacks the distinction made in this way, arguing that primary qualities too are simply ideas in the mind. To some extent, however, Berkeley seems to

have misunderstood the nature of Locke's distinction. Locke does not claim that primary qualities are in the real world and that secondary qualities are ideas, because Locke separates our ideas of primary and secondary qualities from those qualities themselves. Locke's distinction is between primary and secondary qualities, and not between primary qualities and our ideas of secondary qualities.

2.   Even assuming that Locke does accept a representative theory of perception, at least one important part of the primary/secondary quality distinction can be formulated independently of that theory. Primary qualities are the intrinsic properties of all material things, but secondary qualities are powers that can be explained in primary-quality terms. Insofar as the primary/secondary quality distinction is independent of the representative theory of perception, Berkeley's arguments have no force against it.

3.   One possible way of challenging Locke's resemblance thesis is to claim that it involves a reification of the ideas of sense, because it stipulates that ideas, as well as material objects, can be round, square, and so on. This line of argument, however, is not open to Berkeley, who himself is prepared to admit that ideas can be round and who also tends to reify the ideas of sense.

Berkeley has another way of trying to undermine Locke's primary/secondary quality distinction. He says that the concept of the primary quality, extension, which exists independently of the mind, must be an abstract idea. As we have seen, Berkeley argues that there are no abstract ideas. Extension in objects must be an abstract idea because such extension is neither great nor small, since the terms *great* and *small* relate to the conditions of perception. This argument depends on the argument from illusion to show the relativity of perception; it also depends on Berkeley's attack on abstract ideas.

Sensible Objects

Houses, rivers, and mountains are all sensible objects. According to Berkeley, by definition, sensible objects are what we perceive. Given this definition, Berkeley sometimes argues as follows:

1.   No idea can exist unperceived.

2.   We can only ever perceive our own ideas.

3.   Sensible objects are what we perceive.

4.   Therefore, sensible objects are only collections of ideas and cannot exist unperceived.

We have already seen how Berkeley tries to defend premise 2 by arguing that we perceive nothing but sensible qualities and by giving a series of arguments to show that sensible qualities are nothing but ideas. In the first dialogue, Philonous tries to block a possible objection to premise 3. It might be objected to premise 3 that we should distinguish between mediate and immediate perception. Granted that we can only ever immediately perceive our own ideas, it could still be claimed that external objects are perceived mediately and, therefore, that external objects can be distinguished from our own ideas. To defend premise 3, Philonous rejects this distinction and argues that the senses can only perceive what they perceive immediately, because the senses cannot make any inferences. Through the mouthpiece of Philonous, Berkeley is trying to force Lockeans into a dilemma: either objects are immediately perceived, in which case they are ideas; or they are not perceived at all and are the unperceivable causes of our perceptions, which are supposed to be known by inference and reason.

Hylas accepts the first horn of this dilemma, and—finding it difficult to resist Philonous's arguments for the contention that sensible qualities are ideas—is drawn to the conclusion that objects cannot exist unperceived. Later in the second dialogue, Berkeley examines the second horn of the dilemma: that objects are the unperceivable causes of our ideas.

External Objects

Berkeley says that the supposition of external bodies is not necessary to explain the production of ideas. In Part 1, section 18 of the *Principles,* he says that we could never know of the existence of such bodies. Such knowledge would have to come either from the senses or from reason. But it could not come from the senses, because they only inform us of our ideas; therefore, it must come from the inferences of reason. But this is impossible, too, because we cannot infer that unperceivable objects are the cause of our ideas (since there is no necessary connection between such objects and our ideas). Berkeley concludes that it is possible for us to have ideas without their being caused by objects. Since it is impossible for us to know whether external bodies exist, it is not necessary to postulate such bodies as the cause of our ideas.

While it might be admitted that bodies are not strictly necessary to explain the production of ideas, one might still argue that postulating material objects is the best or most simple explanation available of how the ideas of perception are caused. In section 19 of the *Principles,* Berkeley answers this objection. He claims that the existence of material bodies cannot explain our ideas, because it is impossible to explain how material substances could ever have any causal effect on immaterial substances or spirits. This criticism of Locke's theory of perception echoes the criticisms of Descartes's dualism given in Chapter 3 and by Spinoza: how can two unlike substances causally interreact?

Berkeley concludes that, if there were external objects, we could never know this, and if there were no external objects, we would have exactly the same reasons for believing in them as we do now. To this he adds in the *Dialogues* that, if there is no reason for believing in something, then there is sufficient reason for not believing in that thing's existence.

Berkeley tries to establish that there are no external objects. As we shall see later, he adopts different strategies for doing this. Sometimes, he seeks to show that the supposition of external objects is meaningless. At other times, he argues that the notion of matter is contradictory.

Material Substance

Berkeley produces a strange argument to show the inconceivability of an object independent of the mind. He says that one cannot conceive of an object existing outside of a mind. Of course, it is possible to conceive of an object that is not being perceived by anyone, but to do that you must think or conceive of the object yourself. However, what you conceive of must be an idea existing in your mind, and therefore you cannot conceive of an object that exists outside of a mind.

The crucial step in this argument is the assertion that what is conceived must be an idea in the mind. This assertion is ambiguous; the phrase "what is conceived" could refer to the conceiving, or it could refer to what the conceiving is about. In effect, Berkeley is confusing an idea with its subject matter. Take the sentence "One cannot conceive of an object existing without the mind." This could mean either of two things:

1. Without the mind, it is impossible to conceive (of an object).

2. It is impossible to conceive that an object exists independently of the mind.

Establishing assertion 1 does not demonstrate the truth of assertion 2.

Berkeley also tries to show that the notion of material substance is contradictory. He says that material substance is an inert, senseless substratum in which extension, motion, and other qualities subsist. Berkeley then argues that extension, motion, and other sensible qualities are ideas that exist only in the mind, and he claims that an idea can only resemble another idea. Consequently, extension, motion, and anything like these ideas cannot exist in an inert senseless substance. Such a supposition is a contradiction in terms.

But if we do not agree that sensible qualities are ideas, argues Berkeley, the concept of matter is meaningless and hence unacceptable. The concept of matter has two parts: sensible properties and a substratum that supports them. This notion of a substratum that supports properties is incomprehensible. In the *Dialogues,* Philonous argues that, if substratum is supposed to support the mode extension, then substratum must in itself be extended, since the notion of a support presupposes extension. Consequently, every material substance that supports extension must itself have another type of extension if it is to be capable of this support. But this other type of extension must in turn be supported; and so on to infinity. Hence, argues Berkeley, the notion of an inert substratum leads to absurdities. Hylas tries to respond to this argument by claiming that the notion of a support should not be taken literally. However, he finally admits that a nonliteral notion is empty and meaningless.

This argument of Berkeley's appears to be misdirected. Even if it does show that Locke's notion of a substratum is confused, this fact does not amount to an argument against the notion of matter. The concepts of matter and substratum are distinct; we do not have to define a material object in terms of Locke's substratum, and it is not even clear that Locke would want to do that.

Conclusion

Berkeley, like Locke and Descartes, accepts the claim that we can only perceive our own ideas. Indeed, Berkeley explicitly offers the argument from illusion to support the claim. He uses the claim to criticize Locke's primary/secondary quality distinction and eventually to argue against the notion of material substance.

Berkeley attempts to show that on Locke's Empiricist principles, one of three conclusions must be reached:

a.   The idea of material substance involves a contradiction.

b.   Material substance is utterly unknowable.

c.   The idea of such a substance is really vacuous.

In other words, Berkeley tries to show that Locke is committed to a contradiction or to scepticism or to a vacuous thesis.

Many of Berkeley's arguments involve the claims that all sensible qualities are only ideas and that we can only perceive our own ideas. The general form of these arguments can be summarized as follows. Locke must assert one of the following alternatives:

i.   External objects have sensible qualities or something resembling them.

ii.   They do not.

If Locke chooses option i, Berkeley's strategy is to argue for alternative a, on the grounds that it is a contradiction to suppose that an idea could exist in anything but a mind and that the only thing that can resemble an idea is another idea.

On the other hand, if Locke chooses alternative ii, Berkeley's first strategy is to argue for option b, based on the premise that something unperceivable cannot be known. As a second strategy, he argues for option c, on the premise that something unperceivable and unknowable cannot be significantly talked about.

Study Questions

1. How and why does Berkeley argue against Locke's theory of abstract ideas?

2. What is the argument from illusion, and how does Berkeley use it in his criticisms of Locke?

3. Critically assess the argument from illusion.

4. What are Berkeley's arguments against the primary/secondary quality distinction?

5. Does Berkeley misinterpret Locke's primary/secondary quality distinction? If so, are these misinterpretations important to the argument?

6. How does Berkeley argue that all sensible objects are merely collections of ideas?

7. What is Berkeley's argument for the claim that the concept of material substance is self-contradictory?

Discussion Questions

1. Can we only ever perceive our own ideas?

2. Is Locke's Empiricism incompatible with the claim that we know that material objects exist?

CHAPTER 14

Berkeley: God and Minds

So far, Berkeley's philosophy has been presented as consisting largely of arguments directed at refuting the views of Locke. But Berkeley is also concerned to advance and defend his own positive theories, especially two of these: his contention that sensible objects are simply collections of ideas whose essence is to be perceived, and his belief in the existence of God.

Answers to Some Objections

In the *Treatise Concerning the Principles of Human Knowledge*, Part 1, sections 34 to 84, Berkeley raises and answers objections to his idealism.

It might be objected that Berkeley's idealism banishes real things from the world and implies that there is no distinction between real things and illusions. To this Berkeley replies that he only denies a philosophical conception of matter, not the existence of real things. Real things are simply ideas, which exist only in the mind. This does not imply that there is no distinction between reality and illusion, but only that both illusions and reality exist in the mind.

To explain the distinction between reality and illusions, Berkeley appeals to the differences between sense and imagination. He says that ideas of sense differ from ideas of imagination in at least three ways. First, ideas of sense are stronger and more lively; second, they are ordered and have a coherence; third, they do not depend on our will. Since ideas of sense, unlike those of imagination, do not depend on our will, they must have some other cause.

Berkeley admits that it sounds strange to say that we eat and drink ideas, but he dismisses this as unimportant and stresses his point that all we know are ideas and that these are real things.

If extension and shape exist only in the mind, does it not follow that the mind must be extended and shaped? Berkeley denies that this is an implication of his theory. He argues that if it were, it would be also reasonable to say that, because redness exists only in the mind, the mind must be red. Extension and shape exist in the mind only as ideas, not as attributes or characteristics of the mind itself.

Berkeley explains how it can be said that distant things outside us exist in the mind. He points out that we see things at a distance in dreams, and that it is agreed that such objects exist only in the mind. More positively, he says that it is necessary to explain how we perceive distance by sight, because the very sugges-tion of external space poses problems for the contention that things exist as ideas in the mind. To explain the perceiving of distance, Berkeley refers to his earlier work, the *Essay Towards a New Theory of Vision*. We do not directly perceive distance; instead the idea of distance is suggested to us by certain clues in our perceptual experience—for instance, by our ideas' being blurred, out of focus, shades of color, and so on. On the basis of such clues and by their connection, which we learn through experience, we can explain the apparent three-dimensionality of our visual experience, despite the fact that we perceive only our own ideas.

Common Sense

Rather than trying to defend himself against common sense, Berkeley claims that his views vindicate common sense. He takes philosophy—especially that of Locke—to violate common sense, because it is a consequence of Locke's empiri-cism and his ontology that real things exist hidden and unknown. For Berkeley, common sense tells us that real things, like chairs, are not unknowable but are directly experienced. According to Berkeley, philosophers like Locke first raise the dust and then complain that they cannot see. Although Locke has little patience with scepticism and stresses that doubts about the existence of external things have no basis, Berkeley argues that Locke's philosophy leads inevitably to scepticism.

Berkeley denies scepticism by taking it to its limits and then turning the tables against it. First, rather than doubting the existence of unknowable material substance, he argues that matter is impossible. Secondly, instead of saying that real things are distinct from our ideas, Berkeley identifies the real with our ideas. With these bold steps, he claims to make scepticism impossible and to defend common sense.

However, Berkeley's defense of common sense is Janus-faced. He says that we should think with the learned and speak with the vulgar. Sometimes Berkeley is prepared to admit that his views run contrary to "the prejudice of mankind." In Part 1, section 4 of the *Principles,* he says that it is an opinion strangely prevalent among men that houses and the like have an existence distinct from their being perceived, and then he argues that this opinion is contradictory.

In fact, Berkeley's idealism is less in accordance with common sense than he ever admits. It is a consequence of his views that different people must always perceive numerically distinct things. Berkeley tries to escape this implication by saying that different people can have the same ideas. However, this reply confuses numerical and qualitative identity, since different people may have ideas that are qualitatively the same, but they cannot have numerically identical ideas.

Unperceived Objects

Given that sensible objects are only ideas, and that the essence of an idea is to be perceived, surely objects cease to exist when I do not perceive them. If the chair I now perceive consists simply of my ideas, how can it continue to exist when I close my eyes?

Berkeley seems to give three different answers to this question. First, he suggests that the chair does exist even when it is unperceived by me, because I would have certain ideas under certain conditions. For instance, the table in the other room can be said to exist, although I do not perceive it now, because I would perceive it or would have certain ideas, if I were to go into the next room (*Principles*, Part 1, section 3). At *Principles*, Part 1, section 58, Berkeley comments that we can say that the earth moves, despite the fact that we do not perceive this movement, because if we were correctly placed we would perceive the earth moving. In these passages, Berkeley adopts phenomenalism—the view that objects are logical constructions out of possible sense data, or that statements about objects are equivalent to counterfactual or hypothetical statements about sense experience. However, phenomenalism is incompatible with Berkeley's usual and considered position. Berkeley's usual position is that the essence of objects consists in their *actually* being perceived. The phenomenalist, on the other hand, holds that the essence of objects consists in their being perceivable rather than actually being perceived.

Berkeley also gives a second answer to the question of how an object can exist unperceived by me. He says that such an object can be said to exist because it is perceived by other minds, including that of God. In the third dialogue, Berkeley claims that the difference between him and the materialists is not whether things have a real existence independent of any particular mind, but whether they have an absolute existence independent of all minds, including that of God. According to this reply, sensible objects can exist independent of any single finite mind, but they must exist in some mind or other, since they are ideas. Berkeley claims that sensible objects that are not perceived by any person or finite mind, must be perceived by God. God eternally knows all objects, and therefore all things may be said to exist in His mind, even when no human mind perceives them. In the *Dialogues*, Berkeley uses this point to try to establish the existence of God, as we shall see later.

Finally, Berkeley seems to give a third and slightly different reply to the problem of unperceived objects, combining elements from the previous two. According to this version, our ideas of perception are caused or put into our minds directly by God. Unobserved objects exist in the sense that it is God's intention or will that, in the right circumstances, an observer would have certain ideas. Unperceived sensible objects continue to exist in the sense that God is ready to put certain ideas in our minds if we are in the right circumstances. This third answer appeals to the will of God—that is, to His willingness to put certain ideas in our minds under the right conditions. In this way, it differs from the first reply, which does not mention God. The third answer also differs from the second. The second appeals to God's perceptions, or to God as a cosmic observer of all things at all times. The third appeals to God's will.

In summary, Berkeley is aware of the potential objection to his theory—namely, that it implies that the object I am now perceiving cannot exist if I am not perceiving it. In the *Dialogues,* he gives three replies to this objection. However, it is not clear which of the three replies he thinks best, nor even that he distinguishes them. For example, he is not aware of phenomenalism as an alternative to his own idealism, nor as an alternative that attempts to overcome the problems inherent in the representationalist theory of perception presented by Locke.

A Causal Argument for God

Berkeley gives two arguments for the existence of God. The first, given at *Principles* section 29, is based on the assumption that our ideas of sense must have a cause. Effectively, Berkeley argues that the only possible cause of our ideas of sense is God. He does this in two steps: first, he tries to show that the ideas of sense must be caused by another mind, by ruling out alternative explanations; and second, he tries to show that, given the nature of the ideas of sense, the other mind in question must be God.

1. First Step

a. Our ideas of sense must have a cause.

b. Ideas of sense, unlike those of imagination, do not depend on our own will, so they must have some other cause.

c. Ideas of sense are not caused by material objects, since matter does not exist.

d. Ideas of sense cannot be caused by other ideas; since ideas are inactive and have no power or agency, they cannot be the cause of anything.

e.   Therefore, our ideas of sense must be caused by some other mind, since this is the only other possible explanation.

2. Second Step

To establish that the mind in question is indeed God, Berkeley appeals to the nature of the ideas of sense. First, the ideas of sense are always internally consistent, and this shows that they are the product of only one mind. At the same time, they are incredibly complex and varied, and this demonstrates the unimaginable power of the mind in question. Third, notwithstanding their complexity and variety, the ideas of sense are regular and ordered in such detail that we can rely on this regularity even in minute scientific investigations. This degree of regularity and order demonstrates the benevolence of the mind that produced these ideas. In conclusion, the mind that causes the ideas of sense must be unique, unimaginably powerful, and benevolent.

Berkeley posits God as the cause of our ideas in much the same way as Locke posits material objects. Why should Berkeley consider his hypothesis better than Locke's? To this question, Berkeley gives three replies:

1.   He points out that, according to Locke, God creates matter and matter causes ideas in us. Berkeley claims that this implies that God had to create matter in order to put ideas in our minds. Berkeley claims that his own explanation of our ideas is simpler than Locke's: God directly creates ideas in our minds, without the need for matter.

2.   Berkeley claims that the idea of matter is a contradiction and is utterly incomprehensible. On the other hand, God is a mind and the concept of a mind is neither incoherent or obscure, since each of us is himself a mind.

3.   Berkeley contends that it is impossible to explain how matter could ever influence unextended nonmaterial minds. Spinoza gives a similar criticism of Descartes's dualism, arguing that two unlike substances cannot causally interact. Berkeley's own view escapes this problem by having a mind—namely, God—directly cause our ideas.

By arguing that God is the direct cause of our sensible ideas, Berkeley attempts to make God the center of our lives and to destroy the atheism that he thinks is inherent in Locke's philosophy. Locke actually argues that God exists, but His existence plays no central role in Locke's philosophy.

According to Berkeley, the relation between God and the world is more intimate than it is for Descartes and even Leibniz. For Descartes, the world is a physical mechanical system, inhabited by nonmaterial souls, which God started. For Leibniz, the existence of God is required to preestablish the harmony between the perceptions of the infinity of monads. For both philosophers, the existence of God is needed to set the system in motion. On the other hand, for Berkeley, in a way, the world we see actually consists of God's ideas.[61]

Another Argument for God: Continuity

Berkeley has a second argument for the existence of God, which Bennett calls "the continuity argument."[62] The argument runs as follows:

1. All ideas must be perceived.

2. Sensible objects are collections of ideas.

3. Objects continue to exist even when they are not perceived by any finite minds.

---

4. Therefore, there is a nonfinite spirit or mind which perceives objects.

Several points can be made about this argument. First, the argument depends on the truth of premise 2, or Berkeley's idealism. Second, the argument depends on the claim that objects continue to exist even when unperceived by finite minds (premise 3). Let us call this assumption the continuity claim. Given Berkeley's idealism, what possible evidence could there be for the continuity claim? It seems there can be none. It is tempting to think that Berkeley might appeal to common sense to defend the continuity claim. There is, however, a danger of circularity in such an appeal. As we saw earlier, to defend his idealism against the charge that it is contrary to common sense and the continuity claim, Berkeley appeals to the existence of God: he says objects can exist unperceived by us because God perceives them all the time. It appears circular for Berkeley to appeal to the existence of God to save common sense and continuity, and then to appeal to common sense and continuity to establish the existence of God.

The question of whether Berkeley is entitled to the continuity claim invites a brief comparison with Hume. Starting with a view of perception and other ideas similar to Berkeley's and Locke's, Hume argues that there is no rational justification for our belief in the continued existence of objects. This is one reason why it is often claimed that Hume reveals the full force of the sceptical implications inherent in the Empiricist view of perception and knowledge.

A Nonstandard Interpretation

Contrary to the standard interpretation of Berkeley, Bennett contends that Berkeley never has any serious use for the continuity argument. According to Bennett, Berkeley is not concerned to defend the ordinary person's view that objects exist unperceived, even by invoking the existence of God.[63] Bennett says that, for Berkeley, we are not entitled to our ordinary conviction about the continuity of objects existing unperceived. Bennett's view is based on a detailed argument about how certain passages in Berkeley should be read, which need not concern us here.

However, it is worth noting one point in favor of his interpretation and one against it. In favor of the Bennett view is that, when Berkeley talks about the Creation of the Universe in the third dialogue, he does so by appealing to phenomenalism rather than by appealing to God's perceptions. However, against Bennett's interpretation is the fact that Berkeley seems to state the continuity argument more than once—for example, toward the beginning of the second and third dialogues (see II.16 and III.13).

The Spirit or Mind

According to Berkeley, the only substances are spirits or minds. A spirit is a simple undivided active being. Insofar as a mind perceives ideas, it has understanding; insofar as it produces ideas, it is a will. Berkeley's conception of spirit or mind is similar to Descartes's notion of mental substance, except that Berkeley stresses the active nature of the mind.

Berkeley's claim that mind is the only kind of substance in the universe resembles Leibniz's. Both Leibniz and Berkeley reject Descartes's substance dualism. They both argue for the conclusion that matter is not real, although their arguments for this conclusion are very different. Leibniz's arguments are based upon the definition of substance, which implies that all substances must be simple and on the fact that matter is infinitely divisible. Berkeley's arguments are ultimately based on the claim that we can only perceive our own ideas and on an Empiricist view of knowledge. Despite these differences, Berkeley and Leibniz accept the claim that minds are the only substances in the universe.

Berkeley claims that we can have no idea of spirit or mind, yet he also says that the term *spirit* is intelligible. It is impossible for us to have an idea of spirits or minds, because all ideas are passive and inert, and spirits or minds are essentially active. But according to Berkeley, although it is impossible to have an idea of a spirit or mind, we still know what the word *spirit* means, because each of us is a spirit and is directly aware of his own being. Berkeley says that, although we have no idea of spirit, we do have the notion of a spirit. Unfortunately, this distinction between ideas and notions does not help us much in trying to understand Berkeley's position, since to have a notion of a spirit is simply to know what the term means.

Berkeley's claim that we do not have an idea of mind seems to make the existence of minds as problematic as the existence of matter. This unclarity divides into three questions:

1. If Berkeley denies the existence of matter, logically should he not also reject the existence of minds? He answers this question negatively for the following reason. He claims that the concept of matter is contradictory and that there

can be no reasons for positing material objects. On the other hand, the notion of a mind is not contradictory.

2.   Given that we can have no idea of the mind, do we have any reason for supposing that the mind exists? In reply to this, Berkeley argues that there is a reason for me to suppose that I am a mind or spirit. He asserts that there must be something that has ideas or perceives them. Ideas cannot be perceived by other ideas and they cannot exist on their own; therefore, there must be a mind that perceives these ideas. If there is perceiving, then there must be a mind doing the perceiving.

3.   Given that we have no idea of the mind, how do we acquire a notion of the mind at all? In reply to this question, Berkeley says "I have a notion of spirit, though I have not, strictly speaking, an idea of it. I do not perceive it as an idea, nor by means of an idea, but know it by reflection" (p233). In the third dialogue, he says "My own mind and own ideas, I have immediate knowledge of" (III.17).

In Chapter 1 we saw that Descartes's Cogito argument, "I think, therefore I am," appealed to similar claims. It assumed that, if there are ideas, there must a substance that has those ideas. As we shall see in Chapter 17, Hume argues that we are not rationally justified in making this assumption. Furthermore, he claims that we not aware of the mind as a substance. Like Berkeley, he contends that there is no idea or sense impression of the self. Unlike Berkeley, Hume does not assume that there is a self or a mind. Hume asserts that the idea of the mind cannot be derived from experience by applying Empiricist principles. This is another reason why it is often claimed that Hume reveals the full force of the sceptical implications inherent in the Empiricist view of perception and knowledge.

Other Minds

At most, Berkeley's contention that if there are ideas then there must be a mind to perceive those ideas demonstrates that, individually, I can logically infer the existence of my own mind. But by what reasoning, according to Berkeley's system, should we suppose that other minds exist? It appears that Berkeley cannot provide any satisfactory answer to this question. I can only perceive my own ideas; therefore, someone else's body (as I perceive it) is simply a collection of ideas existing in my mind. Furthermore, these ideas in my mind are put there directly by God. Therefore, there is no good reason for me to think that the movement of your arm is caused by your will. There is no good reason for me to think that any changes in the sensible things I perceive are evidence for the existence of other human minds.

Berkeley appears not to appreciate the force of this problem, because he says that we see signs and effects which indicate the existence of other finite spirits. But how can my own ideas be signs for the existence of other finite minds, especially considering that God directly causes me to have these ideas? Berkeley's system, which is designed to avoid scepticism by doing away with material substance, itself seems to lead to scepticism at least with regard to other minds.

Conclusion

The first sentence of Berkeley's *Principles of Human Knowledge* says in part: "It is evident to anyone who takes a survey of the objects of human knowledge that they are either ideas actually imprinted on the senses or . . . such as are perceived by attending to the operations of the mind." Although Berkeley rejects Locke's notion of abstract ideas, he still accepts many of the basic principles of Empiricism inherent in Locke. In particular, he accepts the claim that we can only perceive our own ideas, which Locke inherits from Descartes.

Berkeley explicitly offers the argument from illusion for that claim, and he uses it to criticize Locke's primary/secondary quality distinction and eventually to argue against the notion of material substance. Berkeley attempts to show that, by Locke's Empiricist principles, material objects are either utterly unknowable or require the contradictory notion of material substance. In other words, Locke must be committed either to a contradiction or to scepticism.

Berkeley uses this result to advance his own idealism and theism and to argue that ideas are caused directly by God. In so doing, he implictly endorses the Empiricist principles accepted by Locke.

Now, the question arises of whether Berkeley is entitled to idealism and theism insofar as he accepts Empiricist principles. In other words, if Empiricist principles lead to scepticism about material objects, why do they do not also lead to scepticism about the mind and God? Let us look at two examples:

1. *Cause:* One of the reasons Locke gives in favor of the existence of external objects is that our ideas must have a cause. The principle that everything must have a cause is a tenet of Rationalism, and it is not clear how it can be known, given an Empiricist view of knowledge. Neither is it clear whether the idea of cause can be derived from experience. Berkeley, however, also relies on this principle in his first proof of God's existence.

2. *The Mind:* Like Descartes, Locke assumes the thesis that, if there are ideas, then there must be substance that has those ideas. (Unlike Descartes, Locke does not argue that this substance or the mind must be nonmaterial; on this issue, Locke professes agnosticism.) It is not clear whether the claim "If there ideas, then there must be a mind that perceives those ideas" can be known, given an Empiricist view of knowledge. Neither is it clear that the idea of the mind can be derived from experience. However, Berkeley relies on this claim to establish his idealism (that the only kinds of substances are mental).

Essentially the same points can be put in a different way. To argue for idealism and theism, Berkeley has to assume that we have a priori knowledge of certain

Rationalistic principles, like "Ideas must have causes" and "If there is an idea, then there must be a mind to perceive that idea." He also has to assume that we are justified in using the notions of "mind," "cause," and "God." Furthermore, he has to make these assumptions while simultaneously maintaining that we can only perceive our own ideas. These assumptions are challenged by Hume.

Study Questions

1. How does Berkeley respond to the claim that his idealism is contrary to common sense?

2. How does Berkeley defend the assertion that objects can exist even when unperceived?

3. What are Berkeley's two arguments for the existence of God?

4. Is Berkeley's attempt to explain sensible ideas causally in terms of the existence of God any different from Locke's attempt to do so in terms of the existence of matter?

5. Why does Berkeley say that we have no idea of the mind?

6. What problems does Berkeley have in establishing knowledge of the existence of other minds?

Discussion Questions

1. Compare the role of God in the philosophies of Descartes, Spinoza, Leibniz, and Berkeley.

2. Compare Leibniz's arguments for idealism with Berkeley's.

David Hume (1711–1776)

David Hume was born in Edinburgh in 1711, into a family with a strong legal tradition. He was probably educated at home by private tutors and was a keen reader from childhood on. His studies at Edinburgh University included languages, mathematics, philosophy, and the new Newtonian physics. It had been assumed that he would pursue a legal career, but Hume discovered within himself "an insurmountable aversion to everything but the pursuits of philosophy and general learning." He did not take a degree, and by the time he left Edinburgh he had lost the religious convictions of his Calvinist upbringing and begun to reflect more on classical pagan writers than on Christian sources.

In 1729 Hume became so involved in his philosophical explorations that he eventually made himself ill. By the age of twenty-three, he was seriously depressed. For a brief period he attempted to abandon philosophy and go into business with a Bristol merchant. Apparently he quickly tired of this, and in 1734 his passion for literature is said to have prompted him to go to France for three years' study. In Rheims, he spent some time learning French, and writing. He might have wished to live amidst the intellectual stimulation of Paris, but accommodations at Yvandeau, La Flèche (Descartes's old college), were apparently more suited to Hume's modest means. While there, he used the Jesuits' library and argued with the monks about miracles. At La Flèche, he completed the *Treatise on Human Nature*.

Back in England he edited the *Treatise*, removing some antitheological passages before publishing Books I and II anonymously in January 1739. It is thought the cutting of the text was a precaution taken to avoid offending Joseph Butler, whom Hume held in high esteem. Book III appeared in in 1740, as did the *Abstract*, which was an anonymous pamphlet summarizing the main arguments of the first parts of the *Treatise*. Hume was deeply disappointed by the reviewers' reactions to his work, claiming bitterly that it "fell dead-born from the press."

The two volumes of *Essays Moral and Political,* published in 1741–1742, were written in a more popular style, and their comparative success encouraged Hume to continue presenting his philosophical ideas to the public. In 1745 he discovered that his *Treatise* had in fact been noticed more than he had realized, but again the response was not favorable: he was refused the chair of Ethics and Philosophy at Edinburgh on the grounds of his religious heterodoxy. In need of income, Hume became tutor to the Marquess of Annandale and lived in London and at Weldehall near St. Albans. Only one year later, he was no doubt pleased to leave his reputedly mad pupil and accept the post of secretary to Lieutenant-General St. Clair. The general was due to émbark on a military expedition against the French in Canada, but eventually the expeditionary force was ordered to raid the coast of Brittany instead. This proved to be an unsuccessful mission, but Hume came out of it well and was soon invited to join St. Clair again on missions to Ireland, Vienna, and Turin.

Perhaps his newfound financial independence facilitated Hume's return to his studies. In 1748 he published the work later called *An Enquiry Concerning Human Understanding*. Three years later the *Enquiry Concerning the Principles of Morals* was also published. These works contained new, more popular renderings of the ideas from the *Treatise* and were better received, although still not warmly enough to satisfy Hume. He had more success in 1752 with the *Political Discourses,* but in the same year he was again refused a professorship—this time the chair of Logic at Glasgow. Between 1754 and 1762, Hume wrote *The History of England,* which proved much more popular than his philosophical works.

By 1750 the marriage of his brother had prompted Hume to leave the family home near Berwick, where he had mainly based himself during the previous years. He took up residence with his sister Katherine in Edinburgh and became Keeper of the Library of the Faculty of Advocates there for five years. In 1757 he resigned from this post after being found guilty of ordering "indecent Books and unworthy of a place in a learned library."

In *My Own Life,* Hume described himself as "a man of mild dispositions, of command of temper, of an open, social and cheerful humour." The assessment seems to have been an accurate one: he had many loyal friends in Scotland, some of whom came to his defense when the General Assembly of the Church of Scotland threatened to excommunicate him. In 1763 he went to France for three years as personal assistant to Lord Hertford, and here he is said to have been a much sought-after and favorite guest of the salons. Although he was corpulent and clumsy, his charm and wit endeared him to others, especially the ladies. He "took a particular pleasure in the company of modest women," but never married. Amongst his friends in France were Diderot and D'Alembert. Less happily he also befriended Jean-Jacques Rousseau and brought him to England, only to be accused by Rousseau of conspiring to defame him. Another of Hume's famous friends was Adam Smith, best known to us today as an economist.

Hume served as Undersecretary of State, Northern Department, from 1767 to 1769, "a Philosopher, degenerated into a petty Statesman." Back in Edinburgh, where he was to spend his last years, he again lived with his sister Katherine and advised his nephew David on his education. He worked during this period on the *Dialogues* and also on corrections for new editions of the *History*. Towards the end of his life, his philosophical ideas were attacked by James Beattie and Thomas Reid. Hume was evidently humiliated by the popularity of these attacks; he went so far as to disown the *Treatise* publicly as a "juvenile work." He seemed to be dogged by misunderstanding and preferred to avoid controversy when he could.

In 1775 Hume became ill with cancer of the bowel. Although he did not believe in life after death, he was apparently calm in the face of his decline. He asked Adam Smith to arrange the posthumous publication of the *Dialogues Concerning Natural Religion*. Hume died on August 25, 1776, and the *Dialogues* were eventually published by his nephew in 1779.

CHAPTER 15

Hume: Ideas and Impressions

Hume's philosophy has been interpreted in three major ways. First, he has been regarded as an epistemological sceptic. According to this view, Hume accepts the Empiricist principles inherent in Locke and Berkeley and follows them to their logical conclusion—scepticism. According to this interpretation, Berkeley shows that the notion of material substance is incompatible with Empiricist views about the nature of knowledge, which imply that external objects cannot be known; and Hume shows that the sceptical implications of Empiricism extend also to causality and to the mind. Thus Hume supposedly shows that Locke's line of thought leads inevitably to scepticism (a consequence Locke failed to see).

Second, Hume is represented as a naturalist who shows how certain beliefs arise naturally and inevitably in response to regular features of our experience. Our belief in the existence of external bodies, minds, and causality is prompted by the nonrational aspect of our nature. According to this second interpretation, Hume's aim is to explain the origin of such beliefs and ideas in naturalistic terms. According to this interpretation of Hume, his aim is to supply a psychological explanation rather than only a philosophical analysis. Hume's intention is to provide a science of man—a psychological study of human nature based on observation and what he calls "the experimental method of reasoning," by which conclusions are supported by experience.

One of Hume's main objectives as a naturalistic philosopher is to renounce and replace Rationalism. According to the Rationalists, we must attempt to gain knowledge of the self and of the world through a priori reasoning, and all such knowledge must be supported by reason. Hume, on the other hand, claims that all investigation must be experimental—that is, based on observation and introspection. This difference of procedure is based on a different view of human nature itself. Traditionally, a person is defined as a rational animal, a definition that supports Rationalism. Hume challenges this traditional view of human nature by emphasizing our feelings and passions. For example, he claims that "Reason is and ought only to be the slave of the passions."[64] He says that our human nature determines what kinds of judgments we make, as well as how we breathe and feel. He claims that "belief is more properly an act of the sensitive rather than the cognitive part of our natures."[65] In other words, believing is more like having a feeling than we might suppose.

Hume justifies this emphasis on the nonrational or feeling side of our nature by arguing for scepticism. He claims that certain beliefs and ideas cannot be justified either by appeal to reason alone (as the Rationalists would have us think) or by appeals to experience (as in Locke's approach of reasoning from sense experience). For example, Hume argues that none of our beliefs about the future can be justified by appeal either to reason or to sense experience. Hume's negative arguments for such sceptical conclusions have a positive purpose. They show that reason and sense experience are not the foundation of our beliefs, and this clears the ground for Hume's own positive naturalistic explanation of their origin. Such beliefs cannot be philosophically justified, but they can be psychologically explained. Hume's scepticism and his naturalism constitute two aspects of his attack on Rationalism: his scepticism undermines Rationalism, and his naturalism replaces it.

According to a third interpretation of Hume's thought, Hume is primarily interested in conceptual and linguistic analysis, rather than the study of human nature. In other words, Hume's main aim is to provide philosophical analyses of concepts such as "cause," "personal identity," and "external bodies," rather than to give a natural explanation of our beliefs. For instance, Hume draws a distinction between matters of fact and relations of ideas, which we shall examine in the next chapter. Hume's distinction here can be seen as a forerunner to the contemporary distinction between synthetic statements, which are known a posteriori, and analytic statements, which contain no substantive information and are known a priori.

Although Hume's philosophy has significantly influenced twentieth-century linguistic philosophy, we must be careful not to distort his aims as he himself states them in section I of the *Enquiry Concerning Human Understanding*. As his emphasis on replacing a priori reasoning with the experimental method makes clear, Hume is interested in both psychology and philosophy. He gives a naturalistic and nonrationalistic account of the origins of our beliefs after he has argued philosophically that these beliefs cannot be justified by appeal either to reason or to sense experience. This means, however, that we should not attribute to Hume the ultimate purpose of revealing the logical relationships between certain concepts.[66]

Hume sees himself as primarily trying to explain the principles of human nature. He takes human nature to be the center of the other sciences, since people ultimately judge what is true or false even in physics.

Ideas and Impressions

Locke refers to the objects of the mind as ideas. In section II of the *Enquiry,* Hume calls such objects "perceptions." Hume divides perceptions into two kinds: impressions and ideas. The difference between impressions and ideas consists in the force and liveliness with which they strike the mind; impressions are lively and vivid, while ideas are the faint images or copies of these that we have in thinking and reasoning. All sensations, passions, and emotions are impressions; but to think of something is to form an idea of it.

According to Hume, the distinction between perceiving and thinking is the distinction between having an impression and having an idea, which is a difference of force and liveliness. It is therefore a difference not of kind, but of degree.

Hume characterizes the difference between sensation and thought in this manner partly because he believes that this is the most obvious way to do it. The faintness or force of various perceptions is a matter of immediate experience that can be introspected by anyone. And being based directly on the introspection of experience, this way of drawing the distinction requires few assumptions. In particular, it does not presuppose that impressions are caused by external objects.

In the *Treatise,* Hume illustrates the relation between impressions and ideas in the following way: "when I shut my eyes and think of my chamber, the ideas I form are exact representations of the impressions I felt."[67] In other words, to think is to have an idea, and ideas are faint copies of impressions. Hume says that ideas and impressions always appear to correspond; all ideas are copies of impressions. However, as he points out, this description is not accurate, since I can imagine a golden mountain or a monster even though I have never had an impression of one. Clearly, these ideas are not direct copies of impressions. In order to account for these cases, Hume distinguishes between simple and complex perceptions.

Simple and Complex Perceptions

Both impressions and ideas may be simple or complex. Hume says that simple perceptions cannot be divided or separated into further parts and that complex perceptions can be divided into their simple constituents. For instance, the impression of an apple may be divided into separate tastes, colors, and smells that are united together in the apple. The impression of the apple itself is complex.

Given the distinction between simple and complex perceptions, Hume's views about the correlation between impressions and ideas can be stated. There is a universal correspondence between simple impressions and simple ideas: every simple idea has a simple impression, which resembles it, and every simple impression has a simple idea. Hume tries to establish this by introspecting his own mind, by asking his readers to do the same, and by challenging them to produce a simple idea that does not have a corresponding impression.

Hume claims that this universal correspondence between simple impressions and simple ideas cannot merely be due to chance; there must be some connection between them. He notes that simple impressions always come before their corresponding simple ideas. For instance, a blind person cannot have an impression of any color and therefore cannot have any ideas of colors. Similarly, one cannot form an idea of the taste of pineapple without having first actually tasted it. He concludes that simple impressions cause their corresponding simple ideas: all simple ideas are derived from and represent simple impressions.

This result is most important for Hume's Empiricism. According to Hume, to understand the human mind and its limitations, it is necessary to discover the origins of our ways of thinking, and the preceding conclusion is the first step in this direction. Everything in the mind is a perception, and all perceptions are either impressions or ideas and are either simple or complex. Furthermore:

1. All complex perceptions are made up of simple perceptions.

2. All simple ideas are derived from simple impressions.

From this it follows that all perceptions and ideas result from simple impressions.

Simple impressions are the impressions either of sense or of reflection. Impressions of reflection, which include desire, hope, and fear, arise from reflection on previous experience. Impressions of reflection are due to some things' having appeared before the mind. Hume concludes that there could be no impressions of reflection without impressions of sense. It follows then that all perceptions are a result of our first having simple impressions of sensation.

Hume's theory of ideas and impressions provides an important basis for some of his later arguments involving causation, external objects, and the mind. For example, he says, we have no idea of empty space or time without change, because we have no impressions from which these ideas may be derived. Similarly, he claims, we have no impressions of causal power and necessity, and hence no such simple ideas. Therefore, the ideas of causal power and necessity are not derived from sense experience, and our beliefs involving such ideas cannot be justified by appeal to experience.

At the end of section II of the *Enquiry*, having just established the principle that all ideas are derived from impressions, Hume mentions its application to meaning, in terms reminiscent of Locke and Berkeley. He complains about the "jargon" of metaphysical philosophers and says "when we entertain any suspicion that a philosophical term is employed without any meaning or idea, we need to inquire from what impression is that supposed idea derived?" Hume, who discusses meaning and words less frequently than Locke does, appears to assume a view very similar to Locke's—namely, that all meaningful words must stand for ideas.

Hume's theory of ideas and impressions is similar to Locke's. It is more precise, but it inherits similar philosophical assumptions. Hume's theory of impressions is influenced by Newtonian science: simple impressions are supposed to be the atoms of experience. But it is not clear that experience is atomistic, nor what those postulated atoms are. Like Locke before him, Hume does not explain clearly what he means by simplicity. For example, Hume implies that the impressions of color, taste, and so on are all simple. However, a color—say, red—has a particular hue and intensity, and this suggests that it is complex. Even a color patch of uniform hue and intensity can be divided into smaller color patches. Hume does not address these difficulties: his distinction between simple and complex perceptions is inherited from Locke.

Hume's notion of idea, like Locke's before him, seems to blur the difference between concepts and judgments on the one hand, and images on the other. His claim that ideas are faint copies of impressions makes the distinction between concepts and impressions one of degree rather than kind. Kant rejects this. In the *Critique of Pure Reason,* Kant says of sensation and understanding: "these two great powers or capacities cannot exchange their functions. The understanding can intuit nothing, the senses can think nothing" (B75). In other words, he regards the differences between concepts and sense impressions as one of kind, and not merely of degree. This enables Kant to forge a view of human experience and reason very different from Empiricism and Rationalism.

Association

In section 3 of the *Enquiry,* Hume claims that ideas and impressions do not occur haphazardly or at random. They are bound together and united by association, which Hume compares with the force of gravitational attraction. The principle of association works through three types of relations between our perceptions: resemblances; contiguity in time and place; and cause and effect (*Treatise* I.I.IV).

Because of these three relations, the mind passes naturally from one idea to another. For Hume, association provides a gentle force that connects our ideas as a result of experience and helps explain the workings of the mind. For instance, Hume stresses the inevitability of certain beliefs and contends that this inevitability is the result of association.

In theory, Hume's principle of association should explain how all our beliefs, feelings, and ideas are formed; for example, it explains how one thing reminds us of another. As we shall see later, Hume uses the principle of association to try to explain our beliefs in external objects and in the self. For example, he attempts to explain how we come to treat a set of discrete impressions as a continuous experience by using the principle of association. In practice, however, Hume does not always rely on association alone to explain the formation of ideas. Hume conceives of association mechanistically, as the Newtonian analogy shows, but not all mental activities can easily be portrayed in these terms. For example, in the case of imagination, Hume recognizes the difficulty of depicting the free activity of imagining as a simple result of the principle of association. He states that, in the case of the ideas of imagination, the direction of our thoughts is not completely fixed by association.

Belief

Like Descartes and Locke before him, Hume tries to distinguish between entertaining a thought and actually assenting to or believing it. He says that believing does not merely consist in joining two ideas together. In part II, section V of the *Enquiry,* Hume says that we can join the idea of a man's head with that of the body of a horse, without believing that such an animal actually exists.

What, then, is the difference between believing and imagining? According to Hume, the difference is purely psychological; the difference between believing and imagining consists solely "in their feeling to the mind." He says that a belief is "a lively idea related to or associated with a present impression." Belief is distinguished by the fact that its ideas are more vivid, lively, forcible, firm, and steady. In other words, beliefs are ideas that are more like impressions (*Treatise* I.III.VII).

As well as being purely psychological, Hume's view of belief stresses the feeling aspect of believing. He says that belief "is more properly an act of the sensitive than the cogitative part of our natures" (*Treatise* I.IV.I). Again, Hume tries to draw our attention away from the rational side of our nature, which is less important than we might suppose. In addition, Hume often discusses the naturalness of belief and stresses its involuntariness. We cannot help but believe what we do. As we shall see in the next chapter, Hume thinks that many of our beliefs are based on custom or habit and that they cannot be rationally justified. They cannot be justified; but at the same time, he thinks, they cannot be avoided.

Some Problems

According to Kant, many of the mental activities that Hume, Locke, Descartes, and others tend to characterize as ideas in the mind are more accurately described as practical capacities. To have the concept of a dog is to be capable of making certain classifications or judgments. According to Kant, in order to have the concept of a dog it is not necessary or sufficient to have before one's mind a mental image, picture, or idea of a dog. In the *Critique of Pure Reason,* he says at B180: "no image could ever be adequate to the concept of a triangle in general." He regards concepts as rule-governed abilities, rather than as images or copies of impressions. To have the concept of a dog is, among other things, to be able to make and recognize images of dogs. Kant says "the concept 'dog' signifies a rule according to which my imagination can delineate the figure" of a dog (B180).

The difference between Kant's view and Hume's view of concepts and judgments may be illustrated with another example. At *Treatise* I.I.III, Hume tries to characterize the difference between imagining and remembering. He thinks that there is an immediately perceptible difference between the ideas of memory and those of imagination; the former are more vivid and lively than the latter. Now, even if all memory ideas are more vivid than those of imagination, this fact alone does not delineate the difference between remembering and imagining. But in any case, some acts of remembering seem not to involve having ideas at all. For example, I can remember that $2 + 2 = 4$ without bringing any ideas to mind. This point is important because Hume tends to explain all mental activities in terms of having perceptions, and he thinks of perceptions as impressions or the faint copies of impressions (that is, ideas).

A more Kantian approach to distinguishing between imagination and memory would be to describe what capacities are involved in being able to remember something and in being able to imagine something, rather than trying to specify some perceptible difference, or some difference of feeling, between a memory idea and an idea of imagination.

Study Questions

1. Why is Hume called a naturalist?

2. Explain Hume's distinction between ideas and impressions.

3. Why is Hume called an Empiricist?

4. What is a simple impression?

5. What is the association of ideas?

6. Why does Hume think that beliefs are lively ideas?

Discussion Questions

1. Can the differences among imagination, belief, and memory be explained in terms of how these feel to the mind?

2. Is a concept an idea in the mind?

CHAPTER 16

Hume: Causation

Relations of Ideas and Matters of Fact

In section IV of the *Enquiry Concerning Human Understanding,* Hume divides all objects of inquiry into two exclusive and exhaustive types: relations of ideas and matters of fact. Relations of ideas include geometry, algebra, arithmetic, and "every affirmation which is either intuitively or demonstratively certain," such as "a father is a male." Denying such a truth is a contradiction that cannot be distinctly conceived by the mind. Such truths are "discoverable by the mere operation of thought, without dependence on what is anywhere existent in the universe." In other words, such judgments are demonstrably certain, but only because they tell us exclusively about the logical relations between our ideas and nothing about what actually exists.

According to Hume, matters of fact are not intuitively or demonstratively certain, because the negation of a statement of fact does not involve a contradiction and can be distinctly conceived by the mind. Judgments of fact depend for their truth on what exists in the universe.

Hume's distinction between matters of fact and relations of ideas later became known as "Hume's fork," and it has been very influential in twentieth-century analytic philosophy. In terms of Hume's own aims, it is a very important instrument for spearing the heart of Rationalism. It directly denies the central Rationalist assumption that reasoning alone can give us knowledge of the world. It implies that no matter of fact can be known with demonstrative certainty and that the necessary truths of reason cannot give us knowledge of the world, but can only reveal the logical relations between our ideas. It implies that the methods of Rationalism cannot yield knowledge of matters of fact. Hume's distinction is also important for the development of his own arguments regarding causation and substance.

Notice that Hume actually gives two criteria for distinguishing between relations of ideas and matters of fact: knowledge and truth. According to the first criterion, statements about the relations between ideas are known by a priori reasoning or, in Hume's own words, "by the mere operation of thought." Statements of matters of fact are not knowable in this way. According to the second criterion, statements of matters of fact are made true by what exists, and their denial can "never imply a contradiction." Statements involving the relations of ideas are true independently of what exists, and their denial implies a contradiction.

The difference between these two criteria is important in understanding Kant. Kant distinguishes between a priori/empirical and analytic/synthetic. Briefly, a priori truths are known independently of experience, whereas empirical or a posteriori truths can only be known through experience. Analytic truths cannot be denied without a contradiction, whereas synthetic truths can. We shall examine Kant's distinction in Chapter 18.

The Causal Relation

Hume notes that many of our beliefs about matters of fact are not founded on the present testimony of our senses or on memory. How do we acquire beliefs about the future, which we have not observed? Apparently, we make some inference from what we have observed in the past and are now observing in the present to draw conclusions about the future. According to Hume all such inferences are based on the causal relation.

In section IV, part I of the *Enquiry,* Hume attacks the Rationalist conception of a cause, which involves the idea of necessary connection between particular events. According to Hume, if one event *A* causes another event *B,* the two events are logically distinct, and there is no logical necessity that *B* should follow *A*. For example, it is not logically necessary that a stone thrown into the air should fall to the ground. It is logically conceivable that the stone should stay in the air or continue to rise. Of course, this is not what we are accustomed to, and Hume is not denying that the stone actually will fall to the ground. His point is that it is not a logical contradiction to suppose that the stone won't. Hume says: "every effect is a distinct event from its cause." In other words, what connects two distinct events cannot be a relation of necessity. Therefore, according to Hume, the standard Rationalist conception of the causal relation is mistaken.

Hume thinks that this conclusion has an implication for our knowledge of the effects of causes. He claims that deductive reasoning alone can only tell us about the logical relations between ideas, and never about matters of fact. He concludes that we cannot logically infer the effect from the cause by a priori reasoning alone. To know the laws of nature and what the effect of any particular event will be, we must turn to observation and experience. Hume thus denies the Rationalist claim that we can have a priori knowledge of particular effects.

Universal Causal Axiom

Besides denying the Rationalist view of the nature of causation, Hume also argues in the *Treatise* against the Rationalist claim about the scope of that relationship—namely, that every event must have a cause. These two points are different: the first concerns the analysis of the causal relationship; the second concerns the scope or extent of that relationship. The first point requires an answer to the question, "Does causation involve the idea of necessity?" or in other words, "If one particular event is said to cause another, are the two events logically connected?" Hume's negative answer to this question was examined in the last section. The second point requires a reply to the question "Is it logically necessary that every event has a cause?" which we shall now discuss.

The Rationalists regard the principle that every event has a cause as either demonstratively or intuitively certain: anyone who understands the principle will accept it. As we saw in earlier chapters, this Principle of Sufficient Reason (or Universal Causal Axiom) was a vital component in their attempt to secure a priori knowledge of the world. It also had some importance in the philosophies of Locke and Berkeley.

Hume rejects the Principle of Sufficient Reason by arguing that it is impossible to demonstrate the principle that every event has a cause. All necessity has to be demonstrated by reasoning from ideas; and if there were a proof of the Universal Causal axiom, it would have to consist in showing that the principle follows from our idea of an event—in which case it would be impossible for any event not to have a cause. But says Hume, "whatever may be conceived may exist, in whatever manner conceived." The ideas of an event and a cause are distinct; they can be separated, and thus we can conceive of an event that has no cause. According to Hume, the supposition of an uncaused event is not a logical contradiction and, therefore, the Universal Causal Axiom or Principle of Sufficient Reason is not a logically necessary truth. On the other hand, Hume points out that the statement that every *effect* has a cause is a logical truth capable of proof. However, this does not establish that every *event* must have a cause.

The Idea of Cause

In section VII of the *Enquiry,* Hume turns to the idea of a cause itself, and to Locke's attempted explanation of how this idea may be derived from experience.

Given Hume's basic principles, in order to understand the idea of a cause, we must discover from what impressions this idea is derived. Hume notes that a cause and its effect are always contiguous, or in close proximity. When an object appears to affect one distant from it, it does so through a chain of causes. Hume also notes that a cause is always temporally prior to its effect. He concludes that the impressions of contiguity and temporal priority are essential for an idea of causality. However, he continues, these two impressions are not sufficient to give us an idea of a causal relation as traditionally conceived. Two objects might be related by contiguity and temporal priority simply by coincidence. Therefore, some other ingredient must contribute to our idea of the causal relation that allows us to distinguish between the following two cases:

1. *A* and *B* being related merely coincidentally

2. *A* causing *B*

Hume says that the extra ingredient to the traditional view of a cause is the idea of a necessary connection: if *A* causes *B,* then, given *A, B* had to happen. But Hume points out that there is no impression of necessity nor of necessary connection. We can only observe regularities in experience, and thus our idea of causality cannot be derived from sense impressions.

Hume's argument is primarily directed against Locke, who agrees with Hume that all ideas are derived from experience, while at the same time accepting the traditional notion of cause. Locke was aware of the kind of problem raised by Hume, and he tried to solve it by showing how the idea of cause could be derived from introspecting the agency of our own will. According to Locke, we obtain the ideas of causal influence and power not by observing the regularities in our simple ideas of sense experience but by examining the actions of our own will or volition. Hume directly challenges Locke's thesis. According to Hume, even in the case of our own volition, we can only observe regularities and one event following another. We do not observe any impression of necessity.

A Brief Overview

Hume argues against the Rationalist view of cause. He denies that the causal relation can be assimilated to logical necessity, and he denies the Principle of Sufficient Reason. In brief, Hume asserts that the Rationalist view of causation cannot be justified. He also argues that the idea of causation as a necessary connection cannot be derived from experience, as Locke thinks it can.

Hume concludes that the belief in a necessary connection between events cannot be justified. This conclusion leaves us with three questions. First, does this imply that the term *cause* has no significance? Like Locke, Hume thinks that all significant words stand for ideas. Yet he also seems to be saying that there is no idea of cause. Does this mean that Hume should conclude that the word *cause* is empty metaphysical jargon? He raises this question himself in section VII, part II of the *Enquiry.* He says: "the necessary conclusion seems to be that we have no idea of connection and power at all, and that these words are absolutely without meaning." Immediately afterwards, he adds: "But there still remains one method of avoiding this conclusion." Briefly, Hume does not deny that we have an idea of causation; he only denies that this idea is an idea of a necessary connection between events.

Second, if we do have an idea of causation but it is not derived from any sense impression, how do we acquire it? As we saw at the beginning of Chapter 15, Hume's sceptical arguments are only one aspect of his philosophy. They are designed to clear the path for his own positive and naturalistic explanations, which emphasize the feeling and nonrational sides of human nature. Hume must give his own positive account of the idea of cause to replace the Rationalists's and Locke's. This we shall examine later.

Third, Hume began his investigation of causation by asking how we infer from the past and present to conclusions about the future. So far, we have no answer to this question.

Particular Causal Inferences: Inductive Scepticism

After investigating the nature of causation, Hume returns, in section IV, part II of the *Enquiry,* to his original question: how do we acquire beliefs about the unobserved future? We know that inferences from the past and present to conclusions about the future are based on the causal relations between particular events. However, this does not completely answer the original question: what is the nature of the inference from the past and present to conclusions about the future? The inference consists in a chain of reasoning, but what is the chain of reasoning?

Hume claims that the inference cannot be purely deductive. There is no contradiction in supposing that snow might taste salty in the future. He says: "Now, whatever is intelligible and may be distinctly conceived, implies no contradiction and can never be proved as false by any demonstrative argument or abstract reasoning a priori."

Hume claims that present impressions are not enough to justify beliefs about the unobserved. In particular, we cannot logically infer anything about the unobserved future simply on the basis of present impressions. From the fact that one object *A* exists, we cannot logically deduce that it will have a particular effect *B,* since our ideas of *A* and *B* are distinct and can be separated without contradiction.

Hume says that our beliefs about the unobserved future are based on an observed constant conjunction of events. We observe a constant conjunction between events or objects of two kinds; then, when we observe an event of the first kind, we come to believe that an event of the second kind will occur. Hume believes that this is the actual way in which we acquire our beliefs about future events. He then tries to show that we are not rationally justified in making inferences about the future in this way. This argument is the climax of Hume's sceptical position about causation. He extends his general scepticism about causation to inductive inferences and to beliefs about the future.

According to Hume, the past experience of a constant conjunction between A's and B's and a present impression of an A inevitably leads us to believe that a B will occur. In the *Treatise*, Hume argues that there can be no rational justification for this belief; we would be as justified in believing that an event of type B will not occur.

Despite having observed a constant conjunction between A's and B's and now observing an A, we are not justified in believing that a B will occur, although we will inevitably have such a belief. For this conclusion Hume argues as follows. A causal inference from the observed present and past to the future requires the assumption that the course of nature continues uniformly, as it has done in the past. Given this point, Hume argues that there is no reason or justification for believing that the course of nature is uniform—that it will continue in the same way in the future as it has done in the past. In other words, according to Hume:

1. Our beliefs about the future can only be rationally justified if the supposition that nature will continue uniformly can be rationally justified.

2. This supposition cannot be rationally justified.

---

3. Therefore, our beliefs about the future cannot be rationally justified.

Let us look at premise 2 of this argument first. Hume says that beliefs can only be justified by the evidence of the senses or by demonstrative reasoning. The belief that nature will continue in the same way as it has done in the past cannot be justified on the basis of experiential evidence (the evidence of the senses), because the very nature of such justification makes reference only to what has been previously observed. The uniformity principle implies that the future will resemble the past. Any attempt to infer from the past to the future is, according to premise 1, founded on the assumption that the uniformity principle is true. Therefore, no inductive inference from past experience can justify the uniformity principle, because all such inferences presuppose it. In other words, we cannot justify inductive reasoning on the basis that it has worked in the past, without "going in a circle, and taking for granted . . . the very point in question" (section IV, part I). It would be circular to try to justify induction inductively.

At *Treatise* I.III.VI, Hume also claims that we cannot give a deductive proof of the uniformity principle. To give such a proof, we would have to show that the uniformity principle could not possibly be false. Since we can clearly conceive of a change in the course of nature, such a change is not impossible, and consequently the uniformity principle cannot be established by deductive reasoning.

Because the principle cannot be established either by deductive reasoning or by inferences based on past experience, Hume concludes that we have no reason to believe that the principle is true.

The Need for Uniformity

Having seen Hume's arguments to show that the uniformity principle cannot be justified, we must look at why he takes this to imply that our beliefs about the future cannot be justified (at premise 1). Exactly how do our beliefs about the future depend for their rationality on the uniformity principle? To answer this question, we need to examine two intepretations of Hume's thought.

Many writers on Hume claim that our inferences from the past to the future depend on the uniformity principle in order to be deductively valid. Consider the following argument:

4. All observed A's have been followed by B's.

5. An A is observed now.

   ---

6. Therefore, an event B will occur.

This inductive argument clearly is not deductively valid. According to the standard interpretation, Hume's point is that arguments of this form can be made deductively valid only if we assume that the uniformity principle is true. Premises 4 and 5 together do not logically entail conclusion 6, unless we also assume the uniformity of nature and that all A's will be followed by B's. We can give a reason for believing conclusion 6 only if we can give a reason for believing the premises that entail it. Since there is no reason for believing the uniformity principle, and since premises 4 and 5 entail conclusion 6 only if we grant that principle, there is no reason for believing conclusion 6.

This interpretation imputes to Hume the view that all reasoning is deductive or logical, and that an inference is good if and only if it is logically valid.[68] To give a reason for a proposition, one must give a reason for believing all the propositions that together deductively entail it. According to this interpretation, Hume is taken to have shown that, if all reasoning is deductive, none of our beliefs about the future can be justified. Given this interpretation of Hume, to deny his sceptical conclusion that none of our beliefs about the future are justified, one must deny his assumption that all reasoning is deductive. In other words, on the standard interpretation, Hume reaches a sceptical conclusion with regard to our beliefs about the future because he assumes that all reasoning must be deductively valid. To avoid the sceptical conclusion, we could challenge the assumption that all reasons must be deductively sufficient.

According to another interpretation of Hume, given by Stroud, Hume's sceptical argument does not depend on the assumption that all reasoning is deductive.[69] Instead it depends on a self-conscious feature of reasons. Hume asks "when is a belief that event type B will occur reasonable?" According to Stroud, Hume's answer is that it is not enough to have observed a constant conjunction between A's and B's and to observe an A; one must also have reason to believe that these observations are a reason for believing that an event of type *B* will occur. Stroud reports Hume as saying two things: first, that one must have reason to believe that what is and has been observed can be relied on as a guide for the future; and second, that it is not possible to have such a guide.

The Five Strands

In reviewing Hume's scepticism about the idea of necessary relations or causality, it is important to separate five strands of Hume's argument and views:

1. He distinguishes relations of ideas and matters of fact. This distinction is the basis of his anti-Rationalist claim that matters of fact cannot be known with demonstrative certainty. Hume's claim implies that there can be no a priori knowledge of the world.

2. Hume asserts that the idea of causation cannot be derived from our experience, because we have no impression of necessity. This claim clearly depends on his theory that ideas are faint copies of impressions.

3. Hume claims that all events are distinct: given an event *A*, it is not necessary that a particular event *B* should occur. Like all events, *A* and *B* are distinct. In this way, Hume rejects the Rationalists' position that events are necessarily connected through the laws of nature, which are themselves necessary truths. Hume rejects the Rationalists' tendency to assimilate causality to logical necessity.

4. Hume claims that the universal causal principle itself is not a logically necessary truth, because the notion of an event and the notion of a cause are distinct. In this way, Hume rejects the Rationalists' Principle of Sufficient Reason.

5. Hume says that inductive inferences based on causation cannot be justified by appeal to induction or deduction, because they are based on the principle of the uniformity of nature.

The Naturalistic Explanation

Hume has two general and sceptical conclusions:

1. The belief that there are necessary causal connections between events cannot be justified.

2. There is no rational justification for our beliefs about the future; in other words, induction cannot be justified.

However, scepticism is only one side of Hume's philosophy. Having shown that we have no idea of necessary causal connection and that beliefs about the future cannot be justified, Hume must explain how we have an idea of causation at all. Hume's general aim is to replace Rationalist justifications with naturalistic explanations.

He claims that we do have an idea of causation, so he must show how we came to have this idea. Furthermore, we form beliefs about the future, and he must explain this. Since deductive reason cannot be the basis of our inferences about the future, Hume seeks to give a naturalistic explanation of the idea of causation by offering an account of how we form beliefs about the future.

In section V of the *Enquiry*, Hume explains the idea of cause in terms of feelings of expectation that arise from custom and habit. He says: "all inferences from experience are effects of custom, not reasoning." Hume's explanation can be divided into four stages:

1.   Through becoming accustomed to certain conjunctions, we come to expect events to follow in a certain order. This expectation is spontaneous and natural, but it is not justified. Consequently, beliefs about the future arise naturally by habit through repetition in our experience.

2.   Hume claims that this repetition produces a feeling of necessity in our minds. After observing a constant conjunction of A's and B's, when we next observe an A, we are naturally led to believe that a B will occur. But this belief is accompanied by a certain feeling of determination or inevitability. This feeling is an impression of reflection. The impression is simple and does not represent anything; it is not a perception of necessity between events in the mind, but a feeling of necessity. When Hume says that necessity exists only in the mind, he does not mean that there is a necessary connection between distinct mental events. Hume's view implies scepticism regarding the claim that there is a necessary connection between events—even mental events. When he says that necessity exists only in the mind, Hume means that a feeling of necessity arises in the mind.

3.   From this simple feeling, our idea of necessity is derived. The idea of necessity is derived from the feeling of determination or inevitability that arises naturally when the mind is placed in certain conditions.

4.   The mind has a great propensity to spread itself on external objects, by projecting its impressions and ideas onto the external world. For instance, we take the impression of blue to belong to objects because of what happens in our minds. Similarly with the idea of necessity. As far as our perceptions inform us, necessity does not reside in objects or in mental events. However, we do ascribe necessity to events of all kinds, because of the way the mind reacts after observing constant conjunctions and because of its propensity to project itself. The ascription of necessity is literally false; it is a product of the imagination.

The Two Definitions of Cause

In part II of section VII of the *Enquiry,* Hume gives two definitions of cause:

1. "an object, followed by another, where all objects similar to the first are followed by objects similar to the second."

2. "an object followed by another, and whose appearance always conveys the thought to that other."

These two definitions emphasize the two general aspects of Hume's view of causation. The first defines cause as we find it in the world in terms of the constant conjunctions and regularities that can be met in sense experience. The second concentrates on the purely psychological element in the concept of cause—on the feeling of expectation engendered by the constant conjunctions and regularities of sense experience.

Hume insists that we can have no other idea of cause than these two, and hence that we can have no idea of any actual connection between events. The first definition contains no mention of any relation of necessity between events. The second definition refers to a psychological feeling of necessity conveyed by events. Neither definition gives us the idea of a connection between events.

Conclusion

Hume's sceptical attacks on the traditional idea of cause are based on two foundation stones: his theory of impressions and ideas; and the distinction between matters of fact and relations between ideas. The second of these allows him to argue against a Rationalist view of cause; the first, against the assertion that the idea of a necessary connection between events can be derived from sense experience.

Hume's sceptical arguments are based on these two foundational assumptions, both of which are later challenged by Kant.

1. Impressions and Ideas

Hume says an idea is a faint copy of an impression and that we have no impression of necessary connection. Kant objects to both parts of this claim.

First, with respect to ideas, Kant argues that to have a concept is not to have a faint copy of an impression, but to have certain capacities of recognition and judgment. Given Kant's view of concepts, the fact that we have no impression of a necessary connection between events is no argument against our having the concept. I have no impression of the number one million, but I do have such a concept.

Second, with respect to impressions: Kant rejects Hume's view of perception. Hume claims that we have no sense impression of necessity, and this implies that we can never perceive causal relations between events, or one thing affecting another. (For example, I can perceive the stone fly and the window break, but not the stone breaking the window.) What leads Hume to this claim is his atomistic view of perception, according to which impressions are distinct and fleeting momentary existents. In reply to Hume, Kant argues that an experience consisting merely of atomistic impressions is impossible. According to Kant, experience has a unity and cannot be reduced to its component parts. Furthermore, experience cannot consist of raw impressions, because experience requires concepts.

It is important to understand more exactly the difference between Hume and Kant, since they agree on many points. Hume's argument against Locke has the following basic form:

1. Given an Empiricist view of ideas and perception, it follows that we can have no idea of necessary connection.

2. The Empiricist view of ideas and perception is correct.

3. Therefore, we have no idea of necessary connection.

Kant agrees with Hume's first premise. Hume points out that Empiricism leads to scepticism about cause, and Kant agrees with this. But, unlike Hume, Kant rejects the Empiricist view of ideas and perceptions, including Hume's own theory of impressions and ideas. Consequently, Kant rejects premise 2.

2. Matters of Fact and Relations Between Ideas

This distinction is important for Hume's arguments against the Rationalist conception of cause. Hume employs it to argue against the Universal Causal Axiom—the idea that there are necessary connections between particular events, and the claim that we have a priori knowledge of causes and effects. Kant does not argue against Hume's distinction itself, but he does argue that it is not exhaustive. Hume claims that his fork has only two prongs. Kant thinks there is a third prong: synthetic a priori truths.

As we shall see, Kant's notion of synthetic a priori truths permits him to claim that the Universal Causal Axiom—that all events have a cause—is a necessary truth without being analytic. In other words, it is not a statement of a relation between ideas, but neither is it a matter of fact. Kant agrees with Hume that "Every *effect* has a cause" cannot be denied without contradiction (that is, it is analytic), and that "Every *event* has a cause" can be denied without contradiction (that is, it is not analytic). Yet Kant argues that the claim "Every event has a cause" is a universal and necessary truth of which we can have a priori knowledge. According to Kant, the claim is a necessary truth, but it is not analytic; it is synthetic a priori. Kant tries to explain why the thesis "Every event has a cause" is synthetic a priori, by arguing that the concept of causation is a necessary condition of experience. In this way he attempts to save causation from Hume's scepticism.

Study Questions

1. How does Hume distinguish between the relations of our ideas and matters of fact?

2. Why does Hume reject the Principle of Sufficient Reason?

3. How does Hume argue against the claim that causation is a necessary connection between events? What implications does this argument have regarding our knowledge of causal effects?

4. How, according to Locke, do we acquire the idea of causation? What is Hume's argument against Locke?

5. On what grounds does Hume reject the claim that we can have justified beliefs about the future?

6. How does Hume explain our idea of causation?

7. Why does Hume give two definitions of causation?

Discussion Questions

1. In what way does Hume's view of causation depend on his theory of impressions and ideas?

2. Is it possible to have justified beliefs about the future?

3. In what way do Hume's arguments undermine the views of Spinoza?

CHAPTER 17

Hume: Material Bodies and Identity

Hume's account of causality is aimed at explaining how we acquire natural beliefs that take us beyond knowledge of our present impressions and memories. In the *Treatise on Human Nature* (Book 1, part IV, section II), he turns to other beliefs about the unobserved: our belief in the existence of external objects or bodies. Hume says that it is pointless to ask whether such bodies exist, because we cannot help but believe in their existence. Instead, he seeks to explain the origin of this belief. To do this, Hume divides our belief in the existence of bodies into two parts. First, we believe that objects continue to exist when they are not present to the senses; thus, we believe that they have continued existence. Second, we believe that objects have a distinct existence, independent of perceivers.

It is necessary to delineate exactly what beliefs Hume is trying to explain. According to Hume, we are only ever aware of our own perceptions, which are "momentary and fleeting" internal existences. He says that some philosophers distinguish these impressions from the external objects that these impressions are supposed to represent. Hume insists, however, that the natural belief is that our impressions themselves have distinct and continued existence. According to Hume, the ordinary person does not make the philosophical distinction between internal impressions and external objects, but naturally believes that impressions themselves have a distinct and continued existence. It is this natural belief that Hume seeks to explain. Accordingly, when he speaks of our belief in the existence of distinct and continuing objects, he means the belief that our impressions have a distinct and continuing existence, since ordinary people "suppose their perceptions to be their only objects."

Hume's point is that the ordinary person does not make the philosophical distinction between internal impressions and external objects. To that extent, it is misleading even to say that the ordinary person believes that impressions have a distinct and continuing existence, since this seems to impute to the ordinary person the philosopher's conception of an impression. It would perhaps be more accurate to say that the ordinary person believes that what he perceives (trees, stones, and so on) has a distinct and continuing existence. Hume—and not the ordinary person—makes the further point that we only ever perceive our own impressions. It should also be noted that Hume does not acknowledge any absurdity in the claim that impressions can exist independently of the mind that has them; as we shall see later, this is because he argues that the mind itself is nothing but a collection of perceptions.

The Senses and Reason

Hume attempts to explain the origin of the natural and common nonphilosophical belief that objects have a continuing and distinct existence. (Hume's use of the word *object* here simply signifies impressions.) He asks whether these beliefs are due to the senses, to reason, or to imagination. He argues that such beliefs cannot be due to the senses. Obviously, the senses cannot be the source of our belief that objects continue to exist even when unperceived, since, by definition, the continuation of such bodies is unperceived by the senses. Hume also argues that the senses cannot be the origin of our belief in the distinct existence of bodies. First, the senses present us with impressions only, and not with the idea that these impressions are distinct from ourselves. In order for the senses to give us awareness of the distinct existence of objects, we would have to be aware of the bodies, aware of ourselves, and aware of the distinctness of the two. Second, Hume divides the impressions of sense into three kinds: those of primary qualities like solidity and shape; those of secondary qualities like color, smell, and taste; and those of pleasure and pain. Nobody thinks that the third type of impression has a distinct existence, and Hume claims that all three types of impression are on a par as impressions. Since the senses merely give us an awareness of our impressions, they cannot provide the basis for our attributing distinct existence to certain types of impressions and not to others.

Hume concludes that the popular belief in the distinct and continuing existence of bodies is not due to the senses. He argues that it is not due to reason either. If such beliefs were due to reason, they would have to be based on argument and deduction. Hume says that, even if arguments to this effect existed, they would belong to philosophy and the majority of people would never have heard of them. Consequently, such arguments could not justify the belief held by the ordinary person. Furthermore, most people believe that the very things they see (that is, impressions) have continuing and distinct existence. There can be no question of justifying this commonly held belief by attempting to infer the continuing and distinct existence of objects from the existence of impressions. Hume argues that, even if we did make the philosophical distinction between impressions and represented objects, we still could not rationally justify the claim that objects have a continuing and distinct existence. We still would not be able to make justifiable inferences about such objects from our impressions. Such inferences require that there be an observed constant conjunction between our impressions and the objects, and Hume says that such a conjunction between impressions and objects could never be observed, because we can only perceive impressions.

Imagination

Since the ordinary person's belief in continuing and distinct existence is not due to either reason or the senses, it must have its origin in the imagination, says Hume. These ordinary beliefs or convictions must be the result of some interreaction between our impressions and our imagination. Hume claims that we do not attribute continuous and distinct existence to all our impressions, nor do we attribute distinctness and continuity to all lively and involuntary impressions. Descartes noted that certain impressions come to us without our willing them, and he argued that we naturally take these impressions to represent something outside us. Against this, Hume says that pleasures and pains also come without our choosing them, but we do not naturally ascribe continuity and distinct existence to them.

Hume says that the ordinary person attributes distinct and continuous existence to certain impressions, which are subsequently referred to as objects when they exhibit constancy and coherence. Constancy and coherence are features of series of impressions, rather than of individual impressions. These features define a uniformity in our experience.

Constancy and Coherence

When a series of impressions has constancy, the impressions present themselves in the same order and do not change when interrupted. In the *Treatise*, Hume gives this example: when I look at a scene of mountains, houses, and trees and then shut my eyes or turn away, they have not changed when I look again. A series of perceptions has coherence when, after interruption, it presents itself with regular and predictable alterations. In the *Treatise*, Hume gives the example of how a person's fire looks after he has been out: "as is always the case, if his fire is left unattended for a period of time, when he returns there is a pile of ash."

Hume's examples of constancy and coherence already involve the ideas of continuous and distinct existence because they appeal to objects, which are already continuous and distinct. Of course, to use coherence and constancy to explain how we form beliefs about distinct and continuous existents, Hume has to characterize coherence and constancy without appealing to what he seeks to explain. Otherwise the account would be circular. Indeed, Hume sometimes says that the coherence of perceptions is produced by the supposition that currently unperceived objects continue to exist. Hume seems to want to have it both ways: to explain coherence and constancy in terms of continued existence, and to explain continued existence in terms of coherence and constancy.

In Hume's defense, part of his point is that we form a habit of attributing continued existence to impressions because of their coherence and constancy. Once this habit has been formed, it reinforces itself because, by attributing continued existence, we find more constancy, and so on. This explains why the two mechanisms—the coherence and the constancy of our impressions—reinforce our belief in continuous existence. However, it does not explain how the beliefs in distinct and continuous existence arise in the first place. In other words, the mechanisms of coherence and constancy cannot explain our belief in the continuous existence of objects.

Identity

Hume must explain how we acquire the idea of an object's being identical over time. He says that the idea of identity requires the ideas of unity and diversity; we combine these two elements by thinking of things that last through time as having unity and by thinking of the time as being diverse. This idea of identity is not acquired through the senses, because we are only ever aware of momentary fleeting impressions. The idea of identity is a fiction of the imagination that arises because of the natural dispositions of the mind when it receives an uninterrupted series of impressions. During an uninterrupted series of exactly similar impressions, the mind slips so easily from one moment to the other that it supposes that only time is changing and not the fleeting impressions themselves. In this way, an invariable and uninterrupted series of momentary impressions is taken to be an identical object.

Constancy

When a series of impressions is invariable and uninterrupted, the imagination ascribes constancy to that series. A series of impressions with constancy does not change even when it is interrupted; thus it has invariableness with interruption. Hume explains the origin of our belief in continued existence with reference to constancy; for the sake of simplicity, we can divide this explanation into four steps:

1. The imagination is habitually tuned to ascribing constancy to invariable uninterrupted series of impressions. Indeed, it overlooks the interruptions in a series of impressions that have constancy and, on the basis of their invariableness, treats them as if they were uninterrupted. In other words, in a series of im-

pressions like *AAAAAABBBAAAAA,* the mind overlooks the gaps and treats the series as if it were an *AAAAAAAAAAAAAA* series.[70]

2.   This disregarding of the gaps creates a tension in the mind. Although the habit of the imagination leads us to overlook the gaps, we realize that we are doing this and our realization causes us uneasiness in the mind.

3.   We seek relief from this uneasiness by yielding to the smoothness of the invariability. We suppose that the series is uninterrupted as well as invariable, by supposing that it continues in the same way (but unobserved) during the gaps. We suppose that the same thing continues unobserved; and this is how we come to suppose that the object continues to exist unperceived.

4.   We come to believe this supposition of the imagination. According to Hume, any idea that is sufficiently vivid or lively will become a belief. Liveliness can be communicated to ideas from the impressions with which they are associated. In this way, we come to believe in the continued existence of unperceived objects.

Mental Substance

Hume directly challenges philosophers who think that we are immediately aware of ourselves as a mental substance. If the idea of a continuing self is derived directly from sense experience, there must be an impression of such a self. Hume notes that we are only directly aware of particular impressions, and that there is no impression of a self. All that we can find in introspection is a bundle of different perceptions in perpetual flux.

In Book 1, section V, part IV of the *Treatise,* Hume argues that the idea of a mental substance in which perceptions inhere is unintelligible. First, he points out that there is no impression from which such an idea can be derived. Hume says that if the idea of a substance is the idea of a thing distinct from all perceptions, in which all our perceptions inhere, then we can have no such idea. This is because we can only have ideas of perceptions. Second, Hume says that, if substance is defined as that which may exist by itself, this definition fails to distinguish substance from impressions, since each impression could exist by itself. Third, Hume argues that we cannot acquire knowledge of mental substance, nor indeed of any substance, from a priori reasoning. A priori reasoning can only inform us of the relations between our ideas; it cannot inform us of matters of fact.

Hume concludes that the idea of a mental substance cannot be explained by appealing either to the senses or to reason. He says that the idea of such a substance is a philosophical invention designed to explain personal identity through changes in perceptions. Hume clearly regards the postulation of mental substance as an incorrect way of explaining personal identity. The notion of personal identity should be explained without recourse to postulating the existence of a mental substance.

Personal Identity

Rather than attempting to justify the idea of personal identity, Hume thinks we should seek to reveal its psychological origins in the imagination. Hume asks why we have a propensity to ascribe identity to the succession of impressions and thus suppose that a continued, uninterrupted self exists throughout the course of our lives. As in the case of the identity of objects, Hume is not seeking to explain a belief that the self is something distinct from perceptions, but he is seeking to explain how we come to ascribe personal identity to the series of perceptions themselves. When we speak of ourselves as identical through time, we are ascribing identity to the perceptions we have at different times, and not to something beyond or distinct from those perceptions. The perceptions themselves constitute a single mind.

In all cases of ascribing identity, we attribute identity because the passage of thought along a series of momentary and distinct impressions is so smooth and effortless that we mistake this series for a continuous view of the same object. This applies to personal identity, too. Something about our perceptions makes us disregard their momentary nature and treat them instead as constituting a single mind. Hume believes that this happens because of the resemblance between different perceptions and also because of causation. The function of these two relations is to make the mind glide more easily along a series of momentary and distinct impressions and so regard them as a single continuous self, extended through time.

Resemblance helps in the following way: some ideas resemble earlier ones, especially when they are memories of those earlier perceptions, and this resemblance enables the imagination to treat the series of perceptions as a continuous self. However, comparatively few perceptions resemble each other in this way, and Hume says that causality supplements resemblance to give us an idea of ourselves continuing through time. When a series of perceptions seems to form a single causal chain, the mind glides along the series and easily ignores the differences between the perceptions, until it eventually regards the series as a single self, extended through time. In this way, we come to treat our perceptions as constituting a single mind. This is merely a result of the imagination, for actually all perceptions are distinct and momentary existents, and there really is no necessary connection between these distinct perceptions. The idea of personal identity is a natural and inevitable fiction of the imagination.

Some Problems

We can see that Hume's account of personal identity has much in common with his accounts of causality and external objects. In each case Hume adopts a sceptical position, arguing that our beliefs cannot be justified by appeal either to reason or to sense impressions. He then goes on to give a psychological and naturalistic account of how the imagination provides us with these ideas. This type of explanation has special paradoxical implications when it is applied to the self. According to Hume, the imagination or mind is led to believe that there is a mind, when in fact there is only a collection of distinct perceptions. This claim implies that there is no mind and that the very idea of the mind is a fiction created by the imagination. But what is it that comes to believe that there is a mind? If there is no mind how do I ascribe identity to myself?

There are several problems here. First, it is difficult to see how a mere bundle of perceptions could ever perform the mental activities appealed to in Hume's account of the workings of the imagination. Hume could reply to this point by arguing that the mind's activity simply consists in the occurrence of certain perceptions in the mind. But this reply suggests a more fundamental objection. According to Hume, perceptions are really distinct, without necessary connections between them. To account for the idea of causality without using the idea of necessary connections, Hume has to make use of the notion of the mind or imagination, which notices constant conjunctions among impressions and forms habits. But to explain this notion of the mind, Hume appeals to the notion of causality or constant conjunction. Therefore, Hume's explanations seem to involve a circularity.

In defense of Hume, it could be argued that this circularity need not be vicious. The circularity would be vicious if the subject or person herself had to have the idea of her own identity before she could acquire the idea of causality, and if she had to have the idea of causality before she could acquire the idea of her own identity. To defend Hume, one could argue that, on Hume's principles, we do not need to have the idea of our own identity before we can acquire the idea of causality. Hume is not trying to offer us a philosophical analysis of causation, personal identity, or the like; rather, he is trying to give a psychological account of the origin of such ideas.

However, Hume's account leaves us with an inexplicable fact about perceptions—namely, that the range of vision of any one perception does not extend to all perceptions. Or to put this more naturally, each one of us cannot be aware of all the perceptions that occur. Why do perceptions occur in discrete but separate bundles? This would be answerable if perceptions were in themselves connected with other things or had to belong to individual minds. But Hume rejects such explanations because he regards all perceptions as free-floating, independent of all other perceptions, and independent of all minds. Therefore, he cannot account for the fact that the scope of one's experience does not extend to all extant perceptions. This problem in Hume is a consequence of his view of perceptions as discrete independent existents.

Study Questions

1. How does Hume argue that our belief in the distinct and continued existence of bodies is not derived from sense experience?

2. How does Hume argue that our belief in the distinct and continued existence of bodies cannot be justified by appeal to reason?

3. How does Hume explain our belief in the continued existence of bodies?

4. Why does Hume reject the claim that we have knowledge of a mental substance?

5. What is Hume's view of personal identity? How does it differ from Locke's and Descartes's?

6. How is Hume's view of the mind paradoxical?

Discussion Questions

1. What is the relationship between Hume's scepticism and his naturalism?

2. Can the claim that there are independent external objects be justified?

3. How does Hume's view of continued independent objects compare with Locke's and Berkeley's?

Empiricism

Empiricism is the view that all knowledge originates from experience. More specifically, there are five central pillars of Empiricism, in the Modern period:

1. All our ideas are derived from experience.

2. We can only perceive our own ideas.

3. Knowledge consists in the perceiving of ideas.

4. All significant words stand for ideas.

5. We can have no a priori knowledge of the world.

These theses require elaboration, explanation, and qualification, since they are the bones of the Empiricist view of perception, concepts, knowledge, and language.

1. All our ideas are derived from experience.

Locke says that all our complex ideas are derived from simple ideas. Hume makes basically the same point by asserting that all ideas are derived from simple impressions.

In this context, the term *idea* means, roughly, "concept." The Empiricists tend to obviate the difference between concepts and sense impressions, viewing concepts as faint copies of sense impressions. They tend to regard the difference between concepts and sense impressions as one of degree only and not as one of kind. Hume is more explicit in this regard than either Locke or Berkeley.

Implicit in claim 1 is a broadly atomistic conception of experience. All ideas and/or impressions are either complex or simple. Any complex idea is ultimately composed of simple ideas; and by definition, these simples cannot be broken down any further. They constitute the atoms of experience.

Why does the origin or source of our ideas have philosophical importance? One answer is: if an idea cannot be derived from experience, then we are not justified in using it to make judgments about experience. This answer is a motivating assumption in Locke's program for showing how our complex ideas are derived from simple ideas and in his arguments against innate ideas. This motivation also underlies the work of Hume, who argues that, as traditionally conceived, the ideas of cause, substance, and self cannot be derived from experience in the way Locke claims. Hume does not flinch from the conclusion that beliefs based on such ideas are not justified. But he contends that we make judgments employing such ideas in any case—even if we are not justified in doing so—because of human nature.

2. We can only perceive our own ideas.

The given contingent element in sense experience, which Hume calls simple impressions, is directly known with immediate certainty. Together with the ideas of reflection, simple impressions form the building blocks of knowledge. The claim that we can only perceive our own ideas, when combined with an Empiricist view of knowledge, apparently implies that we cannot know anything beyond our own ideas. Of the three philosophers, Hume comes closest to recognizing this.

3. Knowledge consists in the perceiving of ideas.

Hume thinks of belief as consisting in having vivid ideas. Locke defines knowledge as a perceiving of the relations between our ideas. For the Empiricists, all knowledge is derived from our ideas, which are in turn based on experience.

The Empiricist view of knowledge, when combined with the claim that we can only perceive our own ideas, ultimately implies that we know the content of our present sensory experiences with greater certainty than we can ever know anything about the external world, including whether it exists. Ultimately, Empiricism must face scepticism about the existence of the external world. Locke, for example, tries to avoid that scepticism, in part by appealing to the Rationalist contention that our simple sensory ideas must have a cause. Berkeley tries to avoid scepticism regarding matter by denying that it exists, only to face a similar problem with respect to other minds.

In brief, to argue that we can have any knowledge beyond our own present experience (whether concerning the self, other minds, matter, or God), the Empiricists have to rely on Rationalist principles by claiming that we can have a priori knowledge of the world, through a priori principles like "Everything must have a cause," and "If there is perceiving then there must be a mind that does that perceiving."

4. All significant words stand for ideas.

At the end of the section II of the *Enquiry Concerning Human Understanding*, Hume says: "When we entertain any suspicion that a philosophical term is employed without any meaning or idea, we need but inquire, from what impression is that supposed idea derived?"

Also echoing Locke, Berkeley says: "there are many names in use among speculative men which do not always suggest to others determinate particular ideas, or in truth anything at all" (*Principles*, introduction, paragraph 19).

Berkeley argues, against Locke, that if the word *matter* does not stand for an idea, then the term is vacuous. Having argued in this way, Berkeley tries to defend himself against the charge that, since the words *mind* and *spirit* also do not stand for ideas, they too are vacuous. He tries to distinguish between ideas and notions. He also picks up on Locke's claim that there are certain particle words, like *is*, that do not stand for ideas, but rather for actions of the mind.

5. We have no a priori knowledge of the world.

Hume makes this thesis explicit by distinguishing between relations of ideas and matters of fact. For Hume, no reasoning concerning matters of fact is a priori, but such reasoning is based on custom and habit. Only reasoning regarding relations of ideas is a priori, but such reasoning does not give us knowledge of matters of fact—that is, of the world. In other words, we cannot have knowledge of the world through a priori reasoning alone. To have knowledge of facts, we must resort to experience. Hume's distinction undermines Rationalism.

Some Comparisons

Although the preceding five claims articulate the basic pillars of Modern Empiricism, this does not mean that individually, Locke, Berkeley, and Hume give equal emphasis to, or even endorse, each and every one of the five claims. Empiricism is not a school of philosophy that existed in the seventeenth and eighteenth centuries. It is a loose classification, invented after the fact to draw attention to certain general emphases and themes common to these and other philosophers. It is a convenient term that should not blind us to the differences among so-called Empiricists, nor to the ways in which they were not Empiricists.

For example, only Hume comes close to making claim 5 explicitly. Locke and Berkeley allow some a priori knowledge of the world—for instance, when they rely on the principle that everything must have a cause. The views of both Berkeley and Locke imply that we can have a priori knowledge of God's existence. Berkeley also relies on the a priori principle that, if there is an idea, there must be a mind perceiving that idea. He relies on this principle when he claims that I know of the existence of my own mind, even though I do not perceive it. Furthermore, Locke's view of knowledge contains important elements resembling aspects of Descartes's mathematical model of knowledge. Clearly, there are important strands of Rationalism in Locke and Berkeley, who think that we can have some nonempirical or a priori knowledge of what exists.

Although Locke claims that significant words stand for ideas, he also recognizes that structural or particle words like *is* and *but* are meaningful and do not stand for ideas. He argues that such words are marks for some action of the mind. Berkeley affirms that words like *spirit* and *God* do not name ideas at all, since we cannot have passive ideas of active spirits. Berkeley also emphasizes the use to which we put words in communicating.

As another example, Hume does not explicitly define knowledge, although he does seem to rely implicitly on something similar to claim 3. Berkeley contends that we have knowledge of minds and of God, but that such knowledge does not consist in having ideas. He asserts that we have immediate knowledge of the existence of our own minds and that this consists in a direct intuitive awareness, rather than in the perception of ideas. As we have seen, Locke's notion of sensitive knowledge apparently contradicts his definition of knowledge as the perceiving of relations between ideas, since it requires us to compare ideas directly with external objects.

With respect to claim 2, although Locke says that we can only perceive our own ideas, he also thinks that those ideas represent external objects (with respect to primary qualities).

Of the three Empiricists, Hume is the most explicit in endorsing the preceding five principles and is the most consistent in appreciating the impact of their sceptical implications. In other words, Berkeley and Locke are less Empiricist than Hume. Furthermore, insofar as they are Empiricist and do accept the five principles, they are less consistent in appreciating the sceptical consequences of those principles than Hume is.

Development

It is sometimes claimed that Descartes is the least Rationalist of the three Rationalists and that Leibniz is the most. Similarly, it is held that Locke is the least Empiricist of the three Empiricists and that Hume is the most. According to this simplified picture, the Rationalist assumptions implicit in Descartes's philosophy were made more explicit by Spinoza and Leibniz, and the Empiricist assumptions first articulated by Locke were made more explicit by Berkeley and finally Hume.

Locke and Descartes have been called the founding fathers of Empiricism and

Rationalism, respectively. Among other similarities in their views, both concentrate more explicitly on epistemology (the study of knowledge) than do their successors. Despite this, the Rationalists are more generally concerned with ontology and metaphysics than are Locke and Hume. This is why the notion of substance is so central to the arguments of Spinoza and Leibniz. Their primary concern is with what exists, substance, and both Spinoza and Leibniz argue, in their different ways, against Descartes's mind/matter dualism.

Locke and Hume, on the other hand, are concerned more directly with the justification and origin of ideas, beliefs, and knowledge. Despite the fact that Berkeley has similar interests, his main aim is more ontological, and, in this sense, his primary philosophical motivation is more similar to Spinoza's and Leibniz's. Berkeley is primarily concerned to argue that material substance does not exist.

Kant

It is best to begin our examination of Kant's philosophy with an extremely brief and simplified sketch of the Rationalist and Empiricist traditions. However, it is important to bear in mind that Rationalism and Empiricism are convenient but oversimplfed classifications invented after the Modern period, that they do not signify schools of philosophy, and that they indicate only broad similarities among the views of the included philosophers. Nevertheless, these broad generalizations can help us understand Kant, because Kant disagrees deeply with the emphases of both traditions and attempts to bridge them by adopting new starting points for his philosophy.

Central to Rationalism is the Principle of Sufficient Reason, according to which all truths must be capable of rational explanation. Rationalists tend to regard such explanation as equivalent to logical demonstration; and insofar as they do, this effectively implies that truths are necessary. Furthermore, because in theory truths can be demonstrated a priori, it is in principle possible to know them through reason alone, without recourse to sense experience. The Rationalists also tend to treat sense experience as an inferior form of intellectual apprehension.

Empiricism, on the other hand, begins with sense experience and claims that all knowledge must be derived from it. The only truths not derived from experience merely reveal the logical relations between concepts and do not give us any substantial knowledge about matters of fact. Empiricist principles reject the possibility of a priori knowledge of the world. As Hume saw, Empiricism tends to lead to scepticism; for instance, with regard to causation, the thesis that all events have a cause cannot be demonstrated or derived from experience.

Kantian Starting Points

Kant believes that the Rationalist and Empiricist traditions share certain fundamental assumptions that must be rejected if we are to avoid the apparent deadlock between the traditions.

1. The Difference Between Sensation and Understanding Is One of Degree

Both Rationalists and Empiricists treat the difference between sensation and understanding as a difference of degree rather than as a difference of kind. The Rationalists treat sensation as a confused and inferior form of intellectual apprehension (see Spinoza's *Ethics,* Part II, proposition 25). The Empiricists tend to treat the concepts of the understanding as faint copies of sensible impressions (see Kant's *Critique of Pure Reason* A271/B327 on Leibniz and Locke). Kant, on the other hand, regards the difference between the understanding and sensation as a difference of kind. The raw material of experience (which Kant calls sensible intuition) is passively received through sensation and actively ordered by the understanding. Sensible intuition is passive; the understanding is active. The two are sharply separate: the senses can think nothing, and the understanding cannot receive the raw data of sensible intuitions.

2. There is Only One Source of Knowledge

Following from the previous point, the Rationalists tend to assume that, in principle, all knowledge can be known by the understanding. Meanwhile, the Empiricists tend to assume that all knowledge must be derivable from experience. Both tend to assume in their own way that there is only one source of knowledge. Kant, on the other hand, argues that sensation (or sensible intuition) and the understanding are both necessary for experience and knowledge. For experience to be possible, sensible intuitions must be passively received, and these intuitions must be synthesized or ordered by the concepts of the understanding. Neither sense impressions nor the understanding alone suffice for experience. In Kant's own words, "intuitions without concepts are blind; concepts without intuitions are empty" (A51/B75). The intuitions of passive sensation must be conceptualized by the understanding before we can have experience.

3. All a Priori Truths Are Analytic

An analytic truth cannot be denied without contradiction. Any truth that is not analytic is synthetic. An a priori truth cannot be derived from experience and is both necessarily and universally true (for example, 2 + 2 = 4). A truth that is not a priori is a posteriori or empirical. According to Kant, both the Rationalists and the Empiricists tend to assume that all a priori truths are analytic—that is, cannot be denied without contradiction. More accurately, the Rationalists and the Empiricists do not explicitly distinguish between analytic and a priori truths.

However, the Rationalists and the Empiricists do differ in the importance they attach to a priori truths. Leibniz, for instance, thinks that in principle all truths are capable of logical demonstration; he thereby commits himself to the view that we can have knowledge of the world, through reasoning alone. Hume, on the other hand, thinks that reasoning alone only reveals the logical relations between concepts but tells us nothing about matters of fact. Leibniz thinks that demonstrative reasoning can give us a priori knowledge of the world, and Hume denies this.

Kant rejects both viewpoints. Kant argues that not all necessary truths are analytic; in other words, he says that some a priori truths are synthetic. Thus he is able to argue, in support of Hume and against Leibniz, that analytic truths are uninformative. At the same time, he is able to argue, in support of Leibniz and against Hume, that we do have a priori knowledge of the world. According to Kant, a priori knowledge of the world is expressed by synthetic a priori judgments. Kant thinks that the basic principles of mathematics and science consist of synthetic a priori truths. By rejecting the assumption that all a priori truths are analytic, Kant is able to argue against the scepticism of Hume with regard to, for instance, the Universal Causal Axiom—that all events have a cause. Hume notes that this principle is not derived from experience and that it is not a contradiction to deny it. Kant agrees with Hume on both of these points, but he is still able to argue that the principle is nonetheless a priori: synthetic a priori.

Kant's rejection of the above assumption is most important because one major task of the *Critique* is to explain how synthetic a priori truths are possible.

Immanuel Kant (1724–1804)

Immanuel Kant was born in Königsberg in 1724, into the large family of a hard-working saddler. They were devout pietists, part of a reformist movement in the Lutheran church that placed the highest value on duty, work, and prayer. The family's pastor, Franz Schultz (who was also a theology professor), advised that the boy Immanuel should attend a pietist school, which he entered at the age of eight, receiving a thorough grounding in the Latin classics. It was an oppressive education, however, which Kant is said to have referred to later as "child slavery," while a contemporary of his, David Ruhnken, wrote of the "pedantically gloomy discipline" at the school.

When he was sixteen Kant went to the University of Königsberg, where he spent the next six years. One of his teachers was Martin Knutzen, who introduced Kant to the works of Wolff and Newton, lending Kant books that were at that time not yet part of the standard curriculum.

After graduating, he was compelled, for financial reasons, to take work as a private tutor. His tutorial positions were his sole source of income for some time, even though Kant later described himself as possibly the worst private tutor the world had ever known. He is believed to have matured intellectually during this period of obscurity, and to have begun formulating some of the thoughts that would eventually be expressed in his writings.

At the age of 31, he became a doctor of philosophy and an instructor at the university; although this earned him no salary, it allowed Kant to give public lectures and to broaden his reputation. Kant became highly respected as an academic long before his writings became known. It is said that, in order to obtain a place in one of Kant's lectures, it was necessary to arrive an hour beforehand. He lectured on a wide variety of subjects including logic, physical geography, natural history, anthropology, mathematics, and physics. His first published essay, probably written while he was still a student, was *Thoughts on the True Estimation of Living Forces,* an abstract mathematical work concerning the measurement of force. While working as a private tutor, he wrote the *Universal Natural History and Theory of the Heavens,* which was published in 1755.

Between 1756 and 1763, his early teaching years, Kant published relatively little, compared to his later life. But he had an extraordinary capacity for knowledge of diverse subjects (as was shown by his teaching). Kant was apparently able to describe anything he read about extremely vividly. One day, for example, he spoke of Westminster Bridge in such exact detail that an Englishman asked him how many years he had lived in London and whether he was particularly absorbed in architecture. In fact, he never traveled outside Prussia.

At home he was frugal and disciplined; he rose at 5 A.M. to work, ate only one full meal a day, and invariably went for a solitary walk in the afternoon, whatever the weather. A famous story about Kant is that the housewives of Köningsberg could set their clocks by him, he was so regular in his habits. These tendencies toward hard work and routine were undoubtedly a reflection of his background.

To some extent, his austerity was tempered by a sociable nature, and Kant became a highly popular figure in Königsberg society. In his early years he is said to have spent almost every evening out dining with friends, and later in life he customarily invited others to share his midday meal. He was often remembered for his wit and conviviality on such occasions. He enjoyed the company of women but shied away from the idea of marriage.

Until around 1770, Kant's philosophy was greatly influenced by Wolff, who in turn, had been much influenced by Leibniz. But some time after 1770, Kant's philosophical views changed radically. According to his own account, reading Hume interrupted his dogmatic slumbers and led to his writing the *Critique of Pure Reason* and to the intense period of creativity afterward. Only in 1781, when Kant was 57, did the *Critique of Pure Reason,* which Kant said was the fruit of twelve years' reflection, appear. He acknowledged the difficulty and obscurity of some passages, explaining that the actual writing had been hurried. In 1783 the *Prolegomena* was published as an introduction to the ideas of the *Critique.* The revised second edition of the *Critique* was published in 1787.

After 1781 Kant wrote many books that explained the implications of his views of knowledge and metaphysics for ethics, the philosophy of science, religion, and aesthetics. In 1785 he published the *Groundwork of the Metaphysics of Morals,* and in 1786 the *Metaphysical Foundations of Natural Science.* The *Critique of Practical Reason* (concerned with ethics) appeared in 1788. The *Critique of Judgment,* Kant's work on aesthetics and teleology, was published in 1790. In 1793 Kant published *Religion Within the Limits of Reason Alone,* which earned censure from the King's minister and forced Kant to promise to refrain from publicly discussing religion in his lectures and writings.

By 1796, Kant's faculties had begun to decline. Gradually he became more and more melancholy and distracted, and eventually senile. He died in February 1804.

CHAPTER 1 8

Kant: The
Transcendental
Aesthetic

Kant's Aims

In the preface and introduction to the *Critique of Pure Reason,* Kant declares his aims. He points out that, whereas great progress has been made in logic, mathematics, and science, none has been made in traditional metaphysics, which seeks knowledge beyond the bounds of any possible experience. This casts doubt on the possibility of such metaphysical a priori knowledge; and so Kant asks four essential questions.

1. Is Transcendent Metaphysics Possible?

Is it possible to have theoretical knowledge that goes beyond what we could ever experience? Is it possible to make theoretical a priori claims about the existence of God, the immortality of the soul, and the size and age of the universe? Is the kind of metaphysical knowledge sought by the Rationalists possible? Kant argues that rationalistic, dogmatic metaphysics is impossible. In the Dialectic, Kant seeks to demolish such a transcendent metaphysics at its source. This is why Kant's work is called the *Critique of Pure Reason.* He argues that we inevitably aspire to knowledge that transcends or goes beyond possible experience, but that such knowledge is impossible. But to be able to argue this, Kant seeks to explain when and why a priori knowledge is possible.

2. How Are Mathematics and Pure Natural Science Possible?

Since these sciences do exist, it is legitimate to ask how they are possible. Unlike Descartes, Kant is not interested in establishing such sciences as certain; his concern is with their nature and status. If we can discover how such sciences are possible, we may have some way to answer question 1. For this reason, he asks question 3.

3. How Are Synthetic A Priori Judgments Possible?

According to Kant, judgments like "7 + 5 = 12" and "Every event has a cause" are not analytic: we can deny them without logical contradiction. Nonetheless, they are a priori. Since they claim universal and necessary truth, they cannot be derived from experience. Once we deny the assumption that all a priori truths are analytic, we must seek to explain how synthetic a priori knowledge is possible. Since both mathematics and pure science contain synthetic a priori truths, according to Kant, we can answer question 2 by answering question 3. Furthermore, by explaining how synthetic a priori knowledge is possible in mathematics and pure science, Kant hopes to be able to show why such knowledge is impossible in transcendent metaphysics.

4. What Are The Necessary Conditions of Experience?

In much of the *Critique,* Kant investigates the structural limits to what we can conceive of as a possible experience. These are also the limits to any possible object of experience. Roughly speaking, Kant answers question 3 by arguing that synthetic a priori truths define the necessary conditions of experience. For instance, every event must have a cause because an uncaused event could not be experienced and thus could not be a part of the empirical world. The concepts of "event" and "cause" are logically distinct, just as in the way Hume argues, but they are linked through the notion of the necessary conditions of experience. Thus, Kant's major aims are related: by answering question 4, he can show how synthetic a priori knowledge of the world is possible, and he can show how a priori knowledge is restricted to the bounds of possible experience, thus answering question 1 negatively.

When Kant asks "What are the necessary conditions of experience?" his interest is in the necessary forms of experience. Experience must have a certain order or structure. Kant's investigation into these a priori forms of experience divides into two parts. Experience requires both concepts and intuitions, both understanding and sensibility. Both understanding and sensibility have a priori forms. In the Aesthetic, Kant investigates the a priori forms of sensibility; in the Analytic, Kant investigates the a priori forms of the understanding. This defines the format of the positive side of the *Critique,* after which comes the negative aspect—the attack on dogmatic metaphysics in the Dialectic.

Transcendental Idealism

Kant aims to explain how we have a priori knowledge of the world. However, he realizes that even if he specifies the a priori forms of experience, it will not be enough. There remains what might be called the problem of application: how can we know a priori that the world actually conforms to the formal conditions of experience? According to Kant, philosophers usually assume that our knowledge must conform to the world; and given this assumption, we can never explain how we have a priori knowledge of the world. Rather, we should assume that the world must conform to the a priori forms of our knowledge. In other words, we must give up the assumption that the world is totally independent of the character of experience.

According to Kant, giving up this assumption involves adopting transcendental idealism. Transcendental idealism involves drawing a distinction between: things as they appear to us, or phenomena; and things as they are in themselves, or noumena. Transcendental idealism is the view that the world as we know it—the world of tables, chairs, and other spatio-temporal objects—is transcendentally ideal. We only ever know the world of things as they appear to us, and never how things are in themselves.

Transcendental idealism guarantees a fit between the a priori forms of experience and the a priori features of the world, because it involves giving up the assumption that the world is as it is, totally independently of the formal nature of experience. It involves giving up the assumption that the world is transcendentally real (in other words, that the world is composed of things as they are in themselves, or noumena). Having relinquished this assumption, we can explain how a priori knowledge of the world is possible: the a priori forms of experience are the a priori forms of the world that we experience. Kant often makes the point in the following way: he says that we impose the forms of our experience on the world because "we can know a priori only of things we put there."

The Transcendental Aesthetic

In the Aesthetic, Kant examines the a priori forms of sensibility, which are space and time. Sensibility is the faculty whereby we passively receive empirical or sensible intuitions. It is tempting to regard Kantian empirical intuitions as sensations or as Humean sensible impressions. But this would be incorrect, because it is essential to Kant's view that experience not consist of passively received sensations or sense data. The material passively received by sensibility must be conceptualized and ordered by the understanding before it can be experienced. Therefore, Kantian empirical intuitions should be regarded as the passively received material for experience, which is indescribable until it has been synthesized and ordered by the understanding into a structured experience of spatio-temporal objects.

According to Kant, space and time are the forms of sensibility because empirical intuitions become ordered into experience of spatio-temporal objects. They are the a priori forms of sensibility because they are presupposed by our awareness of spatio-temporal objects rather than being derived from that awareness by abstraction. Experience of objects must be spatial and temporal.

Besides saying that space and time are the a priori forms of sensible intuition, Kant also claims that they are themselves a priori intuitions. In claiming this, Kant denies both the view of Leibniz that space and time are relations and the alternative view that they are concepts. Kant claims that space and time are unique infinite individuals: all spaces are parts of the one whole space, and similarly with time. Insofar as Kant makes such claims, he adopts a Newtonian as opposed to a Leibnizian view of space and time. However, contrary to the Newtonian view, Kant also argues that space and time are transcendentally ideal: space and time are not properties of or part of the world as it is in itself, but rather part of the phenomenal world, the world as it appears. Sometimes, Kant expresses the transcendental ideality of space and time by saying that they are "in us," merely as forms of our representations.

The Metaphysical Exposition of Space

In this section Kant gives four arguments. The first two are to show that space is a priori; the second two to show that space is an intuition and not a concept. The arguments run as follows:

1. Kant argues that space is not an empirical concept derived from experience by abstraction. We could not derive our idea of space by abstracting it from our experience of adjacent objects, because, in order to represent objects as adjacent in the first place, we require an idea of space. Therefore, space is not an empirical concept derived from experience but is a priori and is presupposed by our experience of outer objects.

2. Kant argues that we can imagine space as being empty of objects, but not the absence of space itself. From this, Kant concludes that space is in us a priori, underlying and presupposed by our awareness of outer objects. Space is logically prior to the objects that exist in it.

3. Kant points out that we can represent to ourselves only one space as a unitary whole. Different spaces are simply limitations on (or parts of) the whole of space. Therefore, different spaces do not stand in relation to space in general in the way that instances of a concept stand in relation to the concept itself. Thus space is not a concept but an intuition.

4. Kant argues that space is an infinite given magnitude, and therefore that it is not a concept but an intuition.

The Argument from Geometry

According to Kant, geometry contains synthetic a priori truths about space and the things in space. For instance, compare the following two statements:

1. A triangle has three sides.

2. The angles of a triangle add up to 180 degrees.

Both statements can be known a priori and are necessary truths. But whereas statement 1 is analytic, statement 2 is synthetic, because it tells us something about the character of space. Analytic statements merely reveal the logical relations between concepts, but statement 2 does more than this; it tells us something substantive about the nature of space.

In the transcendental exposition of space, Kant argues that the only possible explanation of the synthetic a priori truths of geometry is his own theory. How is this synthetic a priori knowledge possible? It must be by intuition rather than through concepts, because through concepts we can know only analytic truths. A priori intuition, on the other hand, cannot be derived from experience; and geometrical truths are universally and necessarily true and cannot be learned through experience. Thus Kant argues that space must be the a priori form of our sensible intuition. Our perception of objects must be spatial, and all objects must conform to spatial requirements, because this is how experience is ordered. In a way, then, we impose spatiality upon the world; otherwise, we could not experience outer objects. Kant sometimes expresses this by saying that space is a priori in us as the subjective condition of our sensibility. He says that space is not a property of things in themselves: space is transcendentally ideal and not transcendentally real. Kant argues that space is transcendentally ideal because, if it were not, we could not explain how we have a priori knowledge of it.

Non-Euclidean Geometry

Kant assumes that space is Euclidean—that is, that the synthetic a priori propositions of Euclidean geometry characterize space. Does the more recent development of non-Euclidean geometry pose any threat to Kant's theory of space? At first sight, it seems not: Kant regards the propositions of Euclidean geometry as synthetic and thus allows for the logical possibility of non-Euclidean geometry. However, Kant would not have allowed non-Euclidean geometry to characterize physical space, because he simply assumes that space is Euclidean. In itself this does not seem to be a grave defect in Kant's theory of space, and it would misrepresent his aims to claim that he tries to prove space is Euclidean. His task is to explain how the synthetic a priori propositions of geometry describe space, and to this end he argues that space is the a priori form of our intuition. The fact that he incorrectly assumes that space is necessarily Euclidean seems to be an unimportant detail.

The main problem is Kant's commitment to the view that we know the characteristics of space a priori. Yet it was on the basis of empirical observation that space was discovered to be curved rather than being Euclidean. Thus it seems that the nature of space is an empirical and not an a priori matter. This is a damaging criticism of Kant's theory. If it has to be established empirically that physical space is non-Euclidean, this presents a serious challenge to Kant's claim that geometrical propositions are synthetic a priori. It may be argued that geometry consists of two branches: the pure and the applied. Pure geometry consists of formal analytic propositions that say nothing about space. Applied geometry consists of empirical observations about the nature of space. In neither case do we find synthetic a priori propositions.

In *The Bounds of Sense,* Strawson gives a limited defense of Kant's position. He distinguishes between physical and visual space, and argues that, whereas it is an empirical fact that physical space is non-Euclidean, it would be plausible to regard visual space as Euclidean a priori.[71] Space looks Euclidean, and this could be regarded as an a priori truth. In this way, Strawson argues that Kant's position still has plausibility with regard to visual space, although not with regard to physical space. Against Strawson, it could be countered that it is an empirical fact that space looks Euclidean: if physical space were more curved than it in fact is and if we had a more sensitive visual apparatus, then space would appear non-Euclidean. Furthermore, it is doubtful that Kant would distinguish between visual and physical space. He also claims that physical space is transcendentally ideal and that we perceive objects directly in physical space.

Time

Kant argues that time is the a priori form of sensibility—that it is transcendentally ideal. Kant's views on time are parallel to his views on space except for two differences. First, he says that, whereas space is the a priori form of outer intuition, time is the form of inner intuition. Insofar as our awareness is directed inwardly to our own experience, we are aware of a temporal series. But when our awareness is directed to outer things, to objects other than ourself, it must be a spatial awareness. In other words, experience itself must be temporal, but external objects must be both spatial and temporal.

The second difference between Kant's exposition of space and time is this: geometry is the a priori science of space, but it is not clear in the Aesthetic that there is a parallel a priori science of time. Although Kant does claim that there are synthetic a priori truths about time such that it is one-dimensional, there seems to be no parallel to geometry for time. However, there is some textual evidence, later in the *Critique,* for arguing that Kant regarded arithmetic as a body of synthetic a priori based on time.

Arithmetic

Certainly Kant regards propositions like $7 + 5 = 12$ as synthetic a priori. In the introduction to the *Critique*, he argues that such propositions are not analytic. He says that we cannot logically deduce from the concepts of "seven" and "plus five" that this equals twelve. He says that it is more obvious with large numbers that such propositions are not analytic. What then is the relation between arithmetic and time? A rather crude interpretation of Kant is that he regards numbers as generated by the process of counting and that counting takes time. However, this makes the connection between numbers and time empirical, and Kant's view is that the connection is transcendental. In other words, the connection involves an a priori element: arithmetic is about the magnitude of series, and this finds concrete expression in temporal sequences of successive units. Numbers involve the addition of units, and if arithmetic is to have application to the world, these units must be temporal.

Conclusion

To understand a complex work like the *Critique of Pure Reason*, it is important to bear in mind its aims. As the title of the work suggests, Kant wants to critique the claim that reason can give us a priori metaphysical knowledge of the world that goes beyond what we could possibly experience. But to do this, Kant must first investigate how science and mathematics are possible.

Study Questions

1. What are Kant's main aims in the *Critique of Pure Reason*?

2. What are synthetic a priori truths? Why are they important for Kant?

3. What is the application problem? How does it arise, and how does Kant solve it?

4. What does Kant mean when he says that space and time are the a priori forms of intuition?

5. How does Kant answer the question: how are the synthetic a priori truths of geometry possible?

6. How does Locke think that we acquire the idea of infinite space? How does Kant respond to Locke's claim?

7. What does Kant mean when he claims that space is transcendentally ideal? What reasons does he have for making this claim?

Discussion Questions

1. What is the difference between time and space?

2. How does Leibniz's view of space compare with Kant's?

3. Are there any synthetic a priori truths?

CHAPTER 19

Kant: The Analytic of Concepts

In the Transcendental Analytic, Kant investigates the a priori contribution of the understanding to experience: the categories. In order to clarify his aims in the Analytic, Kant distinguishes between two branches of logic (the science of the rules for understanding). General logic consists of analytic truths, which are rules for logical consistency without which no thought is possible; it deals with the logical form of all thought and is abstracted from the content of all knowledge. Transcendental logic deals with the rules for the pure thought of an object—the a priori characteristics that belong of necessity to an object of experience. The word *transcendental* indicates that this branch of logic is concerned with the conditions and possibility of a priori knowledge of objects, as defined by the pure categories of the understanding.

Transcendental logic is divided into two parts: the Analytic and the Dialectic. The Dialectic, which contains Kant's attack on Rationalistic metaphysics, is the subject of Chapter 21. The Analytic itself has three main subsections: the Metaphysical Deduction, the Transcendental Deduction, and the Principles. In the Metaphysical Deduction, Kant tries to isolate candidates for the status of a priori categories; in the Transcendental Deduction, he argues that the categories are necessary for experience; in the Principles, Kant concentrates on particular categories, and how they find application in experience. The Analytic of Principles is the subject of Chapter 20.

Before looking at the Metaphysical and Transcendental Deductions in this chapter, we shall examine Kant's views on concepts in general, and on the categories in particular.

Concepts

Kant breaks with earlier definitions of concepts in not assimilating concepts and intuitions. This allows him to improve on earlier accounts of what concepts are. Kant regards the understanding in terms of our capacity to make judgments and classifications. He identifies the possession of concepts with the capacity to make judgments of a certain kind. To have a concept is to have a rule-governed ability. This view of concepts has three important consequences:

1. It avoids the problems inherent in treating concepts as mental images. If, as the Empiricists tend to assume, to have a concept of an F is to contemplate a mental image of an F, then we still have to explain how the person recognizes his mental image as being one of an F. To be able to recognize the image of an F as such presupposes that one already has a concept of an F; therefore, merely contemplating it cannot constitute having a concept of an F. This is one of the problems inherent in the Empiricist view of concepts: it presupposes what it intends to explain. Regarding the possession of concepts as practical abilities overcomes this. It also overcomes the problem of general and abstract concepts—concepts that are not easily regarded as images, such as the concept of infinity, a square root, a cause, or the like. Kant recognizes that there can be no image equivalent to such concepts.

2. Kant's view of concepts also avoids the dichotomy of thinking that concepts either must be acquired by abstraction from experience or must be innate. If to have a concept is to have a practical ability to make certain judgments and classifications, we can say that concepts can be learned in the same way one learns and acquires other practical skills. We can avoid the view that concepts either are acquired by abstraction or are innate. In fact, it is difficult to see how concepts could be acquired by abstraction; in order to define what all dogs have in common that distinguishes them from, for instance, cats, it is surely necessary to have some prior concept of a dog. It is thus difficult to see how one could ever acquire such a concept by selective attention or abstraction. If to have a concept is to have an ability to classify and recognize, we do not acquire such abilities through abstraction but learn them through corrected performance. Kant himself does not explicitly make these points; in fact, he believes that empirical concepts are acquired through abstraction. However, he does come close when, for instance, in A133–35 he emphasizes that concepts involve practical skills. Furthermore, he never says that a priori concepts are innate. It is important to remember these points when looking back to the views of the Empiricists (see, for instance, Chapter 12 on Locke).

3. The strength of Kant's view of concepts is apparent when he elucidates them in terms of the function they perform. For example, he says that the concept of an object prevents our modes of knowledge from being haphazard. His view allows him to see that certain concepts have a special status. Concepts are used to make judgments, but judgments must have a certain form; they must be catego-

rical, hypothetical, or something else. The concepts that define the form of judgment must be necessary if one is to use other concepts. Kant is able to classify such concepts by classifying the forms of judgment. This is the basis for the way in which he isolates the categories in the Metaphysical Deduction. Ordinary empirical concepts form the content of our judgments. The categories, on the other hand, relate to the form rather than to the content of our judgment. Categories provide the form for organizing the content of experience and judgment, rather than being part of their content.

The Metaphysical Deduction

The Metaphysical Deduction of "the clue to discovery of all pure concepts of the understanding" is an obscure passage of the *Critique*. Kant's aim is to isolate the categories and find some way of listing them. His intention is not to argue that the categories are necessary for experience; he does that later in the Transcendental Deduction. In the Metaphysical Deduction, Kant intends to list the a priori forms of the understanding, which he will later show are necessary for experience; such a list should be made according to some principle. Kant points out that the only use the understanding can have for concepts is to make judgments by means of them. He argues that certain concepts are more basic than others, and furthermore he argues that these basic concepts can be identified by means of the forms of judgment. Thus, by isolating the forms of judgment, we can list these basic concepts, which will later be shown to be categories necessary for experience.

Certain concepts are more basic than others for Kant, because they relate to the forms rather than to the content of our judgments. For instance, the concept of a property of a thing is more basic than the concept of red. This is because the concept of an object's property forms part of the framework for our ordinary judgments, and more simple concepts, like red, depend in part on this framework for their meaning. The more basic concepts can be isolated by listing the forms of judgment. Notice that Kant is not yet arguing that these basic concepts are necessary for experience; he is simply arguing that the forms of judgment will provide a complete list of the categories, if there are any categories. Clearly Kant believes that there is a parallel between the forms of judgment and the categories. The main function of the categories is to organize the manifold intuitions into experience by the process of synthesis. This organization of synthesis is akin to judgment, and therefore the logical forms of judgment provide a guide to the categories.

The Transcendental Deduction

To deduce the categories is to offer a justification for them—to show that we are entitled to use them. Since the categories are a priori, we cannot deduce them empirically by showing how they are acquired from experience; a transcendental deduction is required. To answer Empiricist philosophers such as Hume and Locke, who deny the possibility of a priori concepts, Kant argues that the categories are necessary to facilitate experience, and that all objects must be thought of as conforming to the categories.

The main argument of the Transcendental Deduction may be summarized as follows:

1.   I have experiences.

2.   All my experiences belong to the same single consciousness.

For instance, my experience of a ten-word sentence is not at all the same as ten separate consciousnesses each aware of one word.

3.   In order for my experiences to belong to one consciousness, it must be possible for me to think of those experiences as mine.

Kant calls the requirement that I should be able to think of my experiences as mine "the transcendental unity of apperception." He says that the possibility of "I think" must accompany all my experiences; otherwise, such experience "means nothing to me" or "is less than a dream." This transcendental unity of apperception is not an awareness of a mental self; it is a formal condition of experience that one should be able to think of one's experience as one's own. Without this condition, experience could not belong to a unified consciousness, and experience would be impossible. This unity of consciousness, as defined by the transcendental unity of apperception, is necessary for all awareness, including ordinary self-consciousness and introspection. Ordinary empirical self-consciousness and introspection about one's experience already presuppose that it is oneself having the experience; and since they already presuppose the unity of consciousness, they cannot explain it.

4.   The ability to think of my experiences as "mine" requires the capacity to make judgments, which have various logical forms.

It is an analytic truth that all my experiences are mine. But to be able to point this out, to be able to think of one's experiences as such, requires a certain conceptual complexity in experience. Kant says that the ability to think of my experiences as mine necessitates synthesis. His point is that my experiences are not an aggregate or association of unconnected items: as the thoughts and experiences of one's mind, they must be interconnected or bound together in one mind. As we shall see later, this binding element is the categories. For experience to be possible, it must belong to a unitary consciousness. This unity of consciousness requires the possibility of thinking of one's experiences as such, and this requires that experience should be rule-governed and connected by categories.

5. The categories are the logical forms of judgment; and since these forms are necessary for experience, so are the categories.

The categories are necessary for the possibility of experience, and all experience must be subject to the categories; otherwise, experience could not be subject to the transcendental unity of apperception. And without such unity, experience is impossible. Since all experience requires the categories, these must be a priori and cannot be derived from experience.

The above interpretation of Kant's argument is stated as a piece of conceptual analysis of the requirements of experience. However, Kant himself states his argument in a psychological idiom, as if he were describing a psychological process. (For reasons we shall return to later, this cannot be Kant's true intention.) He states the argument in the following way (see B143):

1. The manifold intuitions must belong to one consciousness if they are to constitute experience.

2. This means that they must be subject to the transcendental unity of apperception: it must be possible for me to think of them as mine.

3. This requires that the manifold intuitions be synthesized by the understanding. To be subject to the transcendental unity of apperception, intuitions must be united in one consciousness by the synthesis of the understanding.

4. This synthesis is governed by the logical forms of judgment, or the categories.

5. Therefore, the manifold intuitions must be subject to the categories, in order for experience to be possible.

In brief, Kant argues in the Transcendental Deduction that all experience and knowledge must be subject to the Transcendental Unity of Apperception, because otherwise a person's experiences could not belong to one single consciousness. Kant also argues that this unity in experience would be impossible if experience did not conform to the categories. Therefore, he concludes that all experience must conform to the categories and that a priori concepts are possible.

The Transcendental Unity of Apperception

This bold argument depends on the difficult notion of the Transcendental Unity of Apperception, by which Kant means a formal unity of consciousness. Kant's idea can be illustrated with an analogy. Suppose that you hear 20 notes played in sequence that constitute a tune. Twenty separate experiences each of one note, each in a separate consciousness, do not constitute the experience of a tune. So your experience of tune presupposes that your experience of each of the notes belongs to the same consciousness. Kant thinks that all experience must have such unity of consciousness, and furthermore that this unity of consciousness would be impossible if one could not think, "This is my experience." In other words, Kant believes that experience must provide room for the thought of experience itself. In order for my experience to belong to one consciousness, I must be able to think of my experience as mine. This is the crucial step in the argument, because the ability to think of my experiences as mine requires judgment and (hence) the categories. This crucial step in the argument can be challenged: it means that we cannot say both that animals do have experience and that they do not have the ability to think of their experiences as belonging to them. Arguably, animals do have experience and do not have a sense of themselves as owning their own mental states. This contradicts Kant's claim that consciousness requires the possibility of self-consciousness. In defense of Kant, however, it can be argued that we cannot think or conceive of what it is like to have such experience. As soon as we try to imagine what it is like to have the experience of an animal that is not capable of being self-conscious, we must implicitly ascribe self-consciousness to the animal, because we must imagine what it is like for it to have the experience. To imagine what an experience is like is to reflect upon that experience as an experience. Therefore, it is difficult to conceive of what it is like to lack self-consciousness; and in this sense, Kant does set a limit to what we can conceive of as an experience.

It is important to remember that Kant's notion of the Transcendental Unity of Apperception is simply the ability to think "This is my experience." It is not equivalent to ordinary self-consciousness and introspection. It is neither knowledge of the self as empirical object nor knowledge of the self as noumenon. (Kant argues against Descartes's notion of mental substance later, in the Paralogisms.) Kant thinks that knowledge of the self as noumenon is impossible. Ordinary empirical knowledge of ourselves, like knowledge of anything else, already presupposes the Transcendental Unity of Apperception and therefore cannot be equivalent to it.

Objectivity and Experience

Kant's main argument in the Transcendental Deduction seeks to show that the Transcendental Unity of Apperception (and hence the categories) constitutes a necessary condition of experience. However, Kant also argues that experience must be of an objective world, consisting of things that exist independently of our perception of them. He thinks that the idea of an object that exists independently of our perception is a necessary condition of experience.

Kant calls the pure idea of an object "the Transcendental Object = X." He says that this idea prevents our modes of knowledge from being arbitrary (A104). He means that, when we ascribe different representations to the same object, we assert a unity among those representations. For example, we do not see red and feel heat, but we judge that the red object before us is hot. We judge that the redness and the heat are representations of an object, and this concept of an object is a focus around which these and other possible representations are united. The notion of an object gives experience a certain order and coherence, without which appearances would "crowd in upon the soul" and could not constitute experience. Because of the notion of an object, experience is rule-governed and ordered, rather than haphazard. For example, our experience at different times and through the various senses can be referred to the same object, as when we look at and touch an object from different angles. Kant claims this rule-governed unity is necessary for experience.

When we judge that the red object before us is hot, the objectivity of the judgment is expressed by the copula "is." The judgment asserts that the object is red no matter what the state of the subject is (B142). When we judge that an object is circular, we judge that it really is circular, even if it appears to be oval from some angles. In other words, the judgment is objective.

Kant asserts that the unity in experience provided by its objectivity features the same unity required for the "I think" to accompany all our experiences (A105). This is why he says that objectivity is a necessary condition of experience. Objectivity and the Transcendental Unity of Apperception are two sides of the same unity. Both are required for experience, and both require the categories. Kant develops this theme with regard to the category of causation in the Analogies. There he argues that, without the category of cause, experience could not be of an objective world; consequently, there could be no Transcendental Unity of Apperception and hence no experience.

There are several important points to note about the notion of Transcendental Object = X. First, Kant denies Berkeley's claim that objects are collections of ideas when he asserts that experience must be of objects that exist independently of our perceptions of them (see B142, B276, and A820). He also rejects the Lockean thesis that objects exist behind a veil of perception because, unlike the Empiricists, Kant rejects the claim that we can only know our own ideas directly. Indeed, in the Refutation of Idealism, he argues that we are directly aware of the existence of outer objects (B277). Second, Kant agrees with Hume that the notion of an object that exists independently of our perceptions of it cannot be acquired from experience by abstraction. Like Hume, Kant denies that the notion of an object is an empirical concept. But unlike Hume, Kant also denies that our use of this notion is unjustifiable; he argues that it is an a priori formal concept and a presupposition of experience itself. He also denies that the necessary unity of experience can be achieved through the contingent association of ideas (B142). Third, Kant distinguishes the idea of the Transcendental Object = X from the idea of a noumenon (see A253). The notion of noumena (or things as they are in themselves) should be contrasted with phenomena (or things in space and time). Kant claims that we directly perceive phenomena and that we cannot know noumena. He says that the notion of noumena is an empty limiting concept. On the other hand, the pure notion of the Transcendental Object = X is not empty but provides a formal unity in experience that enables our experience to be of an objective world.

Recently some philosophers have tried to follow Kant by arguing that experience must involve experience of an objective world, or that our experience must include awareness of objects that exist independently of our perceptions of them. The argument can be summarized as follows:

1. Experience requires the possibility of the thought of experience itself. A person who is having an experience must be able to think "I am having this experience."

2. In order to be able to have the thought "I am having this experience," I must be able to distinguish how things seem to be (through the lens of my experience) from how things really are. I must be able to distinguish the experience ascribable to me from the objective world, which is distinct and independent of my experience.

3. The thought of experience itself requires the concept of something distinct from experience.

Noumenal Psychology

Many passages in the Transcendental Deduction are presented in a pseudo-psychological idiom. Kant says, for example, that the intuitions we passively receive must be actively synthesized or combined by the understanding and are thereby united into one single consciousness. Such statements imply that synthesis is an act of the understanding, but this implication has serious difficulties. Synthesis cannot be an ordinary empirical event that occurs in the phenomenal world; therefore it must be thought of as a noumenal nontemporal act of the understanding. (Remember that all temporal events either are merely phenomenal or are transcendentally ideal, because time is the a priori form of inner intuition.) If synthesis is a noumenal act of the noumenal understanding, this contradicts Kant's claim that we cannot talk positively about noumena. In brief, insofar as the Transcendental Deduction involves psychological claims, these cannot be ordinary empirical psychological claims, but must be assertions about the psychology of the noumenal self. But on Kant's own admission, noumenal psychology should be impossible. These and other problems relating to Transcendental Idealism will be dealt with in Chapter 20.

Conclusion

In many ways the Transcendental Deduction is the heart of the *Critique*. Therefore, it is appropriate to review some of the major themes of the Deduction and to inspect how Kant tries to break away from both the Empiricist and Rationalist philosophies.

At the beginning of the chapter, we saw the novelty of Kant's theory of concepts. Because he thinks of concepts as rules, he is able to break away from the Empiricist tendency to view concepts as images. This enables Kant to argue for a priori or nonempirical concepts and avoid Hume's scepticism.

The categories or nonempirical concepts govern and unify our experience. They enable Kant to escape the Empiricist view of experience as a collection of discrete impressions. He argues that an atomist view of experience is impossible because experience must have a conceptual element. Experience must have a unity and coherence. For this reason, Kant rejects the idea of passively received sense data. Kant says that intuitions without concepts are blind. They are also impossible, because they cannot be subject to the Transcendental Unity of Apperception.

Kant also rejects the view that we are only directly aware of our own ideas. Instead, he argues that we directly perceive objects in space and time, which exist whether we perceive them or not. In this way, he differs fundamentally from the Empiricists and from Descartes.

Study Questions

1. How does Kant distinguish between an intuition and a concept?

2. What are categories?

3. What is the aim of the Metaphysical Deduction? How does it achieve that aim?

4. What is the aim of the Transcendental Deduction?

5. What is the Transcendental Unity of Apperception?

6. Explain Kant's notion of Transcendental Object $= X$.

7. What reasons does Kant have for thinking that objectivity is a necessary condition of experience?

8. Is the Transcendental Unity of Apperception the same as the idea of a noumenal self? Is the Transcendental Object $= X$ the same as the idea of a noumenon?

Discussion Questions

1. Does experience require the thought of experience itself?

2. Why does Kant think that intuitions without concepts are blind?

3. Is Kant right to claim that experience must include a direct perception of objects that exist independently of our perception of them?

4. Why does Kant reject the claim that we can only perceive our own ideas?

Kant: The Analytic of Principles

Kant uses the argument of the Metaphysical Deduction to isolate the forms of judgment, or to list the categories. In the Transcendental Deduction, Kant argues that categories are necessary for experience, but he does not argue that the particular categories listed in the Metaphysical Deduction are necessary. In the Principles, Kant examines individually the particular categories, like those of causation and substance, and shows how they make experience possible. Kant thinks that, when the categories are applied to temporal experience, they yield synthetic a priori principles.

Before he argues that particular principles are necessary for experience, Kant seeks to show that the categories can be applied to temporal experience; he attempts to do this in the Schematism.

The Schematism

In this section, Kant argues that the categories must be schematized, or given a temporal interpretation, so that they can be applied to experience. One of the difficulties of the Schematism is to know exactly what problem Kant is trying to solve here. His aim is obscure: why does Kant think that the categories have to be schematized?

The categories have their seat a priori in the understanding. Unlike empirical concepts, categories are not acquired from experience. They are derived from the forms of judgment rather than from the content of judgment. Kant believes that principles like "Every event must have a cause" are synthetic a priori and thus are quite unlike general empirical statements—for example, "Every raven is black." Unlike synthetic a priori principles, general empirical statements are neither necessarily nor universally true. Kant recognizes that the idea of synthetic a priori truth is problematic and likely to be challenged by Empiricist philosophers. He anticipates that Empiricists will argue that the categories have no application to experience. Thus, the Schematism is designed to answer such an argument.

Kant says that empirical concepts are homogeneous with appearances, because they contain a sensory element. In other words, it is part of the concept of a dog that a dog should look a certain way: a dog is a dog partly because of the way it appears. On the other hand, the categories are not homogeneous with appearances, because they do not contain a sensory component. It is not part of the concept of a cause that the cause should look a certain way. The problem of the schematism is that we cannot apply the categories on the basis of how things appear. Because of their purity, or because they lack a sensory component, the categories may not be applicable to experience. In the schematism Kant attempts to reply to this argument.

According to Kant, time is the mediator between pure categories and appearances. Because time is the a priori form of sensibility, it is both a priori and sensible. Thus Kant argues that the categories apply to experience only insofar as they determine the necessary structure of our consciousness of time. The categories have legitimate empirical application in relation to time. Although this answer seems vague, it becomes clearer when we consider the particular categories of cause and substance.

Even though we have overcome the difficulty regarding the aim of the Schematism, some further points about it need to be made:

1.   Kant implies that only the categories need to be schematized, because there is no problem about the application of empirical concepts to experience. However, he fails to realize that some empirical concepts (for example, the concepts of entropy and of a republic) do not have a sensory component—that is, do not apply to things because of the way they appear. This suggests, contrary to Kant's implication, that some empirical concepts need to be schematized.

2.   Another way of expressing the same criticism of Kant is to say that he accepts an Empiricist view of all empirical concepts, even though he rejects Empiricism with regard to the categories. Concerning the categories, he rejects the assumption that a concept must apply to an observable feature of experience if it is to have meaning. But he accepts this assumption with respect to all empirical concepts.

3.   In the Schematism, Kant rejects the idea that concepts are images. He says that the schema for an empirical concept is a rule that enables us to produce an image but is not itself an image. This claim enables Kant to free himself from the problems associated with Locke's theory of abstract ideas, as presented by Berkeley.

The First Analogy

For Kant, the category of substance represents the absolutely permanent. In the first analogy, Kant tries to prove that "in all change of appearances, substance is permanent; its quantum in nature is neither increased nor decreased." In other words, Kant seeks to prove that there can be no change in the amount of substance that exists and that all changes are merely a transformation of substance. It would be incorrect to say that Kant is trying to prove the Principle of Conservation of Matter, since he does not argue that substance is matter. How does Kant argue for the principle that something permanent (namely, substance) persists through all change, and that the quantity of this substance cannot vary?

One common interpretation of Kant's argument traces the following steps:

1. Time itself cannot be perceived, and time must be represented in the empirical world. Kant's point here is that we cannot objectively date events just by looking at them, because time cannot be perceived. Thus, there must be something that represents time or enables us to date events objectively.

2. We can only give events an objective position in time in relation to regular changes—for instance, in relation to the regular movements of the sun.

3. We can only identify changes as regular against a background of permanence. Therefore, without a background of permanent objects, it would be impossible to date events objectively.

4. If the objective dating of events were impossible, it would also be impossible to distinguish the subjective time order of our perceptions from the objective order of events; and without the subjective/objective distinction, experience could not be subject to the Transcendental Unity of Apperception.

Strawson claims that the preceding argument is valid and comes close to representing Kant's thought.[72] However, it proves much less than Kant wants to prove. It only shows the need for a relatively permanent background of enduring objects; it does not show the need for an absolutely permanent substance. How then does Kant think he has proved the necessity for an absolutely permanent substance? There are two possible explanations, but both involve a confusion.

First, Kant says an awareness of change requires something that persists through that change, and he argues that the transitory is only a mode of the permanent. This suggests a confusion of the following two assertions:

1. Through every change, there is something permanent.

2. There is one thing that is permanent through all changes.

In other words, Kant confuses the claim that each change requires the existence of something permanent (although not necessarily the same permanent) with the stronger claim that one thing remains permanent through all changes—something absolutely permanent.

Second, Kant claims that we cannot perceive time and that time needs to be represented. He also says that time does not change. Kant could argue that, because time is unchanging, it needs to be represented by something unchanging or absolutely permanent. However, the sentence "Time does not change" is problematic. Things change with respect to time, and therefore it appears illegitimate to assert of time itself that it does or does not change. With respect to what does time itself change or not change?

When Kant passes from the claim that there must be a relatively permanent background against which we can describe change to the conclusion that there must be something absolutely permanent, he commits one of the two fallacies contained in the two preceding explanations.

Another Argument

Kant seems to have another argument for the absolutely permanent. At A186, Kant says that the creation of new substances would make the unity of time impossible. The idea behind this claim is that permanent substance represents the unity of time. By "the unity of time," Kant means that an event occurring at any time has a determinate temporary relation to any other possible event. If a new substance could be created, the unity of time would be impossible, and there would instead be two unrelated time sequences. In addition, without the unity of time, there could be no unity of experience.

Kant's argument can be rephrased as follows:

1. If experience is to be subject to the Transcendental Unity of Apperception, there can be only one time sequence; that is, time must be a unity.

2. This one time sequence is represented by the absolutely permanent. All change must be considered as the alteration of this substance. No change can be considered as the creation or destruction of substance, because a change in the quantity of substance would destroy the unity of time. In other words, the concept of a change in the quantity of substance can have no application in experience, and in this sense the universe is a closed system.

Substance

There are three significant features of Kant's notion of substance in the first analogy:

1.   The unschematized category "substance" can only be thought of as a subject and never as a predicate of something else. How does this definition relate to the definition of the schema substance as the absolutely permanent? Kant says that the substance cannot be created or destroyed. Hence, all change must be conceived of as an alteration of the properties of the permanent substance. For Kant, things that can be destroyed or created, like ordinary objects, cannot be substances and must be reducible to properties of the permanent. In this respect, Kant's notion of substance is similar to Spinoza's.

2.   Sometimes Kant talks of substances in the plural, rather than of substance in the singular. This is puzzling and requires explanation. If the quantity of the one substance cannot be reduced or increased and if we divide the one substance into equal units, then the number of substances cannot be increased or decreased.

3.   Locke says that substance is that in which all properties inhere and, therefore, that substance cannot be reduced to a set of properties. However, Locke also asserts that all our concepts are derived from our experience of simple sensible properties. This makes it impossible for Locke to explain how we could ever acquire the concept of substance. Kant avoids this problem because, for him, the notion of substance is not empirical but a priori.

Causation

Hume rejects the claim that the causal axiom "All events must have a cause" is an analytic truth. In this respect Kant agrees with Hume, but unlike Hume he argues that the causal principle is still a necessary truth because it is synthetic a priori. Hume also challenges the notion of a cause on the ground that such an idea could not be derived from impressions. Kant rejects the claim that all concepts are derived from impressions; for Kant, categories, like the notion of cause, are nonempirical. In the second analogy, Kant defends the notion of causation against Hume's scepticism. By arguing that the notion of causation is a necessary condition of experience, he tries to vindicate its a priori or nonempirical status and defend the claim that an uncaused event is impossible (although not analytically impossible). Kant's aims in the second analogy are relatively clear, but the exact nature of his argument is not.

A Necessary Order

The category of cause, like all the categories, plays a twofold role: first, it provides the necessary unity of consciousness; second, it gives our experience objectivity features. For Kant, these are two sides of the same unity—a unity that is necessary for experience.

Kant notes that we distinguish between the temporal sequence of our perceptions and the objective temporal sequence of events. Without this distinction, experience could not be of an objective world and hence experience would be impossible. Kant also points out that all of our perceptions are successive, and he asks: how can successive experiences be perceptions of both objective alterations and objectively coexistent objects? What character of our experience enables us to count perceptions (which always succeed each other) as the perceptions of objects (which do not)? Kant answers these questions in terms of whether our perceptions lack or possess the feature of order indifference. When I perceive the coexistent parts of a house, my experiences could have occurred in the opposite order; thus, they possess the feature of order indifference. But when I perceive an objective alteration, like the movement of a boat downstream, my perceptions lack this feature of order indifference; my perceptions could not have occurred in a different order. Kant claims that the concept of an objective alteration depends on use of the idea of a necessary order.

According to Strawson, Kant passes from the following claim (1) to the subsequent conclusion (2):

1. When we perceive an objective alteration, our perceptions necessarily have a certain order.

2. An objective change has a necessary order, or it is causally determined.

This shift from 1 to 2 involves two fallacies. First, claim 1 says that, when we perceive an objective alteration $A \rightarrow B$, it is logically necessary that our perception of A precede our perception of B. But claim 2 asserts that the change from A to B is causally necessary. Therefore, passing from claim 1 to conclusion 2 involves changing the sense of the word *necessary*. In addition, claim 1 addresses the order of our perceptions, but claim 2 concerns the order of objective events. So Kant cannot argue from his claim about the necessary order of our perceptions to the truth of the causal axiom.

The Second Analogy

Another argument is offered in the second analogy. Kant asks what conditions are necessary in order for a change in our perceptions to be the perception of an objective change. Clearly, the change in the perceptions cannot be due solely to a change in the observer's position; they must be due to a change in the object. Therefore, we must be able to tell in principle whether the relative position of the object has or has not changed. To be able to determine this, we must be able to apply criteria that allow us to reidentify objects. This means that objects cannot change out of all recognition, because if they did, it would be impossible for us to tell which objects have retained their position and which have altered their relative position. Therefore, changes in objects must be regular, or subject to causal laws. If they were not, we could not reidentify objects following changes in them, and we could not identify objective alterations.

This argument establishes the need for regularity of changes. If we assume that the regularity must be causal, the argument shows that most events should have a cause. The argument fails, however, to prove the principle of the second analogy—that every event must have a cause.

The Third Analogy

In the third analogy, Kant claims that objects must interact causally in order to coexist in space. As we have already seen, Kant thinks that the unity of the natural world is the counterpart of the necessary unity of consciousness. The unity of the natural world requires the unity of space and time. Space and time would be a disunity if any part of space or time did not have a determinate spatial or temporal relation to every other part of space or time. In the third analogy, Kant argues that, since space and time cannot be perceived, their unity must be known through the unity of their contents. In other words, the unity of space and time must be represented by the causal interaction of objects.

Kant claims in the third analogy that objects not causally related to other objects could not be assigned a definite date. Such objects could not belong to the same temporal sequence as other objects. An unrelated object could not be simultaneous with other objects, because it could not be part of a single time sequence. What Kant has in mind is not difficult to grasp. When we see a distant star explode, we can determine precisely when this happened only because we can deduce details about how the star stands in causal relation to other objects on earth and our own perception. Only because the star causally interacts with other objects can we give it a definite date.

Refutation of Idealism

In the Refutation of Idealism, Kant argues that we are directly aware of external objects, which exist independently of our perceptions of them. In so doing, Kant distances himself from earlier philosophers who held that we can only ever be directly aware of our own ideas. Kant says that he has turned the game played by idealists against itself. This can be explained as follows. Idealism assumes that our knowledge of our own inner experiences is more certain than any belief we could have about the external world. Kant rejects the heart of this assumption by arguing that we can only be aware of our own experiences if we are directly aware of external objects. The existence and knowledge of things outside me is necessary for my awareness of my own experience. Kant tries to bury Descartes's assumption that the experiences of a solipsistic mind would be indistinguishable from those of a mind that perceived objects. Kant rejects the assumption central to the Cogito that I can have an immediate and certain knowledge of my ideas. His argument is as follows:

1. I am conscious of my own existence in time. In other words, I know statements of the form: "I am in state P at time t."

2. All time perceptions require something permanent in perception. By this, Kant means that time determinations are only possible in relation to something permanent.

3. This permanent thing is either a perceptual experience or one or more external objects that are not perceptions.

4. The permanent in perception cannot be a perceptual experience.

5. Therefore, it must be outer objects.

The crux of Kant's argument is premise 2. Kant's point is that we can only date an inner state in relation to a framework of outer things that are relatively permanent. Kant is not arguing here for the notion of an absolutely permanent substance, as he did in the first analogy. Premise 4 assumes that even a relatively permanent perception itself requires an objective time position, and thus requires a permanent thing that is distinct from it. In other words, we cannot assign a determinate date to an experience or inner state by appeal to further inner states.

Transcendental Idealism

In the Refutation of Idealism, Kant argues against both problematic and dogmatic idealism. Problematic idealism asserts that we have no immediate knowledge of objects in space, but only of our own ideas. It says that, at best, the existence of objects can only be inferred as the cause of our ideas. This type of view was held by Descartes and is inherent in the philosophy of Locke. It leads to the position that the existence of external objects is dubious. Dogmatic idealism is the view held by Berkeley that objects are collections of ideas and have no existence outside the mind. Whereas problematic idealism calls into question the existence of the external world, dogmatic idealism denies its existence.

But can Kant distinguish his own transcendental idealism from these other types of idealism, especially the dogmatic idealism of Berkeley? The main differences between Kant's and Berkeley's idealism are that Kant asserts while Berkeley denies that objects exist independently of our perceptions and that Berkeley asserts while Kant denies that we can only perceive our own ideas. This is why Kant calls himself an Empirical Realist; he thinks that spatio-temporal objects are empirically real. However, he also thinks that they are transcendentally ideal, and we must examine what he means by this.

Transcendental idealism involves the distinction between phenomena and noumena and the assertion that things in space and time are phenomena and not noumena. Transcendental idealism has at least two important roles in the Analytic:

1. It explains how we can know a priori that the world actually conforms to the a priori forms of experience (that is, how we can know that the world consists

of spatio-temporal objects, given that our experience must have these features). It is designed to solve what we have called the application problem.

2. It prescribes the limits of knowledge. Kant claims that space and time only apply to phenomena and not to noumena. Thus, noumena are nonspatial and nontemporal. Kant also claims that all concepts, including the categories, only have meaning in relation to possible experience and the objects of possible experience—that is, to phenomena and not to noumena. This claim is important for Kant's attack on transcendental metaphysics in the Dialectic.

To understand Kant's transcendental idealism, we must understand the nature of the phenomena/noumena distinction and, thus, the claim that ordinary empirical objects are phenomena and not noumena.

Phenomena and Noumena

Many writers on Kant explain the phenomena/noumena distinction and transcendental idealism in one of two ways. The first way makes Kant's view seem very close to Berkeley's. According to this interpretation, noumena are special nontemporal, nonspatial objects about which we can know nothing, and phenomena are merely constructions from experience. In other words, we construct phenomena by imposing the a priori forms of our experience (space, time and the categories) upon the noumenal world. We, as nontemporal beings, construct the phenomenal world when we synthesize the raw data of experience to produce experience of spatio-temporal objects. These objects are merely constructions out of our experience—unlike noumena, which exist unknown beyond the bounds of experience.

If this is Kant's view, it has many difficulties. Most obviously, Kant seems to be arguing on the one hand that we cannot have knowledge of noumena, while on the other hand he seems to be advancing such knowledge, as when he makes claims about synthesis and the faculties of sensibility and understanding. Furthermore, this reading of Kant's view seems very similar to Berkeley's claim that objects are merely collections of ideas, and it seems to inherit all the problems associated with Berkeley's position. Third, this interpretation of Kant's view seems to contradict his own claims that objects in space and time exist independently of us—that is, are objective.

The other interpretation of the phenomena/noumena distinction is less extravagant and more plausible. Exponents of this interpretation claim that Kant does not regard noumena as nonspatial, nontemporal objects. The concept of a noumenon is not the concept of an object at all. The notion of a noumenon merely serves to draw our attention to the limits of human knowledge and to the impossibility of going beyond those limits. According to this view, Kant is saying that all objects are the spatio-temporal objects, which we can experience. When Kant calls these objects "phenomena," he is simply emphasizing that, when we talk about the world, we can only talk about the objects of possible experience and, therefore, that we must regard the world and all objects as necessarily conforming to the a priori forms of our experience (space, time, and the categories). According to this weaker and much more acceptable form of transcendental idealism, Kant does not intend the phenomena/noumena distinction as an ontological distinction between two types of existents: noumenal and phenomenal objects. This is not Kant's intention, because he does not regard noumena as objects.

Having briefly examined the two major interpretations of transcendental idealism, we must ask which of these two interpretations is the more accurate reflection of Kant's views in the *Critique*. Unfortunately, we can find many passages to support each interpretation. In favor of the first and stronger version of transcendental idealism, we can find Kant claiming: "objects are nothing but representations"(A371); space and time are "in us"; "what we call outer objects are nothing but mere representations" (A30). Moreover, whenever Kant adopts a psychological idiom to express his views, this entails the stronger interpretation of transcendental idealism. For example, this occurs whenever Kant describes synthesis as an act of the understanding or whenever he characterizes the faculties of understanding and sensibility as cooperating to produce experience. The stronger interpretation is required in such cases because the faculties and synthesis cannot be features of the spatio-temporal world. Hence, they must be ascribed to the noumenal world, and we must think of noumena as nonspatial and nontemporal objects.

In favor of the weaker interpretation, we have Kant's claims that the notion of a noumenon is not the concept of any kind of object and is simply an empty limiting concept (A255–57). We also have Kant's claims that spatio-temporal objects exist independent of our perceptions of them, which implies that, after all, they are not literally representations.

Since we can find plenty of passages to support either of the two interpretations, it might be fair to conclude that Kant would prefer to propound the weaker form of transcendental idealism, but does not always state this view clearly, and sometimes ends up asserting a much stronger doctrine.

Study Questions

1. What is Kant's aim in the Schematism?

2. How do the aims of the Metaphysical Deduction, the Transcendental Deduction, the Schematism, and the Analogies differ?

3. What is the argument of the first analogy?

4. "A substance is that which can only be thought of as a subject and never as a predicate of something else." How does this traditional definition of substance relate to Kant's claim that substance is the absolutely permanent?

5. What are the similarities and differences between Hume's and Kant's views of causation?

6. What is Kant's argument for the claim that an uncaused event is impossible?

7. How does Kant argue in the Refutation of Idealism against Descartes's Method of Doubt?

8. How is Kant's transcendental idealism supposed to differ from both problematic and dogmatic idealism?

Discussion Questions

1. How can Kant distinguish between phenomena and noumena, without denying that objects in space and time are objective?

2. How does Kant's view of causation compare with Hume's, Locke's, and Spinoza's?

3. Does Kant succeed in explaining how synthetic a priori truths are possible?

CHAPTER 21

Kant: The Transcendental Dialectic

The Analytic and the Aesthetic explain how a priori knowledge of the world is possible. In the Dialectic, Kant attacks the speculative metaphysics of philosophers like Descartes, Spinoza, and Leibniz, who claim to have a priori knowledge of the soul, God, and the limits of the universe. Kant argues that such knowledge is impossible. It is impossible to have knowledge that transcends the bounds of possible experience, because categories and concepts only have meaning in relation to possible experience: "Concepts without intuitions are empty."

The Dialectic has a negative side and a positive side. The negative side is more than just an attack on the speculative metaphysics of the Rationalists. Kant also tries to diagnose the errors of such metaphysics, and in so doing he introduces a new faculty, reason, which makes inferences or reasons. According to Kant, reason searches for a complete explanation of everything and thus searches for the unconditioned—that which does not depend on any further condition. In seeking a complete explanation, reason is led inevitably to use ideas that have no application to possible experience. The ideas of pure reason overstep the limits of possible experience and thereby produce an illusion. Kant believes that this illusion continues to deceive us even after it has been exposed, because it is an inevitable product of reason.

Kant's positive aim in the Dialectic is to describe the proper function of reason. Briefly, the ideas of reason lay down heuristic maxims. The error is to suppose that these heuristic maxims constitute experience, like the Principles, and give us a priori knowledge of the world.

Paralogisms

In the Paralogisms, Kant attacks "rational psychology," a pseudo-science of a priori knowledge about the soul built on the single proposition "I think." For example, from the "I think," Descartes tries to prove the existence of a simple, unitary, nonphysical substance, the soul. Kant claims that the "I think" is just the formal unity of consciousness. It is therefore, a necessary condition of experience and does not designate a special object. Kant says that Descartes mistakes this formal unity for the awareness of a substance, the soul. In opposition to Descartes, Kant argues that the "I think" cannot be experienced as an object, because every experience must already be subject to the "I think" or Transcendental Unity of Apperception. Kant agrees with Hume that we cannot find an abiding self in the flux of experience, because there is no impression of the self. However, according to Kant, the search for the self in experience is misguided, because any seeking must be done by the self, and hence what is sought is already presupposed in all experience and knowledge. Therefore, the self is neither an experience nor an item to be experienced. This is why Kant says that Descartes mistakes "the unity of experience for the experience of a unity,"[73] or in other words mistakes the unity for a soul. Descartes mistakenly takes the Transcendental Unity of Apperception, a formal unity of experience, to be an object—the soul or mind.

The First Paralogism: Substance

The word *paralogism* means fallacy, and the paralogisms are fallacious arguments in support of rational psychology. The first paralogism runs as follows:

1. Substance is a subject of predicates and is not a predicate of any other subject.

2. I, as a thinking or conscious being, am not a predicate of some other thing.

3. Therefore I am a substance.

Kant says that this argument rests on an empty notion of substance. The concept of a substance can only have meaningful application to objects of possible experience. The "I think" is not an object of possible experience, since it is a necessary condition of experience; consequently, in the preceding argument, the notion of a substance is misused, because it lacks empirical content. For this reason, to say that the I is a substance is to make an empty statement that misleads us with the pretense of an insight. Because the statement "the I is a substance" is without content, we cannot use this statement to prove the immortality of the soul or to distinguish the subject from external objects.

The Second and Third Paralogisms

The second paralogism concerns the claim that the soul is a simple. It asserts that a simple is a thing whose actions cannot be regarded as the actions of an aggregate, and that the soul is such a thing. For example, a body is not a simple, because the motion of a body can be regarded as the combined motion of its parts. On the other hand, the thoughts of a person cannot be regarded as the combined thoughts of an aggregate, because the thoughts of one person must belong to a single consciousness; therefore the soul is a simple. Kant rejects this argument on the ground that the transcendental unity of consciousness does not designate an object and, therefore, does not designate a simple. According to Kant, Descartes confuses the unity of consciousness with the richer idea of a simple soul. For Kant, the unity of consciousness is a necessary condition of all experience and cannot be an object of experience. But the notion of a simple has meaning only in application to the objects of possible experience, and therefore the claim that the soul is a simple is vacuous and without meaning. For this reason, Descartes cannot use this claim to try to establish his dualism.

As we saw in Chapter 3, Descartes uses the claim that the I must be a simple to show that the I or the self must be a nonmaterial and nonspatial substance distinct from the body. The claim that the soul is simple also has an important role to play in the philosophy of Leibniz. For Kant, the claim "the soul is simple" is empty, and on this ground he disputes that it can be a basis for a priori knowledge.

The third paralogism asserts that a person is that which is conscious of its numerical identity through time, and that the soul is such a thing. Kant replies that the claim that the soul is conscious of its numerical identity through time merely expresses the necessary unity of consciousness. This unity of consciousness is not an object we can experience, and the notion of numerical identity through time has meaning only in application to the objects of possible experience; hence, for Kant, the claim that the subject is numerically identical through time is empty and without meaning. In fact, at A363 Kant says that, even if there were soul substances, there could be no guarantee that a person might not consist of as many souls as he has experiences rather than of one soul. There can be no guarantee that a person has only one soul. Kant's point here is that the notion of an identical soul cannot work because it contains no criteria for identity, unlike the notion of a spatio-temporal object. My experience could inhere in 2,000 souls, but the experience would still be mine because it would remain subject to the Transcendental Unity of Apperception. As we saw in Chapter 11, Locke makes a claim similar to Kant's in his discussion of personal identity.

The basis of Kant's arguments in the Paralogisms is that rational psychologists inflate the "I think" to yield conclusions that do not follow. Kant says that the unity of consciousness (the "I think") is not an object of possible experience, and that the categories have meaning only in application to objects of possible experience. Therefore, we cannot meaningfully say that the I is a simple, numerically identical, nonmaterial substance. In this way, Kant tries to defuse the

Cartesian assumption that the "I" in "I think" has a purely inner reference to a mental substance. At B400 he says that the "I think" has no special designation. In other words, it does not refer to an object.

Kant is not denying that I can have empirical knowledge of myself. I can have knowledge of my own body, but this is like the ordinary knowledge we can have of any external object. I can also have knowledge of my own experiences, through introspection or inner sense, but this too is empirical rather than a priori knowledge. Furthermore, for Kant, unlike Descartes, introspection requires the immediate perception of external objects (see the Refutation of Idealism in Chapter 20). Since all forms of self-knowledge require the Transcendental Unity of Apperception, this unity itself does not constitute knowledge of the self.

The Antinomies

An antinomy consists of a thesis and an antithesis that assert contradictory propositions that can both be supported by equally valid proofs. The arguments for both the thesis and antithesis assume a certain view of reason and its demand on the world. When we accept this view of reason, we find ourselves entangled in the antinomy, with equal grounds to assert the thesis and its contradiction.

Kant advances four antinomies:

1. THESIS: The world has a beginning in time and limits in space.

   ANTITHESIS: The world has no beginning in time and no limits in space.

2. THESIS: Nothing exists in the world except simples or composites composed of simples.

   ANTITHESIS: There are no simples in the world.

3. THESIS: Natural events have free causes as well as ordinary natural causes.

   ANTITHESIS: All causation is natural, and there is no freedom in the world.

4. THESIS: There belongs to the world, either as its cause or as its part, an absolutely necessary being.

   ANTITHESIS: No absolutely necessary being exists either in or outside the world.

Kant claims that the four theses represent the assertions of dogmatism and the four antitheses represent the rejoinders of empiricism. However, it is more accurate to say that the theses represent the views of Leibniz and the antitheses the views of Clarke. For both the thesis and the antithesis of each antinomy, Kant claims there is a convincing and sound argument. In fact, however, few of the arguments are compelling.

Kant's general solution to each antinomy is to give up or reject the view of reason on which both sides of the antinomy are based. Kant claims that this original view of reason entails transcendental realism and that, once we adopt transcendental idealism, the antinomy is solved. He also claims that the details of the solution to the first two antinomies differ from the details of the solution to the last two. In the case of the first two, which he calls the mathematical antinomies, we must give up the assumption that the world exists in itself as a whole. Having rejected this assumption, we can see that both the thesis and the antithesis are false. For the first antinomy, the world is neither a finite nor an infinite given whole. For the second antinomy the world is neither finitely nor infinitely divisible.

The third and fourth antinomies are called the dynamical antinomies. Whereas in each of the mathematical antinomies Kant claims that both the thesis and the antithesis antinomies are false, in each of the dynamical antinomies he claims that the thesis and the antithesis are both true: the thesis is true of noumena, and the antithesis is true of phenomena only. For instance, in the third antinomy, Kant claims that the only causes we find in the natural or phenomenal world are natural causes. Everything in the phenomenal world is causally determined. Hence, the antithesis is true of the phenomenal world. On the other hand, free causes exist in the noumenal world only.

Kant's aims in the antinomies are to reveal why speculative metaphysics is so seductive and to uncover its error. He tries to advance beyond the claim that such metaphysics is empty by showing that it involves a contradiction, and in the process he provides an indirect proof of transcendental idealism. We shall concentrate our examination on the first and third antinomies.

The First Antinomy: Time

According to some commentators, Kant's argument for the thesis that the world has a beginning in time is as follows. If the world has no beginning, then up to the present moment an infinite number of seconds has elapsed. But a completed infinite series is impossible; therefore, an infinite number of seconds could not have elapsed. Hence the world must have a beginning in time. As the commentators point out, this argument begs the question.

The argument for the antithesis attempts to show that it is impossible for the world to have had a beginning. Before the first event, there existed nothing at all, and so there was nothing to explain why the world began when it did. Thus, the world cannot have had a beginning and must be infinite in time.

Time and Reason

Kant claims that the antinomies depend on a faulty view of reason (B452). He also says that this is why there is no antinomy concerning the future series of events and time itself. Kant says that we may think with entire indifference about whether the series of future events is infinite or not. This suggests that the series of past events generates an antinomy only because any event depends on and should be explained in terms of what happened before it. This suggests an alternative interpretation of the argument for the thesis concerning time.

Kant sums up the demand of reason as follows: if the conditioned is given, then the unconditioned is also given. In other words, reason demands a sufficient and complete and exhaustive explanation of an event, and thus it ultimately presupposes the existence of something that does not require explanation—that is, the unconditioned. The first antinomy regarding time is generated by reason through its implicit claim that the unconditioned must be either the whole infinite series of events or the first member of a finite series of events. However, the thesis argument shows that the unconditioned cannot be the whole infinite series of events, and the antithesis argument shows that it cannot be the first member of a finite series. In this way the antinomy is generated.

What alternative reading of the thesis argument can be given? Kant could argue that, since each member of an infinite series of events depends on an earlier member that itself needs explanation, the whole infinite series cannot be a complete explanation of any single event. The idea behind this argument can be illustrated with an analogy. Suppose that a man is leaning over. Suppose that he is supported by another man who is also leaning over. Suppose that he in turn is supported by yet another man who is also leaning over; and so on. It is natural to suppose in such a case that the series of men leaning over cannot be infinite and that there eventually must be a support such as a wall.

The Solution

The solution to the antinomy is to deny the premise shared by the arguments for both the thesis and the antithesis. This premise is the assumption made by reason that something must exist that corresponds to the idea of the un-conditioned (B501). Once we reject this claim of reason, the antinomy can be defused. This faulty view of Reason can be replaced by one that sees reason as setting us an indefinite task rather than making an imposition on the world. Reason presents us with a directive, rather than making a claim as to what exists.

Kant says that the unconditioned can never be experienced (B511). Since (according to Transcendental Idealism) the world of things in space and time is phenomenal and must consist of objects of possible experience, reason's demand that the unconditioned must exist entails transcendental realism. Once we reject transcendental realism and replace it with transcendental idealism, we can see that reason's demand can never be satisfied. In detail, reason claims that the un-conditioned exists and that it is either the infinite series of events as a whole or a finite series of events as a whole. Kant claims that the notion of the whole series of events (whether finite or infinite) is empty because there is no experience to which these words could apply. For instance, no experience could count as the discovery of the first event ever, and therefore the notion of the whole finite series of events has no possible application in experience. Similarly, no possible experience could ever justify our using the words "the infinite series of events as a whole." At A483 Kant claims that experience can only justify our using the term *whole* in a comparative sense. In referring to the series of events as a whole, we use the term *whole* in a noncomparative sense. This use has no application in experience and hence is empty. In the words of Strawson, "we must not think of the endless task of investigation as a task of investigating the endless."

This is the essence of Kant's solution to the first two antinomies. There is, however, an important tension in Kant's thought. He claims that reason's demands require us to apply concepts that exceed the range of possible experience and as such are empty and without meaning. This assertion conflicts with the claim that reason's demands are contradictory. Reason's demands cannot be both empty and contradictory.

The First Antinomy: Space

Kant's argument for the thesis that the world must have limits in space is weak. He says that the thought of an infinitely extended world involves the thought of its being possible to complete a temporally infinite process of surveying. He claims that the notion of a completed infinite task is contradictory, and therefore that the world cannot be infinite in space.

There are two problems with this argument. First, Kant is wrong to assert that a completed infinite task is impossible; such a task is impossible only on the assumption that it has a beginning. Second, why should Kant assume that the size of a thing involves the thought of our being able to survey it?

The argument for the antithesis is as follows: if the world were finite, it would stand in a special relation to the space outside it—that is, it would be limited by empty space—but empty space is nothing at all, and therefore there is nothing for the world to be limited by, and it must be infinite in space.

The Second Antinomy: Simples

The thesis claims that composites have indivisible numbers of simple parts, because it is impossible for an aggregate or composite to be made up of aggregates that are themselves made up of aggregates and so on without end. This is impossible because at bottom there would be nothing to make up any of the aggregates. Therefore, there must be indivisible simples.

In the antithesis, Kant argues for the impossibility of composites' being made up of simples. This is impossible because every part of a composite occupies space, and space is infinitely divisible. Therefore, anything that occupies space is infinitely divisible and cannot be made up of simples. Kant's argument for the antithesis fails because it only shows that extended things are conceptually infinitely divisible—not that they are really infinitely divisible (that is, breakable). It also assumes that a particle cannot have a position or occupy space without being extended. But unextended particles could occupy space by virtue of the fact that they generate a forcefield.

Notice that the arguments for both the thesis and the antithesis here can be found in Leibniz. Leibniz uses the argument of the thesis to show that substances must be simples; he then uses the argument of the antithesis to show that nothing extended can be a substance and to conclude that the only substances that can be extensionless are nonspatial minds or monads. However, Kant rejects the notion of a monad, because he argues against the notion of a mental substance in the Paralogisms. Kant also rejects the claim made by Leibniz that extensionless monads fill space through aggregation.

Kant's solution to the second antinomy is to reject the assumption that matter in space is given as either a finitely or an infinitely divisible whole. Matter in space is indefinitely divisible and presents us with an endless task of investigation. Once again this endless task of investigation should not be confused with a task of investigating the endless.

The Third Antinomy: Freedom

The third antinomy consists of the thesis that there is both natural and free causation and of the antithesis that there is only natural causation. In solving this antinomy, Kant tries to reconcile the doctrine of determinism with the idea of freedom. Kant cannot abandon the principle that every event has a cause, because this is a necessary condition of experience. Therefore, every event is completely determined when we view it as a member of a chain of phenomenal events. However, Kant also claims that we can think of ourselves as noumena, and that we can view our actions as free. This means that we can regard ourselves in two ways. First, we can regard ourselves as a part of the natural or phenomenal world, and in so doing we must regard our actions as being causally determined by previous events in the natural world. Second, we can regard ourselves as noumenal beings who do not belong to the spatio-temporal phenomenal world. In so doing we regard our actions in the phenomenal world as having a noumenal cause—that is, as being freely willed by us as noumenal agents. Because we can regard ourselves in two ways, the doctrine of determinism and the idea of freedom can be reconciled, and the third antinomy can be solved. In the phenomenal world all causes are natural, but free causes can exist in the noumenal world.

Kant's discussion of the idea of freedom is directed toward his moral philosophy, which asserts that moral imperatives apply to rational beings as such. However, moral imperatives apply only to free agents, so as rational beings we must be free agents. This point leads Kant to equate the faculty of reason with the free will. The free will must be outside time, because all temporal events are causally determined; therefore, in regarding ourselves as rational beings suscept-ible to moral imperatives, we regard ourselves as noumena.

There are at least four major problems with Kant's attempted reconciliation of determinism and freedom:

1. Heretofore, we have encountered transcendental idealism as a mostly negative doctrine—that is, as supporting the claim that the concepts and the categories only apply meaningfully to things in space and time, and not to things as they are in themselves. Kant's views on freedom seem to require a stronger version of transcendental idealism—one that claims that nontemporal, noumenal objects exist. This appears to conflict with the claim that concepts can only have meaning in application to the objects of possible experience. Kant tries to avoid this problem by asserting that he does not prove that we really are free noumenal beings, but instead merely shows that it is possible for us to think of ourselves in this way. In so doing, Kant attempts to reconcile his views on freedom with the claim that the notion of a noumenon is an empty concept that does not designate an object, and with the claim that we cannot know noumena but only think them.

2. Kant's views on freedom imply that some events can be regarded as having a free noumenal cause. But Kant's views on noumena imply that we could never know which natural events are to be regarded as having a free and noumenal cause, because he must claim that knowledge of noumena is impos-sible. Knowledge of noumena must be impossible because all objects of possible knowledge must be phenomenal and must exist in space and time. This means that we can never tell which events can be regarded as having a noumenal cause and which cannot. Hence, we can never know when to ascribe moral responsibil-ity and when not to.

3. Kant must regard rationality as nontemporal. Otherwise, we could not be free as rational beings. However, we are also committed to seeing rationality in temporal terms—for instance, when we reason about events in the world. It is difficult to see how a nontemporal faculty of reason could ever reason about temporal matters. How could an essentially nontemporal faculty entertain thoughts with an essential temporal content? Kant recognizes this problem and admits that we cannot know how reason is practical.

4. There are problems with the idea that we can think of ourselves as a noumenon. Because noumena are not in space and time, there are no criteria for the identity of noumena. But in thinking of myself as an empirical object in space and time, I think of myself as an object with criteria for identity. How can an empirical object for which there are criteria for identity be identical with a noumenon for which there are no criteria for identity? Kant might reply to this objection by saying that it is exactly with points like this in mind that he claims we can only think or regard ourselves as noumena (rather than know ourselves to be such) and that this is why he claims that the thought of noumena is an empty thought. However, even if Kant says that the thought of our selves' being

noumena and free is an empty thought, he still faces the question: "How can an empty thought be any thought at all?"

The Fourth Antinomy: God

Kant regards the idea of God as an idea of reason. Like all the ideas of reason, the idea of God cannot be exhibited in experience. God is not an object of possible experience and, therefore, cannot be a part of the natural world. So Kant claims that it is impossible to show that God exists. But he also says we can have the idea of such a being as a noumenon, although such a thought can never amount to knowledge. In this way, Kant's views on God have two sides: one, an attack on the traditional proofs of God's existence; and two, an explanation of our idea of God.

Kant claims that all proofs of God's existence can be reduced to three basic arguments: the ontological argument, the cosmological argument, and the physico-theological argument. He attacks the ontological argument on the grounds that existence is not a predicate or property (for details of the ontological argument and how Kant's claim about existence undermines it, see Chapter 19). At A626, Kant claims that existence is not a property. Instead, he says, existence is merely the copula of a judgment. The proposition "God is perfect" contains only two concepts, "God" and "perfect"; the small word *is* adds no new predicate. In other words, there is no difference between the idea of a God who exists and the idea of a God who does not exist. Existence adds nothing to the idea of God, so existence cannot be a perfection (contrary to what is claimed in the ontological argument).

Kant also says that all existential propositions are synthetic and argues against the idea of necessary existence. At A622–23 he says that, even if it is asserted that God is an absolutely necessary being, this does not mean that God necessarily exists. It only means that if God exists then a necessary being exists. It is compatible with this position to deny that God exists.

The cosmological proof of God's existence is as follows. If anything contingent exists, then something necessary must exist. Since something contingent does exist, so does the necessary, and this must be God. Kant concentrates on the last part of this argument—that is, on the move from "something necessary exists" to "God exists." Kant claims that this step of the argument presupposes the ontological argument. The assertion that nothing could be a necessary being but God involves two implicit assertions: first, that if anything is a necessary being then it is God; and second, that if anything is God then it is a necessary being. Kant claims that this second assertion involves the ontological argument.

The physico-theological argument is often called "the argument from design." Kant says that the order in nature does not show the need for a creator; at most it shows the need for a designer. According to Kant, the argument from design presupposes the cosmological argument, because the argument from design moves from the existence of order in nature to the existence of a necessary being, and hence to God. Having rejected the cosmological argument, the ontological argument, and the notion of necessary existence, Kant also rejects the argument from design.

The fact that Kant argues against the various proofs of God's existence does not mean that he wishes to discredit the idea of God. Kant claims that the idea of God, like the idea of freedom, is the idea of something unconditioned, and as such is an inevitable idea of reason. The idea of the unconditioned can never be met with in experience and, therefore, is not an item of knowledge. This is what Kant means when he says that our ideas of the unconditioned are not constitutive but are regulative. Even if it is a mistake to suppose that the ideas of reason can give us a priori knowledge of the world, these ideas are still essential to the way reason functions. In the case of our ideas of freedom and God, our idea of the unconditioned has for Kant a clear role to play in moral reasoning. Kant stresses that we cannot have theoretical knowledge of the unconditioned (including God), but he says that he abolishes knowledge to make room for faith.

Conclusion

As the title of the work suggests, Kant's main aim in the *Critique of Pure Reason* is to criticize the Rationalist claim that reason alone can give us a priori knowledge of the world that transcends the limits of possible experience. In the Dialectic, Kant attempts to show in detail how rationalistic metaphysics fails to give us a priori knowledge of the soul, the limits of the world, and God.

Kant's critique in the Dialectic is based on two major themes of the Analytic and the Aesthetic.

First, to explain how synthetic a priori knowledge is possible, Kant shows that experience must be subject to the categories and the forms of space and time. A priori knowledge of the world is defined by these a priori forms of experience. The categories are simply the ways in which the manifold sensory intuitions are organized; therefore it is vain to hope that the categories can give us any a priori knowledge when divorced from their organizing role in experience. For this reason, Kant says "thoughts without content are empty" (B75). According to Kant, neither intuitions without concepts nor concepts without intuitions can yield knowledge (B74). Rationalistic metaphysics pretends to provide, from concepts alone, a priori knowledge that goes beyond the realm of any possible experience. According to Kant, the categories can only give knowledge when applied to sensible intuitions, within the confines of possible experience. Consequently, rationalistic metaphysics can never give us knowledge.

This criticism of Rationalism does nothing to vindicate Empiricism. Indeed, Kant claims that knowledge requires the cooperation of both sensible intuitions and concepts—an assertion that, in addition to discrediting the Rationalist claim that concepts alone can give us knowledge of the world, rules out the Empiricist contention that we can gain knowledge through sense intuitions alone. Against Rationalism Kant argues that "thoughts without content are empty," but against

Empiricism Kant argues that "intuitions without concepts are blind" (B75). An experience consisting solely of the passive reception of sensory intuitions (or simple impressions) is impossible, because it would not be subject to the categories and the transcendental unity of apperception. Consequently, the claim of Locke and Hume that our ideas are acquired from such an experience is false.

Second, Kant's critique of Rationalism is also based on his transcendental idealism. Kant's most direct argument for transcendental idealism is that it is required to explain how synthetic a priori knowledge is possible. If the world consisted of objects that were transcendentally real, we would never be able to explain how we have synthetic a priori knowledge of it. However, rationalistic metaphysics treats the world as an unconditioned whole that includes objects (like God and the soul) that cannot possibly be experienced. In so doing, according to Kant, it assumes that the world is transcendentally real.

Kant does not merely argue against rationalistic metaphysics; he also offers a diagnosis of why we fall into its errors. Reason seeks complete explanations; and in so doing, it inevitably takes us beyond the limits of possible experience. In our efforts to discover more comprehensive explanations, reason should guide us. But because reason's ideas of the unconditioned lie beyond what we can possibly experience, nothing in the phenomenal world can possibly correspond to them; and since knowledge is limited to the phenomenal world, the ideas of reason do not give us knowledge of the world. Consequently, the proper theoretical function of reason and its ideas is not to give us knowledge, but to guide our investigations.

In the Analytic, Kant tries to explain how the synthetic a priori knowledge that lies at the heart of science and mathematics is possible. He argues that experience must be subject to certain a priori forms and that the world is transcendentally ideal (so that it, too, must conform to the a priori forms of experience). Kant's positive explanations of synthetic a priori knowledge in the Analytic demonstrate the limitations of such knowledge and show that rationalistic metaphysics transgresses those limitations.

Study Questions

1. How do Kant's aims differ in the Aesthetic, the Analytic, and the Dialectic?

2. Why does Kant disagree with Descartes's claim that the mind or the "I think" is a simple mental substance of which we have a priori knowledge?

3. What is an antinomy? What role does transcendental idealism play in solving the antinomies?

4. What are the arguments for the thesis and the antithesis of the first antinomy?

5. How does Kant reconcile the assertion that we are free agents with the claim of the second analogy that all events are caused?

6. Why does Kant think that the existence of God cannot be proved? How does he argue for this claim?

7. How does Kant critique pure reason?

Discussion Questions

1. Does Kant himself violate the claim that concepts without intuitions are empty?

2. Must there be a first event? If not, does this imply that the universe is infinitely old?

3. What is the difference between Kant's notion of an idea of reason and a category?

Suggested Reading

Descartes

T. Sorrell, *Descartes*, Oxford University Press, 1987.

J. Cottingham, *Descartes*, Basil Blackwell, 1986.

E. M. Curley, *Descartes Against the Sceptics*, Harvard University Press, 1978.

B. Williams, *Descartes: The Project of Pure Enquiry*, Penguin, 1978.

M. D. Wilson, *Descartes* (The Arguments of the Philosophers), Routledge & Kegan Paul, 1978.

J. Ree, *Descartes*, Allen Lane, 1974.

A. Kenny, *Descartes*, Random House, 1968.

Spinoza

R. J. Delahunty, *Spinoza* (The Arguments of the Philosophers), Routledge & Kegan Paul, 1985.

J. Bennett, *A Study of Spinoza's Ethics*, Hackett, 1985.

E. M. Curley, *Spinoza's Metaphysics*, Harvard University Press, 1969.

S. Hampshire, *Spinoza*, Penguin, 1951.

H. R. Parkinson, *Spinoza's Theory of Knowledge*, Oxford University Press, 1954.

Leibniz

B. Mates, *The Philosophy of Leibniz,* Oxford University Press, 1986.
N. Jolley, *Leibniz and Locke: A Study of the New Essays on Human Understanding,* Clarendon Press, 1984.
S. Brown, *Leibniz,* University of Minnesota Press, 1984.
G. MacDonald Ross, *Leibniz,* Oxford University Press, 1984.
N. Rescher, *Leibniz: An Introduction to His Philosophy,* Oxford University Press, 1979.
C. D. Broad, *Leibniz: An Introduction,* Cambridge University Press, 1975.
G. H. R. Parkinson, *Logic and Reality in Leibniz's Metaphysics,* Oxford University Press, 1965.

Locke

J. Jenkins, *Understanding Locke,* Edinburgh University Press, 1983.
I. C. Tipton (ed.), *Locke on Human Understanding* (Oxford Readings in Philosophy), Oxford University Press, 1977.
J. Mackie, *Problems from Locke,* Clarendon Press, 1976.
J. Bennett, *Locke, Berkeley, Hume: Central Themes,* Clarendon Press, 1971.
R. Aaron, *John Locke,* Clarendon Press, 1971.
R. S. Woolhouse, *Locke* (Philosophers in Context), Harvester Press, 1983.
J. Yolton, *Locke and the Compass of Human Understanding,* Cambridge University Press, 1970.
D. J. O'Connor, *John Locke,* Dover, 1967.

Berkeley

Dancy, *Berkeley: An Introduction,* Basil Blackwell, 1987.
A. C Grayling, *Berkeley: The Central Arguments,* Duckworth, 1986.
J. Foster and H. Robinson (eds.), *Essays on Berkeley,* Oxford University Press, 1985.
J. O. Urmson, *Berkeley,* Oxford University Press, 1982.
C. Turbayne (ed.), *Berkeley: Critical and Interpretative Essays,* University of Minnesota Press, 1982.
G. Pitcher, *Berkeley* (The Arguments of the Philosophers), Routledge & Kegan Paul, 1977.
I. C. Tipton, *Berkeley: The Philosophy of Immaterialism,* Methuen, 1974.
C. B. Martin and D. M. Armstrong, *Locke and Berkeley,* MacMillan, 1968.
G. J. Warnock, *Berkeley,* Pelican, 1953.

Hume

A. C. Baier, *A Progress of Sentiments: Reflections on Hume's Treatise,* Harvard University Press, 1991.

R. Fogelin, *Hume's Scepticism in the Treatise of Human Nature,* Routledge & Kegan Paul, 1985.

T. Beauchamp and A. Rosenburg, *Hume and the Problem of Causation,* Oxford University Press, 1981.

B. Stroud, *Hume* (The Arguments of the Philosophers), Routledge & Kegan Paul, 1977.

T. Penelhum, *Hume,* St. Martin's Press, 1975.

A. Flew, *Hume's Philosophy of Belief,* Routledge & Kegan Paul, 1961.

J. A. Passmore, *Hume's Intentions,* Cambridge University Press, 1952.

Kant

R. Scruton, *Kant,* Oxford University Press, 1982.

R. Walker, *Kant* (The Arguments of the Philosophers), Routledge & Kegan Paul, 1979.

T. E. Wilkerson, *Kant's Critique of Pure Reason: A Commentary for Students,* Clarendon Press, 1971.

J. Bennett, *Kant's Dialectic,* Cambridge University Press, 1974.

P. F. Strawson, *The Bounds of Sense,* Methuen, 1966.

J. Bennett, *Kant's Analytic,* Cambridge University Press, 1966.

Notes

1. We can explain an object in terms of:

   a. its material cause, what it is made of (for instance, "The ball bounced because it is made of rubber"); or

   b. its formal cause, how it is structured (for example, "The ball rolled down the incline because it is spherical"); or

   c. its efficient cause, what brings it about (for example, "The ball rolled across the floor because it was pushed"); or

   d. its final cause, its purpose (ultimately, we must explain the existence and nature of the ball in terms of its use).

2. See L. Loeb, *From Descartes to Hume* (Cornell University Press, 1981), chapter 1, for criticisms of the division between Empiricism and Rationalism.

3. Robert Cummins and David Owen, *Central Readings in the History of Modern Philosophy* (Wadsworth, 1992), pp. 5–7.

4. Bernard Williams, *Descartes: The Project of Pure Enquiry* (Pelican Books, 1978), p. 54.

5. J. L. Austin, *Sense and Sensibilia* (Oxford University Press, 1962), p. 48.

6. Robert Cummins and David Owen, *Central Readings in the History of Modern Philosophy* (Wadsworth, 1992), p. 3.

7. See J. Cottingham, *Descartes* (Basil Blackwell, 1986), pp. 41–42.

8. Jaakko Hintikka, "Cogito, Ergo Sum: Inference or Performance," *Philosophical Review* 71 (January, 1965), pp. 3–32.

9. S. Haldane and G. T. Ross, *The Philosophical Works of Descartes,* Vol. 2 (Cambridge University Press, 1967), p. 38.

10. Bertrand Russell, *History of Western Philosophy* (Allen & Unwin, 1961).

11. Robert Cummins and David Owen, *Central Readings in the History of Modern Philosophy* (Wadsworth, 1992), pp. 12–13.

12. Ibid., p. 13.

13. S. Haldane and G. R. T. Ross, op. cit., Vol. 3, p. 417.

14. S. Haldane and G. R. T. Ross, op. cit., Vol. 1, p. 443.

15. S. Haldane and G. R. T. Ross, op. cit., Vol. 2, p. 166.

16. Robert Cummins and David Owen, *Central Readings in the History of Modern Philosophy* (Wadsworth, 1992), pp. 13–19.

17. Ibid., p. 15.

18. W. V. O. Quine, "On What There Is," in *From a Logical Point of View,* ed. W. V. O. Quine (Harvard University Press, 1961), p. 1–19.

19. S. Haldane and G. R. T. Ross, op. cit., Vol. 2, p. 92.

20. See A. Kenny, *Descartes* (Random House, 1968), chapter 10; and J. Cottingham, *Descartes* (Basil Blackwell, 1986), pp. 66–70.

21. Gilbert Ryle, *The Concept of Mind* (Hutchinson, 1949), chapter 1.

22. David Armstrong, *The Materialist Theory of Mind* (Routledge & Kegan Paul, 1968).

23. For more recent versions of Materialism, see D. Dennett, *Brainstorms* (Harvester Press, 1978) and P. Churchland, *Matter and Consciousness* (MIT Press, 1988).

24. Robert Cummins and David Owen, *Central Readings in the History of Modern Philosophy* (Wadsworth, 1992), p. 39.

25. See H. H. Joachim, *A Study of the Ethics of Spinoza* (Russell & Russell, 1964) and J. Bennett, *A Study of Spinoza's Ethics* (Hackett, 1985).

26. See E. M. Curley, *Spinoza's Metaphysics: An Essay in Interpretation* (Harvard University Press, 1969).

27. See J. Bennett, *A Study of Spinoza's Ethics* (Hackett, 1985), pp. 92–95.

28. See S. Hampshire, *Spinoza* (Penguin, 1951).

29. Robert Cummins and David Owen, *Central Readings in the History of Modern Philosophy* (Wadsworth, 1992), p. 63.

30.   See G. H. R. Parkinson, *Spinoza's Theory of Knowledge* (Oxford University Press, 1954), chapter 4, section 6; and J. Bennett, *A Study of Spinoza's Ethics* (Hackett, 1985), pp. 64–66.

31.   E. M. Curley, *Spinoza's Metaphysics* (Harvard University Press, 1969).

32.   See R. J. Delahunty, *Spinoza* (Routledge & Kegan Paul, 1985), pp. 183–90.

33.   LeRoy Loemker (ed.), *G. Leibniz: Philosophical Papers and Letters* (Dordrecht, 1969), p. 334.

34.   Ibid., p. 335.

35.   See Benson Mates, *The Philosophy of Leibniz* (Oxford University Press, 1986), pp. 55–56.

36.   See G. H. R. Parkinson, *Logic and Reality in Leibniz's Metaphysics* (Oxford University Press, 1965), chapter 1, sections 3–4.

37.   LeRoy Loemker (ed.), *G. Leibniz: Philosophical Papers and Letters* (Dordrecht, 1969), p. 704.

38.   H. Mason (ed.), *The Leibniz–Arnauld Correspondence* (Manchester University Press, 1967), p. 121.

39.   See Benson Mates, *The Philosophy of Leibniz* (Oxford University Press, 1986), pp. 192–95.

40.   See H. Mason (ed.), *The Leibniz–Arnauld Correspondence* (Manchester University Press, 1967), pp. 107, 121.

41.   LeRoy Loemker (ed.), *G. Leibniz: Philosophical Papers and Letters* (Dordrecht, 1969), p. 310.

42.   Ibid., pp. 675–721.

43.   See, for example, N. Jolley, *Leibniz and Locke* (Clarendon Press, 1984), pp. 4–6, and R. S. Woolhouse, *Locke's Philosophy of Science and Knowledge* (Barnes & Noble, 1971), pp. 25–32 and chapter 9.

44.   For a comparative study of Locke and Leibniz, see N. Jolley, *Leibniz and Locke* (Clarendon Press, 1984).

45.   See, for example, *Essay,* II.VIII.23–24.

46.   See J. Mackie, *Problems from Locke* (Clarendon Press, 1976), chapter 1.

47.   See Ibid., chapter 2, sections 5–7, and J. Jenkins, *Understanding Locke* (Edinburgh University Press, 1982), pp. 82ff.

48.   For further clarification, see J. Bennett, *Locke, Berkely, Hume: Central Themes* (Clarendon Press, 1971), section 5.

49.   See *Essay*, II.XXIII.37.

50.   See, for example, R. S. Woolhouse, *Locke's Philosophy of Science and Knowledge* (Barnes & Noble, 1971); D. J. O'Connor, *John Locke* (Dover, 1967); and J. Jenkins, *Understanding Locke* (Edinburgh University Press, 1982).

51.   R. Aaron, *John Locke* (Oxford University Press, 1971), pp. 175–76.

52.   See, for example, J. Bennett, *Locke, Berkeley, Hume: Central Themes* (Clarendon Press, 1971), section 1, and J. Jenkins, *Understanding Locke* (Edinburgh University Press, 1982), pp. 156–62.

53.   For a more detailed discussion, see J. L. Mackie, op. cit., chapter 3.

54.   See M. Ayers's article "The Ideas of Power and Substance in Locke's Philosophy," in I. C. Tipton's *Locke on Human Understanding: Selected Essays* (Oxford University Press, 1977), 77–105.

55.   Robert Cummins and David Owen, *Central Readings in the History of Modern Philosophy* (Wadsworth, 1992), pp. 276–84.

56.   G. Pitcher, *Berkeley* (Routledge & Kegan Paul, 1977), p. 67.

57.   Robert Cummins and David Owen, *Central Readings in the History of Modern Philosophy* (Wadsworth, 1992), p. 299.

58.   Ibid., p. 304.

59.   See J. Bennett, op. cit., section 5, and J. Jenkins, *Understanding Locke,* (Edinburgh University Press, 1983), pp. 77–81.

60.   For an alternative view, see F. Jackson, "The Existence of Mental Objects," in J. Dancy (ed.), *Perceptual Knowledge* (Oxford University Press, 1988), pp. 113–27.

61.   See Jonathan Dancy, *Berkeley: An Introduction* (Basil Blackwell, 1987), p. 50.

62.   J. Bennett, *Locke, Berkely, Hume: Central Themes* (Clarendon Press, 1971), chapter 7.

63.   Ibid., sections 37 and 40.

64.   *Treatise of Human Nature,* ed. L. A. Selby-Bigge (Oxford University Press, 1888), p. 415.

65.   Ibid., p. 183.

66.   For more on current interpretations of Hume's aims, see J. Wright, *The Sceptical Realism of David Hume* (University of Minnesota Press, 1983), pp. 1–7.

67.   *Treatise of Human Nature,* ed. L. A. Selby-Bigge (Oxford University Press, 1888), p. 3.

68. For discussion of this point, see T. Penelhum, *Hume* (St. Martin's Press, 1975), pp. 50–53.

69. See B. Stroud, *Hume* (Routledge & Kegan Paul, 1977), pp. 56–67.

70. See Ibid., p. 101.

71. P. Strawson, *The Bounds of Sense* (Methuen, 1966), pp. 281–84.

72. Ibid., pp. 125–32.

73. Ibid., p. 162.

Glossary

abstract idea: An abstract idea is an idea formed by abstracting what a certain class of things have in common.

abstraction: For Locke, abstraction is one of the ways in which general ideas are derived from simple ideas. In abstracting, the mind attends to a common feature of a class of things and ignores all other features.

analytic: A statement is an analytic truth if it is true solely in virtue of the meanings of the words it contains. Kant defines an analytic judgment as a judgment in which the concept of the predicate is included in the concept of the subject.

antinomy: For Kant, an antinomy is a pair of valid arguments that have contradictory conclusions but share the same false presupposition.

a posteriori: This term comes from the Latin and means "what comes after." A posteriori knowledge is knowledge that can only be known and justified with reference to particular experiences.

a priori: This term comes from the Latin and means "what comes before." A priori knowledge is knowledge that can be known and justified without reference to particular experiences. A priori truths are truths that are not empirical (or a posteriori). Kant also uses the term "a priori" to mean that which is both necessary and universal, or without exception.

association of ideas: For Hume, association of ideas is the mechanism by which more complex ideas are constructed out of simpler ideas.

attribute: For Spinoza and Descartes, an attribute is an essential property of a substance.

category: For Kant, a category designates concepts that organize and make experience possible. Because they are required for experience, they cannot be acquired from experience, and therefore they are a priori.

clear and distinct idea: For Descartes, an idea is clear and distinct if it is neither confused with any other idea nor confused in itself.

Cogito, the: The Cogito is Descartes's argument, "I think therefore I am."

complex idea: For Locke, any idea that is not simple is complex. Complex ideas are composed of simple ideas. (*See* **simple idea.**)

contingent: A statement is contingent if and only if its denial is logically possible without producing a self-contradiction.

deduction: A deduction is an argument that makes the claim that, if the premises are true, the conclusion must be true. Hence, a deductive argument claims that its conclusion logically cannot be false if its premises are true.

determinism: Determinism is the claim that all events, including human actions, are necessitated by their causes.

direct realism: Direct realism is the claim that we immediately perceive external objects. According to this view, to perceive external objects, we need not first perceive our own ideas. (*See* **representational theory of perception.**)

dualism: Ontological dualism is the claim that the universe consists of two distinct kinds of substances—minds and matter—that are not reducible one to the other.

empirical: *See* **a posteriori**.

epistemology: Epistemology is the philosophical study of knowledge, including how it is acquired and justified.

essence: For Descartes, the essence of a substance is that attribute that the substance cannot cease to have without ceasing to be what it is.

fallacy of composition: This particular fallacy consists of the invalid inference, from the fact that the parts of something have a certain property, that the whole made up of those parts must have that property.

idea: An idea is any content of the mind. For Descartes, Locke, and Berkeley, ideas are the immediate objects of perception. For Hume, an idea is the faint copy of an impression. For Kant, ideas regulate the functioning of reason.

idealism: Idealism is the claim that reality consists solely of minds and their ideas. This claim is sometimes called "subjective idealism" to distinguish it from Kant's transcendental idealism. (*See* **transcendental idealism.**)

identity of indiscernables: This term identifies Leibniz's claim that it is impossible for two distinct objects to have the same properties.

impression: For Hume, an impression is the immediate data of sensation.

induction: An induction is a nondeductive argument that makes the claim that the truth of the premises gives good reason for the truth of the conclusion; the claim is that, if the premises are true, the conclusion is very likely to be true.

innate idea: An idea is innate if it is built into the structure of the mind rather than being derived from sense experience.

intuition: For Kant, intuition primarily designates the faculty that passively receives raw sensible data that, when organized according to the categories, yield experience. Kant also calls this faculty "sensibility." Kant also defines intuition as the elements of experience that are produced by this faculty. For Locke, Descartes, and Spinoza, intuition is the immediate intellectual apprehension of a self-evident truth.

logical implication: One statement logically implies or entails another if and only if it would be a contradiction to affirm the truth of the first and the falsity of the second.

Materialism: Materialism is the claim that reality consists solely of matter. This view entails the denial of both dualism and idealism.

modification or mode: For Descartes and Spinoza, a mode is a particular specification of an attribute of a substance; for example, being a square is a mode of spatial extension.

monad: For Leibniz, a monad is one of the simple nonmaterial substances that alone compose the universe.

monism: Ontological monism is the claim that the universe consists of only one kind of substance.

necessary: A truth is necessary if and only if its denial is logically impossible. As a consequence, necessary truths are true no matter how the world may change.

Newtonian physics: The physics of Sir Isaac Newton, in which space and the objects in space form a closed causal system of determinate laws that govern all matter in motion.

nominal essence: For Locke, the nominal essence of things is the set of observable characteristics of substances in virtue of which they are called by the same name. (*See* **real essence**.)

noumena: For Kant, noumena are things in the world as they are in themselves, independent of the categories and forms of intuition.

ontology: Ontology is a theory about what exists or the nature of being.

pantheism: Pantheism constitutes the claim that God is identical with everything.

paralogism: A paralogism is generally an unsound argument. For Kant, the paralogisms are unsound arguments that depend on treating the transcendental unity of apperception as an object. (*See* **Transcendental Unity of Apperception.**)

phenomena: For Kant, phenomena are objects in space and time that can in principle be experienced. To be experienced, phenomenal objects must be subject to the categories and the forms of intuition. (*See* **noumena.**)

predicate: In a judgment, the predicate is what is affirmed or denied of the subject of the judgment. For example, in the judgment "The ball is red," "red" is the predicate, and "the ball" is the subject. (*See* **subject.**)

primary quality: For Locke, a primary quality is a property of an object that is inherent in the object itself. Locke claims that our ideas of primary qualities resemble the qualities themselves. (*See* **secondary quality.**)

Principle of Sufficient Reason: This principle makes the claim that everything must have a rational explanation.

real essence: For Locke, the real essence of things is the set of unknown characteristics that cause substances to share observable features. (*See* **nominal essence.**)

reason: Reason consists of the ability to think and make deductive inferences, based on the law of noncontradiction.

representational theory of perception: This theory makes the claim that we can only directly perceive our own ideas, and that these ideas represent external objects.

scepticism: A sceptic is one who doubts the possibility of knowledge in a given area of inquiry. Thus, for example, scepticism regarding the external world is doubt that knowledge of the external world is possible.

scholasticism: Scholasticism is the philosophy of the schools—the Medieval philosophical traditions that often used commentary on authoritative texts as a basis for their arguments.

secondary quality: For Locke, a secondary quality is a power of an object to produce certain ideas in the mind. Locke claims that our ideas of secondary qualities do not resemble anything in the object itself. (*See* **primary quality.**)

sense data: Sense data are the raw materials of any experience that consists simply and solely of sensations.

simple idea: For Locke, a simple idea is an idea that cannot be divided into constituent ideas. To be known, simple ideas must be directly experienced.

subject: The subject is the part of a judgment that designates what the judgment is about. For example, in the judgment "The ball is red," "the ball" is the subject, since the judgment is about a ball.

substance: Substances are things that have properties or attributes but are themselves not the attribute of something else. For Spinoza, substance refers to that which exists independently of anything else. For Locke, substance refers to that in which properties inhere.

substratum: For Locke, substratum is that in which all properties inhere but which itself has no properties.

synthetic: A statement is synthetic if it is true or false in virtue of the way the world is. For Kant, a judgment is synthetic if the predicate is not contained in the subject. (*See* **analytic**.)

tautology: A tautology is a statement that is logically true.

transcendental: Transcendental literally means "beyond experience." Kant uses the term to apply to things that are not a part of experience but are necessary for experience to be possible. Transcendental knowledge differs from transcendent metaphysics in that the former, unlike the latter, can be justified by appeal to the necessary conditions of possible experience.

transcendental idealism: Transcendental idealism represents Kant's claim that objects in space and time are empirically real but transcendentally ideal. These objects are empirically real in that they exist independent of perceivers, who may or may not be perceiving them. They are transcendentally ideal in that they depend on the categories and forms of intuition.

transcendental realism: Transcendental realism is the claim (which Kant rejects) that objects in space and time are either empirically ideal or transcendentally real. They are empirically ideal if they exist only as ideas in the mind of the perceiver. They are transcendentally real in that they do not depend on the categories or forms of intuition.

Transcendental Unity of Apperception: For Kant, the Transcendental Unity of Apperception is the requirement that experience must belong to a single consciousness.

transcendent metaphysics: For Kant, metaphysical claims are transcendent when they cannot be justified by reference to any possible experience of objects. Kant also calls this "dogmatic metaphysics."

valid: A deductive argument is valid if and only if the conclusion follows logically from the premises. In other words, an argument is valid if and only if the conclusion cannot be false, given that the premises are true.

Index

Abstract (Hume), 173
Abstract ideas, 149–151
Adequate Reality, Principle of, 27, 28, 29
Aesthetic, Transcendental, 217–221
Analogies of Kant
  first, 234–235
  second, 237–238
  third, 238
Analysis, finite and infinite, 81–82
Analytic, Transcendental, 223–231
Analytic of Concepts, 223–231
Analytic of Principles, 223, 232–241
Animal souls, 95
Annandale, Marquess of, 174
Antinomies of Kant, 246–253
  dynamical, 247, 250–253
  first, 246, 247–249
  fourth, 246, 252–253
  second, 246, 249–250
  third, 246, 250–252
A posteriori truths, 184
Apperception, Transcendental Unity of, 226–228, 229, 231, 244, 245, 246
A priori judgments, 216
A priori knowledge
  Empiricists on, 110, 205, 206, 210, 211–212

  Kant on, 211–212, 217, 253
  Rationalists on, 8
A priori truths, 184, 211–212, 216
Aquinas, St. Thomas, 2, 3
Argument from illusion, 151–155
Aristotle, 2, 3, 4, 91
Arithmetic and mathematics, 110, 216, 221
Armstrong, David, 47–48
Arnauld, Antoine, 78, 81, 92
Ashley, Lord, 113
Association, 180
Attributes, 64–65
Augustine, St., 2
Austin, J. L., 14
Averroes, 2
Avicenna, 2
Ayer, A. J., 152
Ayers, M., 142

Bacon, Francis, 4, 6, 77, 110
Bare monads, 95
Beeckman, Isaac, 9
Being, levels of, 4
Belief, 180, 181
Bennett, J., 168–169
Berkeley, George, 5, 6, 8, 110, 147–172

Berkeley, George *(continued)*
   on abstract ideas, 149–151
   on argument from illusion, 151–155
   biography of, 147–148
   on common sense, 164–165
   on continuity argument for existence of God, 168
   criticisms of, 154–155
   on denial of matter, 149–161
   direct realism and, 155–156
   on external objects, 159–160
   on God, 166–169, 171–172
   Hume vs., 111, 170, 176, 205–206
   idealism of, 163–164
   on ideas, 149–153, 205
   on ideas of sense, 151, 163, 167
   Kant vs., 229, 240
   on knowledge, 206
   on language, 206
   Leibniz vs., 111
   Locke vs., 111, 120, 121, 130, 149–151, 157–158, 161, 164, 167, 171, 205–206
   on material substance, 160–161
   on mind, 169–172
   on perception, 149–161, 165–166
   on perceptual illusions, 120
   on primary and secondary qualities, 156–158
   Principles of Human Knowledge, 149, 159, 164, 165, 166, 171, 205
   on resemblance thesis, 120, 121
   scepticism and, 164
   on sensible objects, 158–159
   on spirit, 169–170
   Three Dialogues Between Hylas and Philonous, 147, 149, 151, 156–157, 159–161, 166, 169
   Treatise Concerning the Principles of Human Knowledge, A, 147, 149, 163
   on unperceived objects, 165–166
Best, Principle of, 87
Body. *See* External objects; Mind/body dualism
Bounds of Sense, The (Strawson), 220
Boyle, Sir Robert, 112, 115, 119
Butler, Joseph, 173

Cartesian circle, 31–32
Categories, 225, 226–227, 231, 232–237
Causal analysis of mind, 46–47
Causal Axiom, Universal, 185, 193, 212
Causal inferences, 187–188
Causality
   Empiricists on, 98, 131, 171, 183–194, 236
   Hume on, 98, 131, 171, 183–194, 236
   Kant on, 98, 193–194, 236–237, 246, 247, 250–252
   Leibniz on, 60, 93–94, 98
   Locke on, 131, 186
   monads and, 93–94
   Rationalists on, 52–53, 54, 57, 60, 62–63, 93–94, 98
   Spinoza on, 52–53, 54, 57, 62–63
Causal relation, 184–185
Cause
   Hume's two definitions of, 192
   idea of, 185–186
   knowledge and, 52–53
Charles II, king of England, 113
Christianity, influences in Medieval period, 1–3
Christina, queen of Sweden, 11
Church of England, 3
Clarke, Samuel, 90, 102, 246
Classification, 24–26, 118, 139, 140
Coexistence between ideas, 144
Cogito of Descartes, 17–22
   criticism of, 21
   as inference, 20–21
   interpretation of, 19–21
   as intuition, 20
   as performance, 19–20
   thinking substance and, 35–37
Coherence, 197–198
Color, 119, 120–121, 122
Common sense, 164–165
Compendium Musicae (Descartes), 9
Complete concepts, 83–84
Complex ideas
   Hume on, 178–180
   Locke on, 118, 127–135
   simple ideas vs., 118, 203–204
Concepts
   Analytic of, 223–231

complete, 83–84
Kant on, 180, 181, 182, 192, 223–231
Leibniz on, 82–84
primitive, 82–83
Consciousness
Descartes on, 41–43. *See also* Mind/body dualism
Kant on, 43, 227–228, 245–246
Locke on, 132–134
Constancy, 197–199
Contingency
God's free choice and, 86, 87
Leibniz on, 85–87, 100
sufficient reason and, 86–87
Continuity argument for existence of God, 168
Contradiction, Principle of, 84, 86
Copernicus, 3
Cosmological argument of Leibniz, 98–99
Critique of Judgment (Kant), 214
Critique of Practical Reason (Kant), 214
Critique of Pure Reason (Kant), 45, 180, 181, 210, 212, 214, 215, 216, 220, 221, 225, 230, 241, 253
Curley, E. M., 58, 65

D'Alembert, Jean Le Rond, 174
Deduction
Metaphysical, 223, 225, 232
Transcendental, 223, 225–230, 232
Definition, 140
Demonstrative knowledge, 145
De Motu (Berkeley), 148
Descartes, René, 5, 6, 8, 9–48
argument from dreaming, 13, 14–15
biography of, 9–11
Cartesian circle and, 31–32
on causal analysis of mind, 46–47
Cogito of, 17–22, 35–37
criticisms of, 16–17, 21, 30–31, 44–46
on deceiving spirit, 13–14, 15
direct realism and, 155, 156

dualism of, 40–48, 66, 68, 107–108
on existence, 17–22, 35–36, 37
on extension, 36, 38, 100–101
on free will, 33, 74–75
on God, 26–33, 37, 52, 56–57, 97, 167–168
on ideas, 24–26, 31–32, 69, 116, 137
Kant vs., 244, 245, 246
on knowledge, 39, 143
Leibniz vs., 100–101, 106–108
Locke vs., 107, 111, 116, 117, 123, 142, 143, 171
Materialism and, 47–48
on matter, 36–40
Meditations of, 10, 13, 15, 17, 19, 21, 22, 24, 25, 26, 30, 32, 33, 35, 36–37, 40, 43
Method of Doubt of, 12–17, 22, 31–32
mind/body dualism of, 40–48, 66
on observation, 39
on perception, 39–40, 123
on primary and secondary qualities, 39–40
on Principle of Adequate Reality, 27, 28, 29
Principle of Sufficient Reason and, 27, 28
Principles of Philosophy, 11, 19, 37, 38
on proofs of existence of God, 26–29, 30–31
on reason, 39, 72, 110
scepticism and, 12–17, 22
on science, 38–39, 63, 110
on sense experience, 13, 14, 16, 39, 72, 110
Spinoza vs., 52, 56–57, 58, 64, 106–108
on substance, 35–37, 45, 56–57, 58
on thinking substance, 35–37, 45
Determinism
Kant on, 250–252
Spinoza on, 74–75
Dialectic, Transcendental, 223, 243–254
Dialogues on Natural Religion (Hume), 98, 175

Diderot, Denis, 174
Direct realism
    Berkeley and, 155–156
    Kant and, 122, 155
Discourse on Metaphysics (Leibniz), 80
Discourse on the Method for Conducting One's Reason Rightly (Descartes), 10, 41, 46
Divine Nature, 62–63, 74, 75
Divisibility, argument from, 43
Doubt
    in argument for distinction of mind vs. body, 41–43
    Cogito as end of, 17–22
    Method of, 12–17, 22, 31–32
Dreaming, Descartes' argument from, 13, 14–15
Dualism of Descartes, 40–48, 66, 68, 107–108. *See also* Mind/body dualism
Dynamical antinomies, 247, 250–253

Eckhart, Johann Georg von, 78
Elizabeth, princess of Bohemia, 11
Empiricists, 5–6, 110–207
    on causality, 98, 131, 171, 183–194, 236
    comparisons of, 110–111, 120, 121, 130, 131, 149–151, 157–158, 161, 164, 167, 170, 171, 176, 179–180, 186, 193, 205–207
    criticisms of, 78, 121–122, 133–134, 137–138, 154–155
    development of, 206–207
    direct realism and, 155–156
    on existence, 195–198
    on experience, 229
    on external objects, 159–160, 195–198, 229
    five central pillars of, 203–205
    on God, 166–169, 171–172
    idealism and, 163–164
    on ideas, 26, 116–118, 127–135, 144–145, 149–151, 163, 167, 178–180, 192–193, 203–205
    on identity, 131–134, 144, 198–201
    on imagination, 163, 181–182, 197, 198–199
    on impressions, 178–180, 192–193, 195–199
    on knowledge, 5, 110, 142–146, 204–206, 210
    on language, 136–139, 177, 205, 206
    on matter, 39, 40, 64, 119–122, 125–126, 149–161
    on mind, 169–172
    naturalism and, 176–177, 190–191
    on perception, 120, 122–126, 149–161, 165–166, 178–180, 193–198, 204–205
    on primary and secondary qualities, 39–40, 119–122, 125–126, 156–158
    on real and nominal essence, 139–142
    on reason, 110, 177, 196–197
    on representational theory, 122–126
    on resemblance thesis, 119–122, 125–126
    scepticism and, 110, 123–125, 164, 168, 170, 176, 177, 187–194, 210
    on sense experience, 210. *See also* Perception
    on substance, 128–131, 139–142, 160–161, 199–200, 236
    on truth, 183, 184, 211–212
    on uniformity principle, 189–190
    See also Berkeley; Hume; Locke
Enquiry Concerning Human Understanding, An (Hume), 174, 177, 178–181, 183–187, 191, 192, 205
Enquiry Concerning the Principles of Morals (Hume), 174
Epistemology, 4
Ernst August, Duke, 78
Error, Descartes on, 33, 37
Essay Concerning Human Understanding (Locke), 78, 114, 115–124, 127, 128, 131–132, 136–138, 142–146
Essays Moral and Political (Hume), 174
Essay Towards a New Theory of Vision (Berkeley), 147, 164
Essay Towards Preventing the Ruin of Great Britain, An (Berkeley), 148

Essence, real vs. nominal, 139–142
Eternal modes, 63
Ethics (Spinoza), 49, 50, 51, 52, 53–57, 59, 62–67, 71–75
Euclid, 2, 5, 51
Euclidean geometry, 219–220
Existence
   Descartes on, 17–22, 35–36, 37
   of God. *See* God
   Hume on, 195–198
   Leibniz on, 99–100
   of matter, 37, 195–198
Experience
   Empiricists on, 229
   Kant on, 216, 228–230
   necessary conditions of, 216
   objectivity and, 228–230
   See also Perception; Sense experience
Experimentation
   as basis of knowledge, 4, 5
   Spinoza on, 52
Extension
   Descartes on, 36, 38, 100–101
   Leibniz on, 100–101
   Spinoza on, 52, 59, 63–64, 65–66
   thought and, 65–66
External objects
   Berkeley on, 159–160
   Hume on, 195–198, 229

Falsity, 73–74
Finite analysis, 81–82
Finite modes, 55, 57–59, 62–63
Free will
   Descartes on, 33, 74–75
   of God, 86, 87
   Kant on, 246, 247, 250–252
   Leibniz on, 86, 87
   Spinoza on, 74–75

Galileo, 4, 10, 15, 110
Gassendi, Pierre, 6, 26, 30, 113
Geometry, Kantian argument from, 219–220
George I, king of England, 148
God
   Berkeley on, 166–169, 171–172
   Descartes on, 26–33, 37, 52, 56–57, 97, 167–168
   free choice of, 86, 87
   idea of, 26, 52
   Kant on, 30, 31, 246, 252–253
   Leibniz on, 86, 96, 97–103, 167–168
   Locke on, 167
   proofs of existence of, 26–29, 30–31, 53–56
   Spinoza on, 51–60, 64–65
Greek influences, 2, 3
Groundwork of the Metaphysics of Morals (Kant), 214

Hallucinations, 154
Hampshire, S., 64
Harmony, preestablished, 95–96, 99
Henry VIII, king of England, 3
Hertford, Lord, 174
Hintikka, Jaakko, 19, 20
History of England, The (Hume), 174, 175
Hobbes, Thomas, 6, 37, 77, 115–116
Hume, David, 5, 110, 173–202
   on association, 180
   on belief, 180, 181
   Berkeley vs., 111, 170, 176, 205–206
   biography of, 173–175
   on causality, 98, 131, 171, 183–194, 236
   on coherence, 197–198
   on constancy, 197–199
   direct realism and, 155
   Enquiry Concerning Human Understanding, An, 174, 177, 178–181, 183–187, 191, 192, 205
   on existence, 195–198
   on external objects, 195–198, 229
   five strands of argument and views of, 190
   on ideas, 178–180, 192–193, 203–205
   on identity, 198–201
   on imagination, 181–182, 197, 198–199
   on impressions, 178–180, 192–193, 195–199
   Kant vs., 193, 211–212, 229, 236, 244, 254
   on knowledge, 206

Hume, David (*continued*)
on language, 177
Locke vs., 111, 131, 179–180,
    186, 193, 205–206, 207
on mental substance, 199–200
on mind, 170
naturalism of, 176–177, 190–191
on need for uniformity, 189–190
on perception, 178–180, 193–
    198, 204
Principle of Sufficient Reason and,
    185, 186
on reason, 177, 196–197
scepticism and, 168, 170, 176,
    177, 187–194, 210
on self, 21
on senses, 196–197
Treatise on Human Nature, 173–
    174, 175, 180, 181, 185, 188,
    195, 197, 199
on truth, 183, 184, 211–212
on two definitions of cause, 192
Hume, Katherine, 174, 175
Hume's fork, 183
Huygens, Christian, 49, 78
Hylas. *See Three Dialogues Between
    Hylas and Philonous*

Idealism
of Berkeley, 163–164
Kant on, 217, 229, 238–240,
    241, 247, 248, 251
Refutation of, 229, 238–239
Transcendental, 217, 239–240,
    241, 247, 248, 251
Ideas
abstract, 149–151
Berkeley on, 149–153, 205
of cause, 185–186
classification of, 24–26, 118, 139
coexistence between, 144
complex, 118, 127–135, 178–180,
    203–204
Descartes on, 24–26, 31–32, 69,
    116, 137
Empiricists on, 26, 116–118,
    127–135, 144–145, 149–151,
    163, 167, 178–180, 192–193,
    203–205
false, 73–74

formation of, 127–135
God, 26, 52
Hume on, 178–180, 192–193,
    203–205
of imagination, 163
impressions and, 178–180, 192–
    193
innate, 26, 116–117, 134
Kant on, 118, 134–135
language and, 136–139, 205
Locke on, 26, 116–118, 127–135,
    144–145, 149–151, 203–205
logical relations between, 144
Method of Doubt and, 31–32
origin of, 117–118
Rationalists on, 24–26, 31–32,
    68–69, 73–74, 116, 137
real existence of, 145
of sense, 151, 163, 167
simple, 118, 178–180, 203–204
Spinoza on, 68–69, 73–74
Identity
diversity and, 131–132, 144
Hume on, 198–201
Locke on, 131–134, 144
personal, 132–134, 200–201
Identity of Indiscernibles, Principle
    of, 91–92, 103
Illusion
argument from, 151–155
perceptual, 120
Imagination
Berkeley on, 163
Hume on, 181–182, 197, 198–
    199
Kant on, 181, 182
Spinoza on, 71–72
Immediate infinite modes, 63
Impenetrability of matter, 101
Impressions, 178–180, 192–193,
    195–199
Indiscernibility of Identicals, Principle
    of, 41
Inductive scepticism, 187–188
Inertia, 101
Infinite analysis, 81–82
Innate ideas, 26, 116–117, 134
Intuition
Kant on, 211, 216, 217–220,
    224, 225, 227, 254
Spinoza on, 73

Intuitive knowledge, 145
James II, king of England, 114
Johann Friedrich, Duke, 78
Johnson, Samuel, 147, 148

Kant, Immanuel, 6, 16, 209–254
  aims of, 215–216
  analogies of, 234–238
  Analytic of Concepts of, 223–231
  Analytic of Principles of, 223,
    232–241
  on antinomies, 246–253
  on a priori judgments, 216
  on arithmetic, 216, 221
  Berkeley vs., 229, 240
  biography of, 213–214
  on categories, 225, 226–227, 231,
    232–237
  on causality, 98, 193–194, 236–
    237, 246, 247, 250–252
  on concepts, 180, 181, 182, 192,
    223–231
  on consciousness, 43, 227–228,
    245–246
  Critique of Pure Reason, 45, 180,
    181, 210, 212, 214, 215, 216,
    220, 221, 225, 230, 241, 253
  Descartes vs., 244, 245, 246
  on determinism vs. free will, 250–
    252
  direct realism and, 122, 155
  on existence of objective world,
    125
  on free will, 246, 247, 250–252
  on geometry, 219–220
  on God, 30, 31, 246, 252–253
  Hume vs., 193, 211–212, 229,
    236, 244, 254
  on ideas, 118, 134–135
  on imagination, 181, 182
  on intuition, 211, 216, 217–220,
    224, 225, 227, 254
  on knowledge, 211–212, 217, 253
  Locke vs., 229, 233, 236, 254
  on logic, 223
  on Metaphysical Deduction, 223,
    225, 232
  on necessary conditions of experi-
    ence, 216
  on noumenal psychology, 230
  on objectivity, 228–230
  Paralogisms of, 43, 45, 244–246
  on perception, 40, 193, 237–239
  on permanence, 234–236
  on phenomena and noumena,
    240–241, 247, 251
  on reason, 247–249, 254
  Refutation of Idealism of, 229,
    238–239
  Schematism of, 232–233
  on science, 216
  on sensation vs. understanding,
    180, 210–211
  on simples, 249–250
  on soul, 245
  on space, 218–220, 238, 246,
    249
  on substance, 45, 234–236, 244
  on time, 220, 235, 238, 246,
    247–249
  on Transcendental Aesthetic, 217–
    221
  on Transcendental Analytic, 223–
    231
  on Transcendental Deduction,
    223, 225–230, 232
  on Transcendental Dialectic, 223,
    243–254
  on Transcendental Idealism, 217,
    239–240, 241, 247, 248, 251
  on Transcendental Unity of
    Apperception, 226–228, 229,
    231, 244, 245, 246
  on truth, 184, 211–212, 216, 233
Knowledge
  a priori, 8, 110, 205, 206, 210,
    211–212, 217, 253
  bases of, 4, 5, 39
  Berkeley on, 206
  cause and, 52–53
  degrees of, 145
  demonstrative, 145
  Descartes on, 39, 143
  Empiricists on, 5, 110, 142–146,
    204–206, 210
  extent of, 145–146
  Hume on, 206
  intuitive, 145
  Kant on, 211–212, 217, 253
  kinds of, 71–73
  Locke on, 142–146

Knowledge *(continued)*
    Rationalists on, 39, 52–53, 71–75, 143
    sensitive, 145
    Spinoza on, 52–53, 71–75
Knutzen, Martin, 213
Kripke, 141

Language
    Berkeley on, 206
    Hume on, 177
    ideas and, 136–139, 205
    Leibniz on, 80–81, 83–84, 89, 90
    Locke on, 136–139, 206
Latin, 1–2
Leibniz, Gottfried, 5, 6, 8, 77–104
    Berkeley vs., 111
    biography of, 77–79
    on causality, 60, 93–94, 98
    on complete concepts, 83–84
    on contingency, 85–87, 100
    cosmological argument of, 98–99
    Descartes vs., 100–101, 106–108
    on existence, 99–100
    on extension, 100–101
    on finite and infinite analysis, 81–82
    on God, 86, 96, 97–103, 167–168
    on language, 80–81, 83–84, 89, 90
    on Locke, 117
    on matter, 38, 101
    Monadology, 80, 84, 86–87, 91–96
    on monads, 57, 92–96, 103
    ontological argument of, 97–98
    on preestablished harmony, 95–96, 99
    on primitive concepts, 82–83
    on Principle of Sufficient Reason, 84, 86–87, 98, 103
    on Principle of the Identity of Indiscernibles, 91–92, 103
    on reason, 84–87
    on relational propositions, 89–90
    relational theory of, 102–103
    on space and time, 102–103
    Spinoza vs., 60, 80, 83, 94, 106–108
    on subject-predicate propositions, 80–81, 83–84, 89, 90

    on substance, 83–84, 91–95
    on truth, 81–87, 89, 211
Letter Concerning Toleration, A (Locke), 114
Locke, John, 5, 6, 8, 110, 112–146
    Berkeley vs., 111, 120, 121, 130, 149–151, 157–158, 161, 164, 167, 171, 205–206
    biography of, 112–114
    on causality, 131, 186
    on classification, 139, 140
    on color, 119, 120–121, 122
    criticisms of, 78, 121–122, 133–134, 137–138
    on definition, 140
    Descartes vs., 107, 111, 116, 117, 123, 142, 143, 171
    direct realism and, 155, 156
    Essay Concerning Human Understanding, 78, 114, 115–124, 127, 128, 131–132, 136–138, 142–146
    on God, 167
    Hume vs., 111, 131, 179–180, 186, 193, 205–206, 207
    on ideas, 26, 116–118, 127–135, 144–145, 149–151, 203–205
    on identity and diversity, 131–132, 144
    Kant vs., 229, 233, 236, 254
    on knowledge, 142–146
    Kripke vs., 141
    on language, 136–139, 206
    Leibniz on, 117
    on matter, 39, 40, 64
    on modes, 127–128
    on notion of pure substratum, 130–131
    on perception, 120, 122–126
    on personal identity, 132–134
    Plato vs., 138–139
    on primary and secondary qualities, 39–40, 119–122, 125–126
    on real and nominal essence, 139–142
    on representational theory, 122–126
    resemblance thesis of, 119–122, 125–126
    scepticism and, 123–125, 164
    Spinoza vs., 64
    on substance, 128–131, 139–142, 236

Logic, general vs. transcendental, 223
Logical relations, 144
Louis XIV, king of France, 77
Luther, Martin, 3

Malebranche, Nicolas, 6, 78
Manasseh ben Israel, 49
Masham, Esther, 114
Materialism
    Descartes and, 47–48
    Spinoza and, 68
Mathematics
    importance of, 110
    Kant on, 216, 221
    See also Reason; Science
Matter
    Berkeley on, 149–161
    denial of, 149–161
    Descartes on, 36–40
    existence of, 37, 195–198
    impenetrability of, 101
    Kant on, 234
    Leibniz on, 38, 101
    Locke on, 39, 40, 64
    mind and, 37. *See also* Mind/body
        dualism
    nature of, 37–38
    primary and secondary qualities of,
        39–40, 119–122, 125–126,
        156–158
    space and, 36, 38
    See also Substance
Mechanistic view of universe, 4, 46
Mediate infinite modes, 63
Medieval period, 1–4
Meditations on First Philosophy (De-
        scartes), 10, 15
    Fifth Meditation, 30
    First Meditation, 13, 33
    Fourth Meditation, 32
    Second Meditation, 17, 19, 21,
        22, 35, 36–37, 40
    Sixth Meditation, 35, 36, 37, 40,
        43
    Third Meditation, 22, 24, 25, 26
Mental substance
    Descartes on, 35–37, 45
    Hume on, 199–200
Mersenne, 10, 25
Metaphysical Deduction, 223, 225,
    232

*Metaphysical Foundations of Natural
    Science* (Kant), 214
Metaphysics, transcendental, 215
Method of Doubt, 12–17, 22
    criticisms of, 16–17
    elements of, 12–13
    ideas and, 31–32
Meyer, Ludovicus, 49–50
Mind, 35–37
    Berkeley on, 169–172
    causal analysis of, 46–47
    Descartes on, 35–37, 40–48
    Hume on, 170
    matter and, 37
    Spinoza on, 66–69
Mind/body dualism
    in argument from divisibility, 43
    in argument from doubt, 41–43
    criticisms of, 44–46
    Descartes on, 40–48, 66
    Locke on, 133
    problem of identity of mental sub-
        stances and, 45
    problem of other minds and, 45–
        46
    problems of interaction and, 44–
        45
    Spinoza on, 51, 54–55, 66–67
Mirrors, and monads, 94–95
Mixed modes, 128
Modern period, 1, 5–6
Modes
    eternal, 63
    finite, 55, 57–59, 62–63
    infinite, 63–64
    Locke on, 127–128
    mixed, 128
    simple, 128
    Spinoza on, 55, 57–59, 62–64
Monadology (Leibniz), 80, 84, 86–87,
    91–96
Monads, 57, 92–96
    bare, 95
    causality and, 93–94
    dynamic nature of, 103
    mirrors and, 94–95
    points of view and, 95
    preestablished harmony and, 95–
        96, 99
Monism, 57
Monmouth, Duke of, 113
My Own Life (Hume), 174

Naturalism, 176–177, 190–191
Nature, 52, 53, 62–63, 64, 65, 74, 75
Necessary truth, 81, 83, 85, 86
New System (Leibniz), 80
Newton, Sir Isaac, 4, 78, 100, 102, 103, 114, 115, 119
Nominal essence, 139–140
Non-Euclidean geometry, 219–220
Notes Against a Program (Descartes), 25
Noumena, 240–241, 247, 251
Noumenal psychology, 230

Objections (Gassendi), 30
Objectivity, 228–230
Objects
    external, 159–160, 195–198, 229
    sensible, 158–159
    unperceived, 165–166
Observation
    as basis of knowledge, 4, 5, 39
    Descartes on, 39
    Hume on, 176–177
Ockham, William of, 3
Ontological argument, 97–98. *See also* God

Pantheism, 51
Paralogisms of Kant, 43, 45, 244–246
Pascal, Blaise, 6
Passions of the Soul, The (Descartes), 11
Perception
    Berkeley on, 149–161, 165–166
    Descartes on, 39–40, 123
    Empiricists on, 120, 122–126, 149–161, 165–166, 178–180, 193–198, 204–205
    Hume on, 178–180, 193–198, 204
    Kant on, 40, 193, 237–239
    Locke on, 120, 122–126
    Rationalists on, 39–40, 106, 123
Perceptual illusions, 120
Permanence, 234–236
Personal identity
    Hume on, 200–201
    Locke on, 132–134

Peter the Great of Russia, 79
Phenomena, 240–241, 247
Phenomenalism, 122
Philonous. *See Three Dialogues Between Hylas and Philonous*
Philosophical Commentaries (Berkeley), 147
Plato, 2, 138–139
Political Discourses (Hume), 174
Preestablished harmony, 95–96, 99
Primary and secondary qualities
    Berkeley on, 156–158
    Descartes on, 39–40
    Locke on, 39–40, 119–122, 125–126
Primitive concepts, 82–83
Principia (Newton), 100
Principle of Adequate Reality, 27, 28, 29
Principle of Contradiction, 84, 86
Principle of Indiscernibility of Identicals, 41
Principle of Sufficient Reason
    Descartes and, 27, 28
    Hume and, 185, 186
    Leibniz and, 84, 86–87, 98, 103
    Rationalists and, 8, 27, 28, 53, 56, 84, 86–87, 98, 103, 105, 106, 210
    Spinoza and, 53, 56
Principle of the Best, 87
Principle of the Identity of Indiscernibles, 91–92, 103
Principles, Analytic of, 223, 232–241
Principles of Human Knowledge (Berkeley), 149, 159, 164, 165, 166, 171, 205
Principles of Philosophy (Descartes), 11, 19, 37, 38
Principles of the Philosophy of René Descartes (Spinoza), 49–50
Prolegomena (Kant), 214
Proofs of existence of God
    Descartes on, 26–29, 30–31
    Spinoza on, 53–56
Psychology, noumenal, 230
Ptolemy, 2

Quine, W. V. O., 31

Rationalists, 5–6, 8–108
  on causality, 52–53, 54, 57, 60,
    62–63, 93–94, 98
  comparisons of, 52, 56–57, 58,
    60, 64, 80, 83, 94, 100–101,
    106–108
  criticisms of, 16–17, 21, 30–31,
    44–46
  on determinism, 74–75
  on dualism, 40–48, 66, 68, 107–
    108
  on existence, 17–22, 35–36, 37,
    99–100
  on extension, 36, 38, 52, 59, 63–
    64, 65–66, 100–101
  on free will, 33, 74–75, 86, 87
  on God, 26–33, 37, 51–60, 64–
    65, 86, 87, 96, 97–103, 167–
    168
  on ideas, 24–26, 31–32, 68–69,
    73–74, 116, 137
  on knowledge, 5, 8, 39, 52–53,
    71–75, 143
  Materialism and, 47–48, 68
  on matter, 36–40, 101
  on mind, 35–37, 40–48, 66–69
  on mind/body dualism, 40–48, 51,
    54–55, 66–67
  on monads, 57, 92–96, 99, 103
  on Nature, 52, 53, 62–63, 64, 65,
    74, 75
  on perception, 39–40, 106, 123
  Principle of Sufficient Reason and,
    8, 27, 28, 53, 56, 84, 86–87,
    98, 103, 105, 106, 210
  on reason, 8, 39, 72, 84–87, 110
  scepticism and, 12–17, 22
  on science, 4, 38–39, 62–63, 110
  on sense experience, 8, 13, 14, 16,
    39, 72, 106, 110
  on soul, 67–68, 95
  on substance, 35–37, 38, 45, 52–
    60, 65, 83–84, 91–95
  on truth, 73–74, 81–87, 89, 100,
    106, 211
  See also Descartes; Leibniz; Spi-
    noza
Rational souls, 95
Real essence, 139–142
Realism, direct, 122, 155–156
Reason
  Descartes on, 39, 72, 110
  Empiricists on, 110, 177, 196–
    197
  Hume on, 177, 196–197
  Kant on, 247–249, 254
  Leibniz on, 84–87
  Rationalists on, 8, 39, 72, 84–87,
    110
  sense experience vs., 8, 39, 72, 110
  Spinoza on, 72
  time and, 247–249
Reasonableness of Christianity (Locke),
    114
Refutation of Idealism, 229, 238–239
Reid, Thomas, 6
Relational propositions, 89–90
Relational theory of Leibniz, 102–
    103
Relations, logical, 144
Religion Within the Limits of Reason
    Alone (Kant), 214
Renaissance, 2, 3
Representational theory, 122–126
Resemblance thesis, 119–122, 125–
    126
Roman influences, 1–2
Rousseau, Jean-Jacques, 174
Rules for the Direction of the Mind
    (Descartes), 20
Russell, Bertrand, 21, 152
Ryle, Gilbert, 46

St. Clair, Lieutenant-General, 174
Scepticism
  Berkeley and, 164
  Descartes and, 12–17, 22
  Empiricists and, 110, 123–125,
    164, 168, 170, 176, 177, 187–
    194, 210
  Hume and, 168, 170, 176, 177,
    187–194, 210
  inductive, 187–188
  Locke and, 123–125, 164
Schematism, 232–233
Schultz, Franz, 213
Science
  Descartes on, 38–39, 63, 110
  Kant on, 216
  Spinoza on, 62–63
Scientific paradigm, 4

Search After Truth, The (Descartes), 19

Secondary qualities. *See* Primary and secondary qualities

Second Replies (Descartes), 20, 21

Sensation vs. understanding, 180, 210–211

Sense
  Hume on, 196–197
  idea of, 151, 163, 167

Sense experience
  Descartes on, 13, 14, 16, 39, 72, 110
  Rationalists on, 8, 13, 14, 16, 39, 72, 106, 110
  reason vs., 8, 39, 72, 110
  Spinoza on, 72, 106
  See also Perception

Sensible objects, 158–159

Sensitive knowledge, 145

Shaftesbury, Earl of, 113

Short Treatise on God, Man and His Well-Being (Spinoza), 49

Simple ideas, 118, 178–180, 203–204

Simple modes, 128

Simples, 249–250

Siris (Berkeley), 148

Smith, Adam, 174, 175

Sophie, Duchess, 78

Soul
  animal, 95
  Kant on, 245
  Leibniz on, 95
  rational, 95
  Spinoza on, 67–68

Space
  Descartes on, 36, 38
  Kant on, 218–220, 238, 246, 249
  Leibniz on, 102–103
  matter and, 36, 38

Spinoza, Benedictus, 5, 8, 49–76, 105–108
  on attributes, 64–65
  biography of, 49–50
  on causality, 52–53, 54, 57, 62–63
  Descartes vs., 52, 56–57, 58, 64, 106–108
  determinism of, 74–75
  Ethics, 49, 50, 51, 52, 53–57, 59, 62–67, 71–75

on extension, 52, 59, 63–64, 65–66
on finite modes, 55, 57–59, 62–63
on free will, 74–75
on God, 51–60, 64–65
on ideas, 68–69, 73–74
on imagination, 71–72
on infinite modes, 63–64
on intuition, 73
on knowledge, 52–53, 71–75
Leibniz vs., 60, 80, 83, 94, 106–108
Locke vs., 64
Materialism and, 68
on mind, 66–69
on mind/body dualism, 51, 54–55, 66–67
on Nature, 52, 53, 62–63, 64, 65, 74, 75
Principle of Sufficient Reason and, 53, 56
on proofs of existence of God, 53–56
on reason, 72
on science, 62–63
on soul, 67–68
on substance, 38, 52–60, 65
on truth and falsity, 73–74

Spirit
  Berkeley on, 169–170
  deceiving, 13–14, 15
  See also Mind; Soul

Stillingfleet, Edward, 130, 142

Strawson, P., 220, 234, 237, 249

Stroud, B., 189–190

Subject-predicate propositions, 80–81, 83–84, 89, 90

Substance
  Berkeley on, 160–161
  Descartes on, 35–37, 45, 56–57, 58
  Empiricism and, 129–130
  Empiricists on, 128–131, 139–142, 160–161, 199–200, 236
  Kant on, 45, 234–236, 244
  Leibniz on, 83–84, 91–95
  Locke on, 128–131, 139–142, 236
  mental, 35–37, 45, 199–200
  Rationalists on, 35–37, 38, 45, 52–60, 65
  Spinoza on, 38, 52–60, 65
  See also Matter

Substratum, 130–131
Sufficient Reason. *See* Principle of
    Sufficient Reason
Summa Theologica (Aquinas), 2

Theodicy (Leibniz), 78
Thinking substance. *See* Mental sub-
    stance
Thought, and extension, 65–66
*Thoughts on the True Estimation of
    Living Forces* (Kant), 214
*Three Dialogues Between Hylas and
    Philonous* (Berkeley), 147, 149,
    151, 156–157, 159–161, 166,
    169
Time
    Kant on, 220, 235, 238, 246,
        247–249
    Leibniz on, 102–103
    reason and, 247–249
Tractatus Politicus (Spinoza), 50
Transcendental Aesthetic, 217–221
Transcendental Analytic, 223–231
Transcendental Deduction, 223, 225–
    230, 232
Transcendental Dialectic, 223, 243–
    254
Transcendental Idealism, 217, 239–
    240, 241, 247, 248, 251
Transcendental logic, 223
Transcendental metaphysics, 215
Transcendental Unity of Appercep-
    tion, 226–228, 229, 231, 244,
    245, 246
*Treatise Concerning the Principles of
    Human Knowledge, A* (Be-
    rkeley), 147, 149, 163

Treatise on Human Nature (Hume),
    173–174, 175, 180, 181, 185,
    188, 195, 197, 199
Truth
    a posteriori, 184
    a priori, 184, 211–212, 216
    contingent, 85, 100
    Hume on, 183, 184, 211–212
    Kant on, 184, 211–212, 216, 233
    Leibniz on, 81–87, 89, 211
    necessary, 81, 83, 85, 86
    Rationalists on, 73–74, 81–87,
        89, 100, 106, 211
    Spinoza on, 73–74
Tschirnhaus, Ehrenfried Walter von,
    78
Two Treatises on Civil Government
    (Locke), 114

Understanding
    free will and, 33
    sensation vs., 180, 210–211
Uniformity principle, 189–190
Universal Causal Axiom, 185, 193,
    212
*Universal Natural History and Theory
    of the Heavens* (Kant), 214
Universals, 138
Unperceived objects, 165–166

Van Den Ende, Francis, 49

William, king of England, 114
William of Ockham, 3
Wittgenstein, Ludwig, 125
Wolff, Christian, 6, 214